Energy in France

Planning, Politics and Policy

N. J. D. Lucas

Published for The David Davies Memorial Institute
of International Studies
by
EUROPA PUBLICATIONS LIMITED
LONDON

Europa Publications Limited
18 Bedford Square, London, WC1B 3JN

British Library Cataloguing in Publication Data

Lucas, N. J. D.

Energy in France

1. Energy industries—France—History

I. Title II. David Davies Memorial Institute of International Studies

338.4'7'6214   HD9502.F72

ISBN 0-905118-30-8

Printed and bound in England by
Staples Printers Rochester Limited
at the Stanhope Press

Energy in France

To my mother

Acknowledgements

This study was initiated by the David Davies Memorial Institute of International Studies, and I am most grateful for the help of the Institute in the course of preparation. I am especially grateful to the Director, Miss Mary Sibthorp, O.B.E., for her formidable encouragement.

I am indebted to my wife, Danièle, for her determined researches in the chilly peripheries of *L'Institut Français* and the depositories of other London libraries, each with its own peculiarly disagreeable micro-climate.

I wish also to acknowledge the help of the executives of the French energy industries and civil servants who gave me most generously of their time. I should like to thank them by name, but some prefer not to be mentioned and it would be invidious to select. But, I wish to record particularly the help which I received from the personnel of *Electricité de France* (EDF), who often anticipated my requirements in the most astonishing manner and always answered my questions most fully. I am grateful to the staff of the *Institut Economique et Juridique de l'Energie* at Grenoble; some of the ideas of Professor Jean-Marie Martin of the Institute can be detected in Chapter II. I should also like to acknowledge some ideas of Elizabeth Lalanne which have influenced parts of Chapter VII, because she has not, as far as I know, published them. Bernard Bourgeois, Bertrand Chateau and Dominique Finon were also generous with their time and thoughts. Members of the staff of the Foreign and Commonwealth Office kindly gave me interviews or arranged interviews in France; I should like to thank Mrs. Lucy Ismail, Messrs. Antony Goodenough, Adrian Fortescue, Philip Morrice, Michael John Aaronson, J. McCrae and J. Clibourne.

I wish to thank also Miss Esme Allen for successfully typing a hideous manuscript.

Finally, I should acknowledge the role of the vignerons of Bordeaux, Burgundy and Cognac whose produce has been a great help in composition and whose recent prices have provided me with an extra incentive.

Contents

Foreword

Lord Caccia of Abernant

A great many books have been written about energy and about what we should or should not do. Few have attempted to assess how it is that we decide what we should or should not do.

An extreme conception of energy policy might be that it is a choice based firmly on rigorous technical and economic criteria. Such an opinion could scarcely survive in times when the politics of energy are daily made manifest in the tribulations of oil and nuclear power. That politics is at the heart of energy choices is evident; what is rarely recognized is the extent to which the structure of institutions that form and express the political life of a nation also makes its own significant and characteristic contribution to those choices.

This book traces in detail the influence that is brought to bear on the choice of energy technology in France by the institutions which have evolved over centuries for reasons and by forces that are unrelated to present affairs. Just as government policy is a function of the history and structure of institutions, so the popular response to that policy is conditioned by the political nature and traditional forms of expression of the French people. One of the most valuable features of the book is the comprehensive and objective discussion of the French anti-nuclear movement, placing the movement within its proper political and historical context. It is perhaps the most thorough analysis of this type of development yet to be made, and is of particular value and importance as France is proceeding vigorously with a large nuclear programme.

Abbreviations

AEE	Agence pour les Economies d'Energie
BRP	Bureau de Recherches du Pétrole
CDF	Charbonnages de France et Houillères Bassin
CEA	Commissariat à l'Energie Atomique
CES	Commissariat à l'Energie Solaire
CFDT	Confédération Française Démocratique du Travail
CFMU	Compagnie Française des Minerais d'Uranium
CFP	Compagnie Française des Pétroles
CGE	Compagnie Générale Electromécanique
CGP	Commissariat Général du Plan
CGT	Confédération Générale du Travail
CNPF	Confédération Nationale du Patronat Français
CNR	Compagnie Nationale du Rhône
CNRS	Centre National de la Recherche Scientifique
Cogema	Compagnie Générale des Matières Nucléaires
Crilan	Comité Régional d'Information et de Lutte Anti-nucléaire
CRS	Compagnies Républicaines de Sécurité
DEN	Délégation aux Energies Nouvelles
DGE	Délégation Générale à l'Energie
DICA	Direction des Carburants
Digec	Direction du Gaz, de l'Electricité et du Charbon
DUP	Déclaration d'Utilité Publique
EDF	Electricité de France
ENA	Ecole Nationale d'Administration
ENEL	Ente Nazionale per l'Energia Elettrica
ENI	Ente Nazionale Idrocarburi
ERAP	Entreprise de Recherche et d'Activité Pétrolière
ERDA	Energy Research and Development Agency
FDES	Fonds de Développement Economique et Social
GDF	Gaz de France
IEJE	Institut Economique et Juridique de l'Energie
Insee	Institut National de la Statistique et des Etudes Economiques
LCR	Ligue Communiste Révolutionnaire
LWR	Light Water Reactor
MAN	Mouvement pour une Alternative Non Violente
MTCE	Millions of Tonnes of Coal Equivalent

MTOE	Millions of Tonnes of Oil Equivalent
Nersa	Société Centrale Nucléaire Européenne à Neutrons Rapides
Onarem	Office National des Ressources Minières
PCF	Parti Communiste Français
PSU	Parti Socialiste Unifié
PWR	Pressurized Water Reactor
RPR	Rassemblement pour la République
SCSIN	Service Central de Sûreté des Installations Nucléaires
SNEA	Société Nationale Elf-Aquitaine
SNGSO	Société Nationale du Gaz du Sud-Ouest
SNPA	Société Nationale des Pétroles d'Aquitaine
Somair	Société des Mines de l'Air
SPR	Service des Protections contre les Radiations
TDF	Télédiffusion de France
TOE	Tonne of Oil Equivalent
UGP	Union Générale des Pétroles

I

Purpose and Context

A. Objectives

Energy policy in every country in the world is the result of the action of many conflicting economic and political forces which are finally arbitrated either by the market or by political decision supported by legislation or by a combination of both. The length of the future period affected by the policy and its stability will depend on the nature of the process determining the policy and by the nature of the final sanction. Policies evolved by the interplay of private interests sanctioned by the market will contain unstable elements, which the companies will do their best to remove, and will generally deal with the future in unspecific terms. Policies produced by elected representatives in a democratic political system will also contain unstable elements. Policies produced by single party systems or evolved by strong administrations will be comparatively difficult to reverse, but may contain severe economic penalties. The alleged conflict between the priorities of politicians, which are to stay in power and therefore to attend to the immediately urgent rather than the really important matters, and the needs of policy making for a long view and arbitration in the collective interest are nowhere so evident as in energy policy. France offers an especially interesting study because she has had for many years a system for making decisions which has several aspects that are generally respected. The well-known French system of indicative planning permits, on the face of it, the needs of the future to be catered for by men of wisdom and far-sightedness, and permits decisions to be made by a rational arbitration by the same men possessing both complete personal disinterest and a clear perception of the interest of the State.

The contemporary concern with energy supplies and the apparent difficulty of reconciling some of the characteristics of this sector with the operation of free markets has led everywhere to a systematic intervention by government in energy markets; often this intervention has been *ad hoc* and as a result contradictory. Inevitably, therefore, intervention by governments eventually is seen to require co-ordination to achieve specified general objectives, this constitutes an energy policy. Most developed countries are at this stage. Subsequently, one can observe that countries begin to define more specific objectives such as the amounts of energy or of certain fuels which are to be consumed at a future date; the U.K., the U.S.A., the Federal Republic of Germany, Japan and many other countries have attempted to do this. The strength of their conviction in their forecasts, their motives and the exact meaning of their efforts vary enormously and need not concern us; it is only necessary to establish this trend towards practices similar to those that are used in France. It is useful, therefore, to investigate the French experience to determine to what extent the reality lives up to the attractive impression.

French energy policy is interesting also for much simpler reasons. The sheer magnitude of the decisions involved is staggering; the order placed by *Electricité de France* with Framatome in the spring of 1974 for 7 billion FF[1] was the biggest contract ever signed in the world; the construction programme decided by the *Conseil Central de Planification* on 1 February 1973 envisaged an installed nuclear-fuelled generating capacity of about 30 GW(e) by 1985;[2] the investments provided for the construction of nuclear stations and the provision of fuel cycle facilities during the course of the Seventh Plan (1976–1980) amount to over 70 billion FF.[3] Will it be possible for the French heavy electrical and engineering industries successfully to mount this effort, and what will be the effect on other sectors deprived of investment funds?

There are other material factors of direct consequence for other nations. The large domestic construction programme undertaken by the French will enable them sooner or later to export nuclear technology in massive quantities. The extent to which export sales are necessary for the economic viability of the programme, the anticipated volume of sales, the timing and the terms of sale, in particular the terms relating to the provision of the associated sensitive technologies of uranium enrichment and nuclear fuel reprocessing, are all matters which affect the international community and are compelling reasons for following closely developments in France.

The French domestic nuclear programme has not gone entirely without criticism; in some places it has given rise to a lively environmental opposition. As a new social phenomenon this is of great intrinsic interest, but it is still more significant in its quality as a signal of the stresses between the increasing intervention of government in people's lives in the search for greater economic prosperity and political security, and the desire for a more liberal society in which to enjoy those benefits. The conflict, nascent in France, between technocracy and democracy has lessons for all countries.

Finally, and perhaps subsuming all the rest, it is an objective of this study to show how French energy policy is conditioned by the social and political life and history of France. T. S. Eliot reminds us that the technique of cooking cabbages is a manifestation of culture;[4] there are enough excellent books on cookery, mixing anthropology and cuisine, to show that he was right. Energy policy is no less a matter of culture. A French official described to me the reaction of his country to the Yom Kippur War as being 'a caricature of French institutions'. Policy probably is so always and everywhere.

B. Fundamentals

1. SUPPLY AND USE

The structure of energy supplies in France in 1977 is shown in Table 1. The heavy dependence on oil imports is obvious; it is also unattractive to an administration and politicians of markedly nationalistic line. The table also shows how the supply structure has evolved from 1975 and illustrates the progress towards the objectives for 1985 as defined by the Fifth Plan. Table 2 shows how this energy was used. The residential sector is served mainly by oil products; it consumes little electricity. This observation, plus the fact that France consumes little electricity per head by the standards of other industrialized countries, is an important part of the argument for the policy of *tout électrique* (all electric).

Table 1. Evolution of supplies 1975–1977 and objectives for 1985.

	1977 (MTOE)	Change 77/76 (%)	Change 76/75 (%)	Centre Objective 1985 (MTOE)
Solid fuels:				
Hard coal production	14.4	−3	−2	
Hard coal imports	10.3	+13	+26	
Hard coke	7.1	−5	−1	
Sub total	31.8	+1	+11	25
Natural gas:				
Production	6.5	+7	−7	
Imports (NL)	10.2	+10	+14	
Imports (Other)	2.6	−5	+23	
Sub total	19.3	+7	+7	37
Primary electricity:				
Nuclear	4.0	+14	−14	55
Hydraulic	17.3	+56	−19	14
Sub total	21.3	+8	−18	69
Oil:				
Production	1.0	−10	−39	
Imports	115.8	−4	+18	
Sub total	116.8	−4	+18	98
New sources:				
Sub total	negligible	—	—	3
Total	189.2	+6.3	+7.8	232

3

Table. 2. Energy balance, 1976 (MTOE).

	Solid Fuels	Crude Oil and NGL	Petroleum Products	Gas	Nuclear Power	Hydro and Geo-thermal	Electricity	Total
Indigenous production	17.00	1.92		6.06	3.46	10.82		39.26
Imports	15.11	121.99	8.71	12.01			0.84	158.66
Exports	−1.10		−10.30	−0.12			−0.66	−12.17
Marine bunkers and stock change	0.79	−0.58	−7.32	−0.74				−7.85
Total	31.80	123.33	−8.91	17.21	3.46	10.82	0.18	177.90
Electricity generation	−14.56		−13.68	−2.04	−3.46	−10.82	17.49	−27.07
Statistical difference, own use and losses	−2.73	−0.28	−1.60	−0.79			−2.18	−7.01
Gas manufacture	−0.08		−0.34	−0.15				−0.27
Refineries		−123.61	117.04				−0.35	−6.92
Total final consumption	14.42		92.52	14.52			15.14	136.61
Total industry	10.00		27.43	7.46			7.53	52.42
of which:								
Iron/Steel	8.04		2.02	0.94			1.25	12.26
Chemical	0.65		8.31	2.89			1.81	13.66
Other	1.30		17.10	3.63			4.46	26.50
Transport	0.04		29.23	0.01			0.56	29.83
Agriculture			2.77				0.12	2.89
Commerce			0.15	2.87			3.01	6.02
Public service			0.03				0.22	0.25
Residential	4.39		28.14	4.19			3.72	40.44
Non-Energy			4.76					4.76
Electricity generated (TWh)					15.8	49.4	203.4	

Sector / Function	Oil	Gas	Coal	Electricity Supply	Nuclear Fuel	Reactor Construction	New Sources	Conservation
Financial Tutelle	Ministry of Economics and Finance							
Technical Tutelle	Ministry of Industry and Research							
	Délégation Générale à l'Energie							
	DICA		DIGEC		DGE		DEN	AEE
Foreign Policy	Quai d'Orsay							
	Délégation Générale à l'Energie							
	Oil Companies				CEA	CEA/ FRAMATOME	CES	
Planning	Commissariat Général du Plan							
	Commission de l'Energie							
	Commission Peon							
Operating Organizations	CFP SNEA SHELL ESSO BP	GDF SNGSO SNPA	CDF	EDF CNR	COGEMA	FRAMATOME	CES Plus Private Capital	

Fig. 1. A matrix representation of institutional relationships in the French energy sector.

5

Table 3.   The structure of the Operating Institutions in the French energy sector.

SECTOR	Organization	Control	Place in the Industry
COAL	CDF	100% state owned	Monopoly of production
GAS	GDF	100% state owned	78% of sales
	SNGSO	Subsidiary of GDF	22% of sales
	Elf-Aquitaine	70% state owned	96% of production
ELECTRICITY	EDF	100% state owned	80% of production Monopoly of transport Near monopoly of final sales
	CNR	Mixed economy	Hydro-electric production sold to EDF
NUCLEAR	CEA	100% state owned	Research and control of all nuclear activities
	Cogema	100% owned by CEA	Monopoly of fuel cycle processes
	Framatome	51% owned by Creusot Loire	Sole French manufacturer of nuclear steam supply systems
OIL	Elf-Aquitaine	70% state owned	23% of sales of oil products
	CFP	35% state owned but 40% of voting rights	27.30%
	Shell-Française	Royal Dutch Shell 95%	15.6%
	Esso	Exxon 81.6%	12.1%
	Cie. Française des Pétroles BP	BP 70%	11%

2. THE INSTITUTIONS

A useful schematic presentation of the relationships between different parties is given by the matrix shown in Fig. 1. The industrial sector within which the influence is exerted is shown along the top and the function of the institution is shown down the side. A brief note of the structure of the principal enterprises concerned with energy supplies is given in Table 3. The meaning of initials and acronyms is given in Table 4.

These tables suggest some fairly well-known and/or obvious points. There is an enormous State involvement in the energy industries. France, like the U.K., has virtual State monopolies in electricity supply, coal mining and sales of gas, but she is also more directly involved in the oil industry and exercises, as we shall see later, a considerable control by legislation. Moreover, the close relationship which exists between the administration and public enterprise permits the fact of nationalization to be much more effectively employed than in the U.K., to further the aims of government or the administration.

Another impression one gets from studying the matrix of relationships is of the obvious importance of the *Ministères des Finances* and *de l'Industrie* and of the *Commissariat du Plan*; these institutions have particularly strong positions because their functions extend across all the operating organizations. The latter are obliged to compete for scarce resources, the allocation of which is subject to the arbitration of these three bodies. In the course of this competition, the industries invariably expose their problems, put their case, attack the position of others and in so doing transfer the information and understanding which is an essential basis for power in a modern society. The information will all eventually be coded in financial terms and this, together with the implicit importance of money, will give the *Ministre des Finances* great influence. But it is still of significance to the companies to argue their case within the *Ministère de l'Industrie* and the *Commissariat du Plan* in order to obtain the technical sanction for investment programmes and sales targets which will then give them a strong case for obtaining either money from the *Ministère des Finances* or its permission to borrow elsewhere.

References

1. *Nuclear News*, April 1974.
2. *Le Programme Electro-Nucléaire Français*, Note d'Information, Ministère de l'Industrie et de la Recherche, January 1976.
3. *Rapport de la Commission de l'Energie*, Commissariat General du Plan, La Documentation Française, Paris, 1976.
4. T. S. Eliot. *Notes towards the Definition of Culture*, Faber and Faber, London, 1948.

II

The Evolution of Relationships
among Institutions

The relationships among the institutions concerned in energy supply have evolved in a manner conditioned by several factors. Some of these factors are specific to the energy industries, others reflect the wider environment in which the energy industries operate. It so happens that, broadly, one can detect four stages of evolution, the boundaries between which are marked by reasonably distinct changes both in the energy specific and energy non-specific factors.[1,2,3]

The four periods comprise: the period between the two World Wars, the period following the Second World War up until about 1957/58, from then until 1970–1973, and from then until the present. The principal energy specific factors describing these periods are as follows. Between the wars the uses of energy were mostly specific to particular fuels. There was little competition for markets or supplies. Immediately after the Second World War, energy was in extremely short supply, all that could be produced could be sold, foreign exchange was scarce and consequently the production of indigenous energy from high-cost coal resources and hydraulic power was encouraged. Competition between fuels for markets again was negligible. At the end of this period, for many reasons, oil began rapidly to displace other fuels, most especially coal; ruthless competition was the order of the day, energy prices fell and were generally considered likely to go on falling. In 1970/71, the Teheran-Tripoli agreements and the difficulties of the French oil companies in Algeria brought home some of the dangers of relying with excessive confidence on petroleum. The events following the October War of 1973 reinforced this judgement and a new perception of energy supplies became widely accepted.

In parallel with this evolution of the energy market, there were changes in the nature of the relationships between and amongst the various branches of industry and government. The first period was characterized by government

8

control of private industry, mostly proceeding through government departments. After the War the State nationalized large parts of the sector and introduced State agencies into the oil sector. The following period saw mounting discontent among the publicly owned industries, especially EDF, with the irksome and detailed controls of government. New relationships between government and public industry were defined. Private capital began again to be an important part of the energy sector, generally in association with public enterprise.

The final period is characterized by the successful attempts of some of the public firms to control the environment in which they operate. In particular, the companies try to extend their control upstream to ensure supplies and downstream to secure markets, to ensure control of future technologies which they could use or which threaten them, and finally to obtain access to means of finance that would remove them, as far as possible, from the grip of the State. This sort of behaviour is probably what is meant when one hears certain French public firms described as a state within a state, a description frequently met with in France, especially of EDF. The boundaries of the stages described are not strict, they vary from industry to industry and from function to function; events have not always evolved according to this scheme and there have been other currents. It is nevertheless a possible basis from which to start.

These four stages define a historical dimension in which to situate changes. It is also useful to add a sectorial dimension. The energy industries separate into two groups. There is a group whose activities are largely confined to the nation, coal, gas, electricity, nuclear. There is a group whose activities cannot and must not be confined to the nation; it comprises the oil companies. In the first group the principal relations are between industry and state. In the second group the dominant relationships are those between firms; the activities of the French oil companies have always been determined in the first instance by the need to operate in an environment controlled by the oil majors. Each subsector has its own internal dynamics, yet interacts with the other.

A. Between the Wars

The period between the Wars was characterized by competition for space presided over by the State. The end uses for different forms of energy were rather specific; gas for lighting; electricity for lighting and electrochemistry; coal for heating, industrial processes and railways; oil for lubrication and road transport. There was little competition for markets. The gas industry countered the potential threat to their lighting market by buying up the nascent electricity companies; gas and electricity in many areas were provided by a joint enterprise. There was little competition for supplies. Electricity came from hydraulic power or was generated by heavy industry and sold as a by-product; gas was manufactured from coal. The use of coal as a feedstock for the electricity supply industry did not introduce competition where a joint enterprise operated. The industries were all protected from the competition of imported goods or capital; nor did they seek abroad for supplies, technology, capital or markets. In sum, the separate coal, oil and gas/electricity sectors existed with little inter-sector competition for markets or supplies and a small interdependence.

The principal competition was for terrain. To have permitted competition between similar supply industries within the same area would have sanctioned a duplication of expensive supply infrastructures; concessions were therefore allocated by the State both for supply and use. The basic text establishing the regime of concessions for coal mining was the law of 21 April 1810; it conferred on the concessionnaire a perpetual right to the mine, subject to certain general rules. A law of 1919 forbade the use of hydraulic energy resources (waterfalls, tides, rivers, lakes) for generating electricity without a concession from the State. Similar concessions regulated the behaviour of the public services of gas and electricity.

Having created local monopolies it evidently required the vigilance of the State to see that the concessions were not abused. This function was the origin of the great directorates, *la direction des mines, la direction de l'électricité*. The well trained and intelligent engineers of the *grand corps* who staffed these directorates were far more competent and acted more coherently than the 'subsistence capitalists' who ran the industries. Responsibility for control of the sector, initiative and what would now be called policy, passed into the hands of the administration.

The most perfect example of the public powers trying to form the industries to their own designs is the perpetual battle during the interwar period to interconnect electricity and gas supply systems to permit more efficient use of resources. None of the companies had the resources to assure within a single region, and still less throughout the nation, the development and management of an interconnected system of production, transmission and distribution. The syndrome was similar in the U.K. In an attempt to encourage and to constrain the producers to collaborate on the financing of interconnections, the French State introduced a regime of concessions for long distance transmission of electricity. The attempt was only partially successful. In 1937 the State again took the initiative by establishing a national body within which the producers and distributors of electricity should define a plan of development for the means of production and transport of electricity in a national framework. The State also attempted to harmonize tariffs and restructure the industry. Nevertheless, despite these efforts, by 1946 there were still 54 companies producing electricity from 86 thermal stations and 100 companies exploiting 300 hydraulic stations. Long distance transmission was practised by 86 companies and there were some 1,150 distribution companies.[4]

The coal mining industry evolved differently. A mine owner cannot be protected from competition assigning him the sort of local monopoly enjoyed by gas and electricity distributors, but ways do exist, and the generally protectionist French State tolerated them. They were not as good; competition broke through. There was, therefore, a natural tendency for coal production to be concentrated in a few mines.

By 1938 there were 181 workings; within these 11 companies produced over 64% of the total French production; small companies, although representing two-thirds of the numbers, produced less than 2% of the output.[5]

Nevertheless, the degree of concentration was not enough to secure a rational use of resources. In the *Nord* and *Pas-de-Calais* regions, especially, the geological circumstances demanded a common use of services; but the concessionnaires were reluctant to compromise their individualism. Persuasion was inhibited by the existence of the concession in perpetuity. The State did attempt to force concentration by modifying the regime of concession in perpetuity. The State did attempt to force concentration by modifying the regime of concessions. In 1919 it introduced the concept of temporary concession, but it had little effect because most mining rights had been allocated under the old system. The example does show a desire within the administration to concentrate the sector analogous to its initiatives in gas and electricity supply.

Circumstances forced the intervention of the French State in the oil industry to take a quite different turn. France had never managed to secure supplies of oil through the activity of indigenous entrepreneurs. Worse, the known supplies were in the hands of the Dutch and the Anglo-Saxon companies which controlled also the markets and technology. During the First World War the scarcity of fuel supplies to the French troops caused them such distress as to provoke Clemenceau's sad observation that 'a drop of oil is worth a drop of blood'.

To compensate for the deficiencies of its capitalists, the French Government demanded at the end of the War the 25% share of the Deutsche Bank in the Turkish Petroleum Company, dominated by the Anglo-Persian Oil Company, itself the result of an initiative of the British Admiralty. It appears that in this affair the French benefited from a variety of rivalries and grudges. It is alleged that Henry Deterding, the President of Royal Dutch-Shell, helped persuade the U.K. to agree to the transfer to France of the Deutsche Bank holding. He planned, following an idea of Gulbenkian, to create a joint company with the *Banque de l'Union Parisienne* to which the French would be persuaded to attribute their part. In this way Deterding would be on equal terms with the Anglo-Persian Oil Company, then holder of 50% of the capital of the Turkish Petroleum Company, and the ensemble would be dominated by the U.K. But Gulbenkian wanted to frustrate Deterding's ambition and presented to the French Government also the idea of a French company to manage the holding.[6]

Be that as it may, the transfer of the Deutsche Bank holding to France was regulated by the San Remo Treaty in 1920. In 1924 France set up the *Compagnie Française des Pétroles* (CFP) to manage its interests. The concept of the CFP was an innovation in industry–government relationships. The capital of the company came entirely from private sources, but the Government was the source of initiative and retained some control.

The Government nominated the President of the company before it had been formed – Ernest Mercier. In correspondence dated 20 September 1923, the Foreign Minister, Raymond Poincaré, defined the institutional framework of the company:

> As soon as possible the group will take the form of a limited liability company, whose statutes . . . will be approved by the government.

He went on to specify that the objectives of the Government were:

> . . . to create a tool capable of the realisation of a national petroleum policy. The company must be essentially French and remain completely independent. It will do its utmost to develop petroleum production, under French control, in the different producing regions.
>
> . . . it may receive from the government the mission of undertaking such work as the government thinks necessary. If this should not be profitable the state will accord appropriate remuneration.

Similarly the Minister specified four objectives of the company. They were:

1. To exploit the resources and the advantages which the State would obtain by diplomatic effort or otherwise in matters concerning petroleum.
2. To take whatever holdings were necessary in other petroleum-bearing regions, especially Central and South America, in order to maintain a balance of supplies.
3. To take up the problem of the Russian concessions.
4. To develop the petroleum resources of France, the colonies and the protectorates.

The company was to receive the support of the Government and the co-operation of its administrators. The Minister also insisted on the necessity to ensure permanent control of the company by French capital. This correspondence is the real genesis of the CFP; the same ideas were later cast into statutes.

Through its part ownership of the Turkish Petroleum Company, later the Iraq Petroleum Company, the French obtained access to large deposits of oil in Iraq. As this was the result of a diplomatic coup rather than steady industrial and commercial development, it was not easy to dispose of the large quantities potentially available. The CFP had no outlets and was obliged to create them; it could most easily do this in France. Mercier desired also to develop an advanced refining industry in France, counter to the prevailing practice for other European states; for strategic reasons the French Government shared this objective. Government intervention in the market at the time alternated between liberalism and *dirigisme*. After impropriating a monopoly of imports in 1917, the Government returned in 1921 to a free market system which permitted the international societies to strengthen their position and undertake a price war detrimental to the young French company. The majors even imposed a refining quota on the French companies. To help the CFP the French Government drew up some formidable legislation centred around three texts – the law of 10 January 1925 required that petroleum could only be imported by companies so authorized by the State; the law of 4 April 1926 attributes to the State a monopoly of crude imports and the law of 30 March 1928 defines the conditions under which this monopoly would be delegated to the companies accredited by the State. The completion of the legislation was prompted in late 1927 by the well at Baba Gurgur which revealed the first and largest Iraqi deposits and made it imperative for the CFP to prepare outlets.

The law of 30 March required special licences for the imports of crude, for refining, for imports of petroleum products and distribution. The licences for crude oil originally ran for 20 years and were known as A20s. The period was later reduced to 13 years (A13) and now stands at 10 (A10). The licences for refined products ran for three years (A3). The idea was to permit the public authorities considerable control over the sector whilst still leaving the companies an adequate guarantee of continuity to permit them confidently to invest in refinery and distribution capacity.

In return, the oil companies operating in France undertook to construct refining capacity in line with market trends and to build up strategic stock-piles. Later they were also obliged to transport two-thirds of their imports under the French flag.

The first allocation of quotas respected fairly strictly the established market shares of each society, with the exception of the CFP which received, in addition to its own quota, the right to refine the equivalent of one-quarter of the French consumption. This gave the company refined products far in excess of its own outlets, but ensured that its competitors would buy the surplus. The concept of the French policy is clear; French capital was to operate an oil company in the interest of the nation within limits defined by the State. In turn the State would do its utmost to favour the CFP at home. But among the shareholders of CFP were other distributors of refined products, sometimes working for the foreign oil companies. The insecurity of his control over the company led Ernest Mercier into great difficulties. In December 1928 he offered his resignation to Poincaré. To stabilize the company the State took a 25% holding. There were difficulties with Parliament and it was not until July 1931 that the State holding was agreed; by that time it had been increased to 35% with 40% voting rights. The French considered the oil policy to have been a success in the years preceding the War, as measured by the extent of the national involvement in the processing and handling of oil, e.g. the development of refining on French soil: 14 refineries in 1938 processing 8.0 million tonnes of oil compared with 17 much smaller refineries in 1926 processing 0.6 million tonnes; the proportion of oil shipped under the French flag (44%) and the size of the French oil fleet (446,000 tonnes[7]). CFP was responsible for about 50% of crude imports and 50% of all refining done in France, the remainder was controlled by the multinationals.

The issue of licences and the supervision of the petroleum industry was the responsibility of the *Office National des Combustibles Liquides* and later of the *Direction des Carburants* (DICA). But the strong international companies, which it would have been undesirable and indeed impossible to eliminate from the French market, were a different story from the protected 'subsistence capitalists' operating in the other energy sectors. The DICA never achieved a dominance of the oil sector comparable to the analogous directions for coal, electricity and gas.

B. The Time of Nationalizations

At the end of the War the conjunction of political and economic circumstances was favourable to a national co-ordination of energy supplies. The *Conseil National de la Résistance* demonstrated a marked political will to put the commanding heights of the economy into the hands of the State. Six years of armed conflict had gravely damaged plant in all the industries. A financial and technical reconstruction was imperative. The scarcity of fuel made rationing inevitable. The investments to equip new hydraulic stations or to compensate for the neglect of the coal mines between the wars could only come from the State. The logical support for nationalization seemed overwhelming.

The coal industry was nationalized by the law of 17 May 1946 creating nine *Houillères de Bassin* and the *Charbonnages de France* (CDF). The organizations of the first group were regional boards for production, exploitation and sale. The role of CDF was to co-ordinate and direct the ensemble. The group of institutions had a monopoly of the production and treatment of coal.

The gas and electricity supply industries were nationalized by the law of 8 April 1946. *Electricité de France* was assigned a monopoly of the transport of electricity, though not of its production; it acquired most of the generating plant and almost all of the distribution facilities. The original intention was that distribution would be entrusted eventually to particular public enterprises with geographically limited competence. This never happened. Organizations such as CDF and SNCF, which produced electricity for their own requirements, were permitted to sell their surplus to EDF. The *Compagnie Nationale du Rhône* was responsible for the development of hydraulic sites on the Rhône. The national interests in gas production, distribution and supply were assigned to GDF. Because of the existence of many pre-war joint gas-electricity supply companies and because of the strong interest, within the Ministry of Finances, in restricting expenditure, GDF and EDF were given a common personnel for distribution: *Electricité et Gaz de France* (EGF).

The senior management of these public enterprises came, naturally enough, from the great directorates of the State. They could provide men of far greater talent than could the fragmented industries. The policy of the public enterprises was defined by the newly formed *Commissariat du Plan* in its First Plan. The members of this body were also mainly *fonctionnaires*; they and the *fonctionnaires* in the technical directorates shared their priorities and ways of thinking with their colleagues among the senior management of the public enterprise who just the other day had also been *fonctionnaires*. This common background, plus the general atmosphere of working together for renewal, plus the fact that in such times priorities are relatively easy to define, assured a remarkable consensus of opinion. The First Plan, designed by these partners, was a bureaucratic plan; it was never even formally approved by Parliament.

The natural ease of relationships between the administration and the heads of public enterprise has persisted, although strains have arisen from conflicts of substance. In the post-war years, and really ever since, public enterprise has been more attractive than French capitalism for men of value and ambition. The generally higher standards in public enterprise, plus the weight of being a monopoly buyer, plus the historical determinism of the period of reconstruction combined to create a relationship between suppliers of equipment and public enterprise not unlike the *tutelle* which exists between the enterprise and the State. Whether the explanation is convincing or not, the facts about the paternalistic attitude to suppliers are well documented.[8]

The aim of the First Plan was simultaneously to reconstruct and modernize French industry. Coal, electricity, steel, cement, agricultural machinery and transportation were chosen as priority areas for rapid development. Production objectives were assigned to the various sectors, taking care to ensure consistency. Investment programmes and means of finance were proposed after studies as intensive as the limited time allowed. These served as a management framework for nationalized industries. The First Plan is generally considered to have been a great success.[9] It was possible to proceed in this way for two fundamental reasons: the French economy was a closed economy and the economic problem was an initial value problem. That the French economy was closed means simply that large quantities of imports were not available, and in any case there was little foreign exchange to pay for them, so that *internal coherence* was a valid and essential aim of the French economy, i.e. there should be enough coal to make the steel to make the tractors etc. A central planning system should be able to ensure coherence. It takes much management responsibility away from the individual organizations and invests it in the State. That the economic problem was an initial value problem means that the only conditions to meet were to use the available resources and ensure coherence; there was no question of the consumer showing his preference through the price mechanism and thereby requiring some sort of optimum solution in which the constraints both of resource availability and consumer demand were satisfied. Everything was so scarce that whatever could be made could be sold, and there was no means of assessing whether the directions of the Commissariat were substantially out of line with the preferences of the population.

The understanding amongst the enterprises and between them and the administration was reinforced by the relationship of the industries to one another in the economy of the country. All the energy that could be produced at this time was needed; there was essentially no competition for markets and by now a good deal of interdependence; for example the gas industry and the electricity supply industries relied on coal as a feedstock. It follows that the relationships between these industries were characterized by competition for resources, but not markets, and the requirement for congruence in their future plans. Competition for resources did not set energy industry against energy industry as effectively as competition for markets because it was not specific to energy, all industries were competing for the same resources. The requirement for congruence also put limits on the extent to which it would have been healthy for one energy industry to seek resources to the detriment of its supplier or customer.

In broad terms the nature of French public enterprise at this time was therefore akin to that of a branch of the administration. Economic competition was weak, direction was clear and government control tight.

The oil industry was dominated by foreign companies and not susceptible to the same treatment. It could not be made a priority area of the Plan, although the need for reconstruction was as great as elsewhere. Only three refineries in France were intact at the end of the War with a capacity of 1.5 million tonnes. To encourage redevelopment and modernization of the industry, the *Institut Francais du Pétrole* (IFP) was founded in 1944 with the functions of research, education and documentation. It had no control over real resources, but it could assist the initiatives of others. The general perspective of the Plan and its ideas on how the economy would grow, also encouraged the decision of the CFP to undertake the construction of large new refineries benefiting from economies of scale.

The oil industry in France was changing rapidly, and in responding to events in difficult circumstances a certain lack of logic crept into the institional structure. Some days before the War began a fairly large discovery of natural gas was made by the *Centre de Recherches de Pétrole du Midi* (CRPM). At the outbreak of war the *Régie Autonome des Pétroles* (RAP), a State enterprise, was created to succeed the CRPM. In 1941 the *Société National des Pétroles d'Aquitaine* (SNPA) was also created, with the mission of prospecting Aquitaine, except for the concessions attributed to the RAP. It was not possible for the CFP to perform this task because the company had been declared an *ennemi technique* by the U.K. on the grounds that its registered office was in occupied Paris; its interests had been sequestered in London.

After the War the political will of the Resistance to attribute the basic industries to the State could not resist the opportunity of establishing State control over a portion of the oil industry, however small. In October 1945, therefore, was created the *Bureau des Recherches de Pétrole* (BRP), a public enterprise charged with the task of elaborating a programme of exploration and putting it into practice for the exclusive interest of the nation. The BRP was allocated substantial annual subsidies from the specially constituted

Fonds de Soutien aux Hydrocarbones, whose revenues were obtained by a tax on the sales of petrol, gas oil and light fuel oil.

The CFP had not been a great commercial success before the War; it paid one dividend, in 1936. Moreover, it was engaged in difficult negotiations with the U.K. and American oil companies over compensation for its revenue lost during the War.[10] Whether it was these factors or the political will to nationalization which prevailed, the result was several new offshoots of an essentially unchanged French oil policy. Later, still more national companies were created, including Repal in which the Government of Algeria was represented. Investment companies (REPs) were instituted with the intention of mobilizing private capital for exploration. Their shareholders benefited from tax exemptions.

In this way the French Government continued its efforts to mobilize the resources of the country to secure petroleum supplies. Its strategy is in marked contrast to the principles of concentration observed in the other sectors.

The licensing system had been suspended at the outbreak of war; it was re-established in 1950 when the CFP had achieved adequate production levels. In the same year, the State decided to insist that companies possessing the authority both to distribute and refine petroleum should meet at least 90% of their refined product needs from French refineries. The scope of this ruling was large because the companies falling into this class supplied about 95% of the market. The point, of course, was to oblige oil companies to invest in refining capacity in France if they wished to be part of the French market. To give the international companies an incentive to be present on the French market, prices were permitted to be kept high and competition was restricted by the licensing system. The oil policy after 1939 was administered, and largely devised, by the *Direction des Carburants* (DICA) which had replaced the *Office National des Combustibles Liquides*. The DICA was a powerful body at the time.

One of the earliest of the post-war State energy institutions (contemporary with the BRP) was the *Commissariat à l'Energie Atomique* (CEA). It was created in October 1945 and given full responsibility for the promotion and co-ordination of every aspect of nuclear energy, both military and commercial. In practice, its priority was to develop the necessary scientific and technical structures, and for this reason it had more freedom of action than the commercial institutions.

The different structures of the three sectors co-existed peaceably because there was little competition and few tensions.

C. Competition Arrives

The harmonious relationships which existed between the energy industries were disturbed by the events of 1957/58. These years are of critical importance for European energy policies; they are the years when it became impossible not to accept that large quantities of petroleum could be produced from the

Middle East and carried to Europe at a cost much lower than that of mining indigenous coal. The events are well known;[11] briefly they are as follows. A mild recession coincided with a clement winter; the consumption of energy fell for the first time since the War, but imports of coal and oil continued to increase. The final agony was that a wet summer in 1958 allowed exceptional production of hydraulic electricity. Consequently, the effect of the slight fall in energy consumption was amplified many times on the indigenous coal industry.

It was impossible not to accept that the difficulties of the coal industry were the consequence of structural changes. Economies of scale in the oil industry were reinforced by inevitable pressures on the cartel of oil majors to close the gap between price and the cost of Middle East oil. The operating environments of all the energy industries were modified by this penetration, but the most greatly disturbed was the coal industry which was in direct competition with oil for the bulk fuel market. The important question of the time was: how far to let oil penetrate the market to the cost of social stability and political security.

It has been argued by Professor Martin that France had insufficient control over the international oil companies to give systematic aid to the State dominated sector:[3] 'In the absence of effective control over investments in petroleum the public powers have never mastered the rhythm of substitution of energy sources.'

Drawing on the work of Saab, Martin argues that restrictive as the licensing system may have been, it in no way interfered with the fundamental determinants of oil policy, the rate of growth of supplies, buying and selling prices, and rates of profit.[12] As a result there was no control over investment because it was almost entirely self-financed.

This analysis is largely true. The State in principle could have controlled part of the behaviour of the companies by restricting the allocation of licences. But this would have antagonized the major oil companies on whom the State was relying for a secure and stable supply of oil. This basic weakness in the negotiating position of the State has always prevented it from using the legislation of 1928 to its full effect; it has always been careful to favour French companies whilst still permitting the internationals to grow modestly. This procedure has always been possible up to now because the total market has grown.

The argument that France could not satisfactorily solve the coal problem without exercising a politically undesirable degree of control over the oil companies is therefore reasonable. But it is not enough to explain French policy, because they never tried – even in an imperfect way. All European countries offered some degree of protection to their indigenous coal industry; France offered less than any other country. She was the only European country not to put an excise tax on heavy fuel oil; and she even, in 1968, made the Value Added Tax on heavy fuel oil deductible, so that the ex-refinery price of these fuels became the lowest in the EEC. Relative to French coal, therm for therm, the price of heavy fuel oil fell from a factor of 2.3 higher in 1958, to 1.2 in 1973, a reduction of 50%.

France cheerfully embraced the penetration of oil. She did so because a policy of cheap oil suited three powerful groups for three quite different reasons. It suited the *Ministère des Finances* because it brought low prices and demanded no investment from the State. It suited the *Ministère de l'Industrie* because it engendered an international competitive manufacturing industry. It benefited a coalition of Gaullist politicians and oil company executives (not always distinguishable) who perceived an opportunity of creating an extensive and secure structure of oil supplies based on French crude. Let us take these points singly.

The *Ministère des Finances*, like any organization responsible for preserving financial equilibrium, has a near time-horizon. Its priorities are, to keep the external account in balance, to keep the public accounts in balance and to stabilize, if not to reduce, the price index. To an *Inspecteur des Finances*, a cheap petroleum policy was the answer to his prayer. It provided for low cost sources of energy; it made almost no demands on the public purse for investment capital; it assured that the cost of energy in use fell in constant francs.

The *Ministère de l'Industrie* was worried about competition. France had a well-established tradition of non-competitive industries protected by import tariffs, price fixing cartels, tax evasion and like devices. The imminent entry of France into the Common Market and the consequent regime of decreasing barriers to trade was therefore a source of great concern to the State. The Third Plan, published in 1959, makes this point in general terms: 'The period covered by the Third Plan is one of fundamental importance in preparing the French economy for European competition.'

The Minister was not the only worried man. French industrialists were conscious of their weakness, especially the men running the traditional heavy industry. It was precisely in this sector that the links between the politicians and the grand old families of France were strongest. The lobbying was persuasive.

The third element of this triangle of forces was a coalition of the leading politicians with the French oil company executives. The compatibility of their expectations requires some explanation.

The results of the apparently disorganized, but enthusiastic, encouragement by the State of exploration for petroleum were extremely fruitful. In France itself, the SNPA discovered deposits of oil at Lacq in 1949 and then two years later the much more important deposits of gas which lay underneath. In 1951, Esso discovered another small oilfield at Parentis. But the greatest success was the Sahara where large deposits of oil and gas began to be discovered after 1956. Guidelines for the exploitation of these discoveries were given by the *code pétrolier Saharien*. This edict provided for an equal division of profits between the State (France) and the public and private investors. The code also assigned to the State the priority of supply from the franc zone.

The brilliant success of these explorations in the Sahara posed the problem of how to dispose of the oil. As a result of previous policies, France was endowed with a well-developed refining structure. Technically the obvious solution was to sell the oil on the French market. De Gaulle recognized that international independence in all its forms was an essential requirement of political influence; autonomy in energy supplies was much to his liking. The other leading politicians of the day were dedicated Gaullists and acquiesced. It is also significant that the top men in the State oil industry and administration had been put there by de Gaulle and shared his political perspective. The greatest of these was M. Pierre Guillaumat. M. Guillaumat has undoubtedly been a most pervasive and effective influence on all French energy policy. He was a Gaullist from the first; after the Liberation he became Director of the DICA, then Commissaire at the CEA. During the war in Algeria he was *Ministre des Armées*. He was frequently referred to as the *éminence grise* of General de Gaulle in the energy sector, and as the Minister for Oil. He appointed men of similar outlook to strategic posts throughout the industry. Later his protégés penetrated the other energy industries; they have continued to encourage like-minded younger men. As a result, a distinct 'Gaullist memory effect' is detectable throughout the energy industries. The alliance of this coalition of politicians and oil companies with the *Ministères de l'Industrie* and *des Finances* was irresistible.

Some of the oil from the Sahara was sold to international companies refining in France, but to supplement that channel, a new State organization, *l'Union Générale des Pétroles* (UGP) was created, jointly owned by the State producers of crude. In 1960 it organized, with Caltex, a distribution network with a market-share of 5%. In 1962, the year in which Algeria achieved independence, the production of crude oil from the franc zone was 23 Mt of which 17 Mt came from the Sahara; it supplied half the needs of the nation.

The independence of Algeria initiated the long negotiations that would end years later with a dramatic redefinition of relationships. But for the time being the validity of the concept of *pétrole franc* was not in doubt. The Treaty of Evian was signed in March 1962. Those clauses of the agreement which related to oil proposed that Algeria would agree to give priority to French oil companies, in the allocation of permits to prospect and produce, for a period of 10 years. In fact, French diplomacy was later able to exact an agreement for 15 years with the possibility of revision at the end of the first five; this was signed in 1965.

The public powers imposed another element of the policy of *pétrole franc* in 1963 when the licences for refining were renewed. They obliged all refineries on French soil to take a part of the crude produced by ERAP in Algeria, thereby assuring another link between France and French crude.

The objectives of French oil policy were restated by an inter-ministerial Council in November 1964. The producing capacity controlled by French companies had to be permanently equal to French consumption. The origin of the production should be diversified as far as possible. French enterprises should keep more than half the national market in refining and in distribution and should penetrate abroad. These principles were confirmed by the *Ministre de l'Industrie* before the National Assembly in November 1968.

The objectives were largely reached. In 1969, the French companies were producing 80 Mt against a national consumption of 70 Mt; they had slightly more than 50% of the refining and distribution in France and exports of finished products exceeded imports by 14.2 Mt to 5.2 Mt.[7] An indication of the relative prices of selected fuels in France during the last 20 years is shown in Fig. 2. The indicator taken for coal is the average price at Rouen; the indicator for heavy fuel oil is the price at the refinery wall. It is clear how, as a result of the policy of cheap oil, the gap between the prices of coal and heavy fuel oil widened up to 1973 and how phenomenally cheap were oil products compared to other comparable fuels.

The consequences of the policy of cheap oil were multitudinous. The most important were:

the regression of the coal industry;
the frustration of natural gas;
a suspension of interest in commercial nuclear power;
the conversion to oil of EDF;
a complete disregard for conservation;
the destruction of complicity between the State enterprises;
the destruction of the organic union between State and enterprise.

The first five items of this list are technical consequences; the last two are institutional. Let us take them one by one.

The Third Plan had proposed a target of 65 Mt of production by 1965, compared to the actual production of 60 Mt in 1959. The Plan had only been published a few months when the parlous state of the coal industry and the recognition of the consequences of a low cost energy policy made it necessary to prepare a special supplementary plan for the coal industry. This, the Jeanneney Plan, proposed a rapid regression of the industry, and suggested an objective of 53 Mt in 1965. It offered a little protection for coal by requiring oil companies to restrict price reductions from the official price to no more than 5%; this provision was lifted in 1963 as part of the Stabilization Plan, thereafter allowing the oil companies full licence. In the same year the miners reacted violently to the regression of the industry. A long strike followed. The Government instituted a 'Round Table' between themselves, the enterprise and the unions. The State relieved the industry of some of their financial charges, but also fixed an enormous programme of regression, known as the *Plan de la Table Ronde*. The deficit of the industry continued to grow. In 1968 another special plan, *Le Plan Bettencourt*, confirmed the rhythm of regression.

The penetration of oil gravely frustrated attempts to extend the use of natural gas in France. GDF has never had access to the low cost reserves enjoyed by the British Gas Corporation, but this material difficulty was

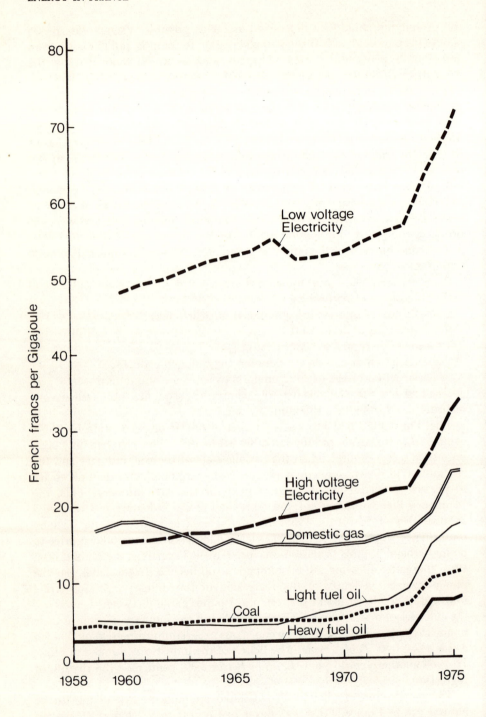

Fig. 2. The evolution of energy prices in France in French francs per Gigajoule.

reinforced by the policy of cheap oil. The low profit margins and slow rate of growth of sales were inadequate to finance the heavy investments required. By the late '60s, GDF was heavily in debt. The *Ministère des Finances* imposed a programme of financial recovery which was successful, but at the expense of investment; the consequences extend to this day.

Nuclear energy became something of a backwater in France. The interest of private industry was muted, what development did take place was non-commercial and largely financed or subsidized by the State. Consequently the arm of the State within this secondary sector became extremely powerful. The CEA was able to impose its designs on the construction industry and had the capacity to elaborate those designs in great detail. The role of the construction industries was reduced to carrying out given instructions and they were unable to develop the expertise and understanding which would have permitted them to have offered the reactor designs on export markets. Considerable resentment against the CEA developed within the construction industry.

EDF was at first unaffected by the penetration of oil. It thought not in terms of particular markets, but in terms of its growth rate of 7–8% a year which had prevailed since the war and which it had come to regard as a natural law. Just as long as it could keep up that rate it was happy. The penetration of oil into Europe was led by sales of petrol for the automobile industry; in refining crude oil to petrol, large volumes of heavy fuel oil are produced concomitantly. This product had no market at the time other than to large boilers for power generation; it was therefore bound to be sold just below the thermally equivalent price of coal. EDF's first reaction was to launch a programme of fuel oil fired generating plant; thirty-seven 250 MW(e) generating sets were ordered and put into service in the period 1956–1974. All the sets up to 1963 had been designed to burn coal. Thereafter, everyone was to burn fuel oil, with the exception of two units on the coalfields. Subsequently CDF negotiated an agreement with EDF to the effect that the annual burn of French coal would reach 15 Mt by 1975, but it was later revised and in the event EDF burnt less than half that figure. EDF began to look at the nuclear programme with an increasingly jaundiced eye. Obsessed now by the criterion of least cost, the enterprise became more and more convinced that the gas graphite line of development being followed by the CEA would have less chance of competing economically with the light water reactors developed in the U.S.A. The last remarks bring us up to the institutional consequences of the penetration of oil.

EDF was the main customer of CDF and the main potential customer for CEA technology. Its views on what its suppliers had to offer did not make for friendly relations. The dispute with CDF was straightforward. That with the CEA had limitless ramifications.

The CEA had developed their technology with great dedication. To understand the full extent of their chagrin it is necessary briefly to review the history of the programme. In 1952, the Chamber of Deputies voted a five-year programme of research and development of the natural uranium gas graphite reactor (UNGG), and the first elements of a reprocessing factory; this was to be implemented by CEA. In 1956, EDF began its first nuclear programme comprising three reactors of the UNGG type, Chinon 1, 2, 3. In 1958, Framatome, a firm owned by Schneider, took out a licence from Westinghouse to manufacture the PWR. In 1960, EDF undertook an experimental programme of diversification and decided to construct a light water reactor at Chooz; Framatome received the order for the nuclear steam supply system. In 1963, EDF undertook a second UNGG programme, Saint Laurent 1, 2 and Bugey 1. After this date the UNGG design became the object of steadily increasing attack by EDF not only for the reasons mentioned, but also because the vast bulk of experience of nuclear reactors in the world lay with the LWRs, so that in the event of trouble the costs of retrieving the situation would be shared amongst many more participants. French heavy industry also favoured the American designs because these offered more scope for export. The improved export prospects were the consequence of three factors:

1. The determination of CEA, as already noted, to maintain complete control over the details of design of the UNGG reactors and the habit of EDF to assure the architecture of its own stations impeded the industry from obtaining 'turn key' experience in the UNGG design. With the LWRs for which they had licences, both Schneider (PWR) and *La Compagnie Générale d'Electricité* (BWR) hoped to construct a trading position in France that would facilitate export.
2. The apparent superior economic viability of the LWR designs and particularly the reduced work needed on site.
3. The dominant position in the market already established by American designs.

The CEA took up a position against the EDF and the construction industry and in favour of their own UNGG designs. There had always been tension between EDF and CEA as a result partly of overlap in their functions and partly of their attempts to control new areas of responsibility as they arose. The original statutes of the two bodies did not assign responsibility for the construction of nuclear stations. A first CEA-EDF protocol in 1956 gave EDF responsibility for the construction of nuclear stations to CEA's design; this led to interminable disputes over, for example, materials. There were also differences of objective: EDF claimed a duty to cut generating costs even if that meant using American technology. The CEA advocated that energy policy should be guided by wider considerations; in this they received top level political support even from de Gaulle himself who was completely opposed to the construction of American designs. When the Director-General of EDF, M. A. Decelle, resigned in 1967, this was widely attributed to his frequently stated belief in the superior merits of American designs, and to the exhaustion of de Gaulle's patience.

The Government sought advice on the choice of reactor from a Consultative Commission, known as the *Commission Consultative pour la Pro-*

duction d'Electricité d'Origine Nucléaire – the *Commission PEON*. The composition and lengthy deliberations of this committee are described in detail in Chapter VI. EDF, with a large pool of able engineers and technologists, operated extremely skilfully within the PEON Commission – as it does within other important committees – to ensure that the decision of the group incorporated the views of the enterprise.

The PEON Commission report,[13] published in December 1968, was couched ambiguously, but essentially favoured the LWRs. It concluded that after Fessenheim 1, 2, at that time planned as UNGG stations, there would be no imminent need for further such stations. The LWR design was thought to provide the cheapest electricity and the Commission recommended building a 600 MW(e) prototype. The report is permeated with discussion of the prospects for exporting reactors and fuel reprocessing plant, matters which were then discussed with less caution than now; it is clear there were an important consideration of nuclear policy.

But de Gaulle was not the man to be unduly influenced by the recommendations of technicians if they went against his political aims. The final obstacle to the LWR programme still remained. Senior French administrators (*les grands commis de l'Etat*), laid siege to de Gaulle and, it is now believed, were on the point of convincing him when he was defeated in the referendum in 1969. The new President, M. Georges Pompidou, was easier meat; by 1970 he was convinced of the need to manufacture American designs. The orders for Fessenheim 1 and 2 were changed to PWRs and given to Framatome.

The last in the list of consequences attributed to the policy of cheap oil was the collapse of the organic union between the State enterprise and the State. In fact, this change in relationships had far wider origins although they were exacerbated by the disorder in the energy markets. The apparatus of control in public enterprise by Ministries is extensive. It is described later. For the immediate purpose all that matters is that they were employed by the State in the 1960s in a most aggressive fashion. This assertion is well documented.[2,14,15] Control was exercised principally by the Ministry of Finance. The power of this department was, and still is, legendary in France. M. Alain Peyrefitte, frequently a Minister under de Gaulle, Pompidou, and recently recalled to the present Government, claims:[16]

> The administrative omnipotence has two stages. There is that of the administration over all that which is not administration. And then there is that exercised by the (Ministry of) Finance on the rest of the administration. The departments which make others tremble, tremble themselves before the rue de Rivoli – who tremble before no one.

Peyrefitte described the considerable control exercised by the Ministry officials over the spending Ministers even after the resources have been attributed to the spending Ministry in the budget. M. J. Chirac, a very experienced French politician and ex-Prime Minister, has also claimed that the State no longer dominates its administration, and has drawn attention to the fact, as he sees it, of the disproportionate power of the Ministry of Finance and inadequate response to the political direction.[17]

One of the institutions most restless under the prevailing regime was EDF, and its complaints mainly concerned the restrictions placed upon it by the Ministry of Finances. One of the matters which attracted most attention was the control, essentially by the Ministry of Finances, of the salaries of the personnel of EDF. It led eventually to a strike in which the supply of electricity was cut. Similarly, input prices and tariffs were fixed by Ministries, either exclusively or predominantly by that of Finances; permission to borrow funds from national or international markets was required from the *Fonds de Développement Economique et Social* (FDES), an institution presided over and controlled by the Ministry of Finance.

These relationships were not untypical of those characterizing public enterprise and government departments. There is, however, one aspect, small but significant, which is particular to EDF. EDF regularly showed an annual growth rate of 7% or more in electricity sales; this roughly meant a doubling every 10 years. As a consequence EDF was obliged to finance every 10 years as many new stations as existed at the beginning of those 10 years, and to replace obsolete plant. This programme called for ever-increasing injections of capital. The response of the Ministry of Finances was that one way to reduce the requirement was to lower the growth rate; it was hostile therefore to all advertising and aggressive commercial behaviour on the part of EDF. As a consequence, the *Contrôleur d'Etat* was careful to restrict the allocations for advertising to 0.5% of the value of total sales.[18] On one occasion a commercial campaign was stopped dead on instructions from the rue de Rivoli. This was especially irritating for EDF who even at that time perceived their greatest opportunities for expansion as lying with sales of electricity for thermal uses. This largely new market could not be penetrated without an extensive and aggressive selling campaign that was denied to them.

The whole question of the direction of public enterprise in France was the subject of a Working Party set up in April 1966 by the Prime Minister, and chaired by M. S. Nora. The need for this study was attributed to concern for the competitiveness of French industry in the environment of the Common Market, concern with the finances of public enterprises and the dissatisfaction of the public enterprises with the existing and tiresome system. The study[19] confirmed that effective power to control the affairs of public enterprise was moving consistently towards the Government, partly to the technical *tutelle*, but mainly to the Ministry of Finances. The Working Party made many recommendations on the whole nature of the relationships involved, but the most essential requirement was seen to be a greater autonomy of public enterprise in pricing policy, salaries and investment. In return the industries would be subjected to more vigorous criteria of management and self-financing.

26

Specifically, it was proposed to re-establish the industries' finances by setting prices at a level that reflected true costs and eliminating the need for transfer payments from the State, and also to allocate clearly the responsibilities of the technical *tutelle*, the financial *tutelle* and the enterprise. The State could ask the enterprise to undertake certain actions for the sake of wider social and political considerations, but the enterprise was entitled to be reimbursed. Responsibilities were allocated as follows:[20]

the enterprise was responsible for developing markets and making best use of its assets;

the technical *tutelle* had the responsibility for elaborating sector policies, particularly in energy and transport;

the financial *tutelle* had the responsibility for reconciling sector policies and maintaining the equilibrium of the economy.

EDF, which had participated vociferously in the protests against the existing system, was chosen as an experiment in the new order, both for the new salary policy and new contractual relationships between the State and public enterprise. In the negotiations leading up to the agreement of the *Contrat de Programme*, a principal objective of EDF was to obtain the right and the duty to promote their product and to pursue an effective commercial policy.[18] By this means EDF hoped to increase sales sufficiently to provide more of its own finance and so to assure its own continuing and growing autonomy. This objective was vigorously resisted by the Ministry of Finance and according to M. P. Delouvrier, the President of EDF, it took six months to agree to this aspect of the contract.[18]

The contract was eventually signed at the end of 1970 and covered the years 1971–1975, which were the subject of the Sixth Plan. The results of this new independence of management were expressed in the official vision of EDF of the 'great commercial turning'. The aim of this initiative was to capture new markets, particularly the domestic space heating market, on the basis of the growing price of oil and the qualities of electricity – cleanliness, convenience, absence of pollution, the possibility of heating each room to the required extent – combined with the relative fall of electricity prices. The campaign comprised modifications to tariffs to encourage bulk users, cultivation of relationships with groups acting on the interface between the electricity supplier and user, e.g. architects, equipment designers and distributors, town planners, and a vigorous advertising campaign with the slogan *tout électrique*.

The severance of the apron strings for which EDF fought so fiercely was forced upon the CEA.[21] After it had been decided to construct American designs of reactor, then the function of the CEA changed; previously the largest part of its commercial work had been directed to research, development and design associated with the UNGG reactor line. The CEA at the time contained many people who were disconsolate with the decision; section heads down to research workers shared a resentment against the selection of foreign technology and a fear of the consequences; the unions were strongly opposed. President Pompidou, making fruitful use of the right to appoint directly the senior positions in French public enterprise, chose as the senior administrator M. André Giraud, a strong and brilliant man, and assigned him the mission of converting the CEA to an economic institution with commercial objectives and a relatively small spending section. The internal structure of CEA was changed and given the form of a central kernel surrounded by seven units each with a relatively homogeneous task and subject to different criteria for good management as became the wide variety of matters under the control of the CEA. The seven units covered radiological security, scientific research, nuclear materials, industrial co-operation on non-nuclear matters, programmes of national interest, industrial application of nuclear energy and military applications. It was foreseen that certain operational units might take the form of private companies in which CEA would have a participation. The organization was further modified by 1975 by the creation of subsidiaries in which the activities with conflicting management needs could each find the best working environment. The *Institut de Recherche Fondamentale* (IRF) was formed to group the units working in basic research, an *Institut de Sûreté et Protection* was formed to cover safety matters and, in August 1975, the CEA received authority from the Government to constitute its activities relating to the full cycle into a new private subsidiary, 100% owned by CEA, called the *Compagnie générale des Matières Nucléaires* (Cogema). The purposes of creating Cogema were to facilitate the management of the CEA's industrial activities on a commercial basis, to provide the State with an instrument for ensuring all the stages in the provision of nuclear fuel and to permit France to enter as easily as possible into international markets both for the purchase of raw materials and the sale of products.[22]

A similar trend to independence can be detected in the oil industry. In order to strengthen the instruments available for the execution of the Algerian oil policy, the functions of the existing public groups, BRP, RAP, UGP, were assigned to a new single public organization, *l'Entreprise de Recherches et d'Activités Pétrolières* (ERAP). ERAP, like its forebears, was created by ministerial decree, it was never voted by Parliament. Credit for the conception and construction of ERAP is universally given to the man who filled the posts of *Président* and *Directeur-Général* for its first 11 years – M. P. Guillaumat.

The analogy between this change in the institutional structure of the oil industry and the later changes in the CEA is striking. Immediately after the war, new institutions were established to keep the State interest in oil and nuclear energy, BRP and CEA. In 1966, the BRP was transformed into a State enterprise to operate in a competitive, international sector; nine years later the commercial interests of CEA were assigned to a new similar institution.

The relations between the State and the major oil companies continued on much the same lines. The licensing system was an irritant to the companies compensated by the high profits on the French market and by the security which the system offered. The issue of licences always anticipated the growth of the oil market. The rapid penetration of oil which was unforeseen by the architects of the Fourth and Fifth Plans was not hindered by any corresponding myopia at the DICA. Prices were controlled, but at levels determined by the world market. Investments were financed without State funds and were not controlled. Again, the Fourth and Fifth Plans grossly underestimated the growth in refinery capacity. The Plans were of no consequence; the oil companies made the running. The pragmatic relationship was lucidly defined by M. A. Giraud, then *Directeur* of the DICA. He explained that the law of 1928 'recognized in a realistic fashion the prime importance of the oil companies and delegated to them the exercise of these activities within a flexible framework, reduced to the essential, in which the State and the companies have discovered their interest'.[23]

The essential process of this period was, then, the almost uncontrolled progression of the oil companies with the connivance of the actors mentioned. The institutional consequences within the energy sector were the emergence of ERAP as an aggressive and independent new force, and the liberation of EDF and the CEA as a reaction to this conjuncture. GDF and CDF, in deficit and timidly managed, remained close to the State.

D. The Nucleocrats

1. DETERMINING INFLUENCES

The fourth stage in the evolution of relationships is characterized by an increasingly clear perception of the difficulties and uncertainties of maintaining cheap and secure oil supplies, and by the emergence of new ideas about the structures preferred for French industry if it were to flourish in an ever more international environment, and perhaps also by the political changes following the departure of the founder and animator of the Fifth Republic.

Awareness of the dangers of relying excessively on oil appear to have been more seriously entertained at high political and administrative levels in France during the late 1960s than they were elsewhere in Europe, and certainly the events in Algeria in 1970 and 1971 gave the French a first-hand experience of the weakness of the position of the consuming nations, and caused them to perceive the beginning of the end more clearly than did other European nations; the Algerians had, of course, 'eaten' all the foreign companies successively between 1962 and 1970, leaving only the French companies CFP and Elf-ERAP. The French companies were eaten last; to be chosen last was, in the eyes of M. P. Guillaumat, a partial success.[24]

Algerian initiatives to control its own petroleum deposits began in 1963 with the formation of its own national oil company, Sonatrach. This company amicably acquired the distribution network belonging to BP, and it then nationalized Esso and Mobil as, or ostensibly as, a political reprisal for alleged

American collusion with Israel in the Six-Day War. The first nibble at France came during the serious disorders in Paris in May 1968; Algeria took the opportunity to nationalize 14 French oil companies involved in distribution of refined products. In the following 10 days, another 45 French companies, non-energy, were nationalized. Détente prevailed and indemnities were agreed for the nationalized companies.

The agreement at Evian in 1965 had foreseen for 1 January 1969 a re-examination of the fiscal claims relating to petroleum. The royalties going to Algeria were considerably lower, on average about half, than those obtained by other producers. Negotiations were postponed throughout 1969, because of France's internal changes, but as soon as M. Pompidou became President he sent the Minister of Foreign Affairs, M. M. Schumann, to Algeria to open negotiations. The delegation from the French Government proposed a reduction in royalties of 4 cents the barrel, in reply to the Algerian proposal of an increase of 57 cents.[25] Negotiations made no progress, and in July 1970 the Algerian Government fixed the reference price of oil unilaterally. In February 1971, Boumedienne announced the nationalization of 51% of the oil production and 100% of gas production, promising France that her security of supply would not be affected. CFP and ERAP withdrew their personnel from Algeria and tried to organize a boycott of Algerian oil.

The French Government approached the U.S. Government for help in seeing that U.S. companies did not ship oil from the French concessions; it also created problems for Algeria in international bodies such as the Common Market and the World Bank. But Sonatrach proved equal to the task of managing the French companies' production equipment and, although the boycott was largely successful, eventually wider political considerations prevailed and the French Government retreated. It did so by announcing that the position of the Algerian Government made the pursuit of oil negotiations between the Governments purposeless, and that, therefore, it would be up to Algeria to talk to the oil companies directly. This formula permitted the companies to salvage what they could. CFP had a comparatively small interest in Algeria and had plenty of resources elsewhere in the world, which they could develop to replace Algerian oil; they were the first to approach Algeria. ERAP had a much larger interest in Algeria; moreover, it had fewer resources elsewhere, and importantly its President and Director-General, M. Pierre Guillaumat, had a strong personal commitment to the policy of *pétrole franc* and to the whole French petroleum policy of which ERAP's presence in Algeria was the pivot and the clearest symbol of success. M. Guillaumat's disappointment was evident.[24] Nevertheless, ERAP eventually signed a settlement, also in September 1971. This account illustrates the way in which the men determining France's foreign policy worked with the French oil companies, especially ERAP. Oil supply is an important aspect of French foreign policy and the Government and the companies worked fairly openly together to ensure success; there came a time, however, when wider considerations of foreign policy intervened, and the Government conceded, leaving the companies isolated and obliged to suffer privations for the fact of being seen as agents for the State.

The events following the October War are well known and do not require elaboration; they undoubtedly reinforced French fears and stimulated their endeavours to develop new secure sources of energy, particularly nuclear. But it was the events of 1970/71 which mark the change in French attitudes, later events really only reinforced the changes set in motion at that time. The other great determining influence on institutional relationships was the prevailing conception of French industrial policy.

One of the best accounts of the preoccupations of the French Government in industrial policy is to be found in an interview which the Prime Minister, M. J. Chaban-Delmas, gave to the business magazine *L'Expansion*.[26] French business was perceived as being increasingly vulnerable to foreign competition, partly because of material superiority of organization and size of unit, and partly because of the independent, aggressive competitive spirit of foreign firms in contrast to the less self-reliant French firms seeking, and provided with, extensive State direction and protection. The aims of the industrial policy were to rectify these disadvantageous operating conditions and attitudes. The means employed varied from sector to sector, according to the precise environment of particular industries and the degree of competition and *regroupement* so far attained, but the general principles were to eradicate the paternalistic *tutelle* of the State, to restructure industry into larger units that would be competitive nationally and internationally and then to sell abroad. The final structure would consist of one or perhaps two great national firms for each sector, for example Pechiney-Ugine and Penarroya-Mokta in non-ferrous metals, and Rhône-Poulenc and ERAP-CFP in chemistry. In practice, the structure tended more and more to single firms dominating sectors as the great firms tended to divide tasks between them. It was at the time envisaged that there should be two constructors of reactors, CGE and Framatome, in order to preserve competition, but in this sector as well a monopoly eventually developed. An especially interesting remark by M. Chaban-Delmas was that: 'In any case, the creation of purely national groups can only be a stage, leaving these groups themselves to negotiate balanced international alliances.' Competitiveness was to be preserved by competition with foreign firms or other international groups or non-European organizations.

The heavy electrical manufacturing industry and turbine manufacturers were a prime target of this policy; three of each shared a French market considerably smaller than that of the U.K. or West Germany served by only two firms. The attempt by Westinghouse to dominate the French market through the purchase of Jeumont-Schneider was prevented by a Government decision; it preferred to constitute European ensembles around two poles: *Compagnie Electro-Mécanique* (CEM) with Brown-Boveri, and Alsthom-CGE, which was also to seek European alliances. Again in the event a monopoly of State contracts developed. Similarly, much of the heavy mechanical engineering industry was grouped into a new ensemble, Creusot-Loire. Part of the rationale for encouraging foreign alliances was to facilitate access to foreign capital. The work on the Sixth Plan had shown a substantial gap between the financial needs of industry to carry out the objectives and the money available in the French economy.

There can be little doubt that the political priorities of President Georges Pompidou contributed greatly to the importance placed on industrialization, and that his attitudes and business experience shaped the form of the policy and assisted its outcome. De Gaulle devoted much of his effort to the industrialization of France, even though it appears that the task bored him, because he recognized it as a necessary basis for his aspirations in international affairs. His nationalist outlook would have certainly directed French industrial policy down different channels. Pompidou had a consuming interest in French industrial policy. Peyrefitte, Pompidou's Minister of Justice in his first government, attributes to Pompidou, a few days after his election, the words:[16] 'We have an objective which must dominate the others: to make of France a great industrial nation. It is within our reach. Let us achieve it without dispersing our efforts.'

There is a persistent rumour among French officials that President Pompidou made extensive use of his relationships with the banking world, gained while he was a Director of the Rothschild Bank, to encourage the French banks to put up money for the restructuring of French industry, especially in strategic sectors, and for the funding of State spending programmes in these sectors, e.g. the nuclear programme. Given the circumstances, there is a good chance that this belief is true.

The events following the October War again reinforced the existing trend. Although not specifically threatening French industry, they were seen, especially by the small group of people responsible for co-ordinating French industrial policy as a particularly striking example of the sort of gross dislocations of the world industrial and economic system which were likely to become increasingly frequent and which only large firms with international markets and international alliances could withstand.

2. THE EFFECTS ON POWER RELATIONSHIPS WITHIN THE INDUSTRY

The material effect of the crises in oil supply were to embarrass the national oil companies and to rejoice the newly emerging EDF-CEA axis. The eventual effect of the rise in oil prices was to depress demand for products well below the refining capacity. The theoretical action of market forces should drive prices down to short-run marginal costs. It did. That itself is bad enough, because there is no way of covering the fixed costs. But in order to preserve established positions, the oil companies are now actually selling below short-run marginal cost, thereby adding an operating loss to the unrecovered capital charges. The problem is especially bad for the European oil companies which have generally poor access to the protected markets outside Europe. Both ELF and CFP have large and increasing debts. They are obliged to borrow to cover operating losses and therefore to cut down on investment. Their problems have caused the *Ministère des Finances* to take an active part in the life of the company; the Ministry obviously stresses the need for financial recovery. The companies cannot therefore prospect for new resources to supply the nation – their *raison d'être*. The State could provide finance, and has done so, but only in small quantities.

The State could also help by using the law of 1928 to restrict the activities of the majors. This has been suggested several times by M. Chalandon, the President of ELF.[27] The Government has not so far fallen to the temptation; it is unlikely to do so for fear of upsetting its European partners or antagonizing the major oil companies on whom it depends for secure and stable supplies.

The genesis of the nuclear programme precedes the crisis in oil supplies. It can be dated to EDF's vision in about 1970 of the 'great commercial turning', consolidated by the Teheran-Tripoli agreements, the choice of LWRs and the restructuring of the CEA. The programme was simply turned up a notch after the October War.

3. THE BEHAVIOUR OF PUBLIC ENTERPRISE

The objectives of public enterprise in this period have been perceptively analysed by Professor J. M. Martin.[2] He asserts that the essential principle of their behaviour is to control the environment in which they operate. Specifically, they seek to extend their control upstream to secure supplies, and downstream to secure markets, to ensure control of future technologies which they could use or which threaten them, and finally to obtain access to means of finance that would remove them as far as possible from the grip of the State. All these four functions immediately after the War, if they had been perceived at all, would have been thought of as the functions of government, suppliers and fate.

The proposition needs two qualifications. First, some companies have been better able to achieve their objectives than others, depending on the power relationship in the industry. Second, the influences which formed the *ideal* of independent institutions modifying their environment have paradoxically led *in reality* to a strengthening of some aspects of control. The conflict is particularly evident in EDF; the nuclear programme has so indebted the enterprise that the *contrat de programme* was rescinded and not renewed and the control of the *Ministère des Finances* has been re-established. It is essential to distinguish between the ambitions of the enterprise, which are as described above, and the constraints, one of which is a contingent submission to old controls.

The CEA is the best example of this new behaviour. By means of its participation in joint enterprises with private firms and foreign capital, it now controls the whole nuclear industry, from uranium prospecting, mining, ore processing, enrichment, fuel element fabrication, to reprocessing. It also has considerable influence within the reactor construction industry. Let us examine its activities within the four functions described. The first function is to secure its supplies. For the CEA this means, in the first place, the access to uranium ore, and through Cogema, usually in association with foreign partners, it is active all over the world.[28]

France has significant uranium resources of her own, but far from enough to sustain her nuclear programme. The chief priority of the CEA is to acquire access to reserves in old French colonies still under the influence of Paris and considered politically secure. The uranium is not actually styled *uranium national* or *uranium franc*, but the motive is identical to the mainspring of French petroleum policy in the 'sixties. Considerable French diplomatic effort goes into maintaining influence in the colonies as demonstrated by the recent airlift by France of troops to Zaire. In April 1974 there was trouble in one of the CEA's most successful prospecting areas – Niger. The President, Diori Hamani, tried to nationalize the uranium deposits and was overthrown by Lt.-Col. Kountche. It is alleged that France had a hand in the *coup d'état*.[29]

Details of French mining activities in Niger are given in Chapter III. Cogema is prospecting also in Gabon, Mauritania, Canada, the U.S.A. and Indonesia in association with the states and various private firms; it holds an exploration permit in Senegal and mining rights in several Australian provinces. Cogema hopes that its initiatives should permit it to market about 5,500 tonnes of uranium by 1980 and about 10,000 tonnes by 1985.

The next function is the control of the energy market; for CEA its final market is the electricity supply industry at home and abroad. At home, any exercise of control that it can have must take the form of pressure, preferably in conjunction with EDF on government policy. Since the reorganization of the CEA and the redefinition of its function, the principal sources of discord between CEA and EDF have been removed; these two powerful bodies, therefore, operate largely together in their attempts to influence government policy. CEA seeks to influence overseas markets for enriched uranium by participating with foreign capital in joint ventures to construct enrichment capacity.

The operating company for the Eurodif plant under construction at Tricastin in the Rhône valley comprises shareholders from five nations: Italy (*Agip Nucleare, Comitato Nazionale per l'Energia*), 25%; Spain (*Empresa Nacional del Uranio*), 11.1%; Belgium (*Société Belge pour l'Enrichissement de l'Uranium*), 11.1%; France (*Cogema*), 27.8%, and Iran through Sofidif (*Société Franco-Iranienne pour l'Enrichissement de l'Uranium par Diffusion Gazeuse*). The last-named group, composed of the CEA (60%) and the Atomic Energy Organization of Iran (40%), holds 25% of Eurodif. It is a little-noted fact that Iran has a blocking minority in Sofidif so that in principle France does not have complete control. A new international consortium, Coredif, will shortly begin construction of another large enrichment unit.

The control of technology is a particularly important function of the CEA; it is concerned both to direct the commercialization of existing technology and to direct the development of new technology; in the former group the important elements are ore treatment, enrichment and reprocessing. Conversion operations are carried out by Comurhex, a company owned 39% by

Cogema, 10% by St. Gobain and 51% by Pechiney Ugine Kuhlmann; the production capacity is at present 7,000 tonnes per year of uranium hexa-fluoride and is to be increased to 11,000 tonnes per year by 1980. This considerably exceeds domestic requirements and it is planned to export these services. The participation of the CEA in the enrichment process has been described. Cogema owns and operates the reprocessing plants at Marcoule and La Hague; it proposes to use the site at La Hague for a new reprocessing project designed to meet the requirements of EDF and to benefit from the likely future undercapacity of reprocessing plant in the world by offering reprocessing services to foreign customers. Cogema is a partner in at least 20 companies with foreign and private capital. The CEA also has a participation in Framatome, the French monopoly manufacturer of nuclear steam supply systems. After several changes of structure it is owned at present by Creusot-Loire (51%), Westinghouse (15%), the CEA (30%), and others including Jeumont-Schneider (4%). The CEA in participation with French and foreign capitalism in Framatome and Comurhex does not interfere with the management in any detail, but it provides political direction.

For the purposes of controlling new technology, the CEA has a wide variety of subsidiaries, the most important of which are:

Novatome: 15% Alsthom-Atlantique
           34% CEA
           51% Creusot-Loire
           to be responsible for the engineering, industrial architecture and construction of fast reactor plant;
Serena: 65% a joint subsidiary of Novatome and CEA
           35% the West German society KUG controlled by Siemens and in which participate the *Belgo-nucléaire* and Neratom (Netherlands).

This company has the exclusive right to commercialize a combined French and West German technique and will have three licences, Novatome and West German and Italian concerns.

An especially fascinating example of this behaviour is the attempt by the CEA to acquire the technology of solar energy. It had 20% of a company called Sofretes in which Renault had a large share. The company made solar powered water pumps, technically exciting but commercially disappointing. A large increase of capital was a necessary (but not sufficient) condition to make the company profitable. Renault would not take the risk; the CEA bought their holding and became majority shareholder. The operation was brought rapidly to fruition a few days before the formation of a *Commissariat à l'Energie Solaire* which might have considered itse'f a more suitable candidate to hold the State interest.

The final function suggested was the control of finance. Although the capital requirement of the CEA is not high compared to EDF, the rapid rate of growth of its activities, their relatively long lead times and its relative youth as a commercial organization do not permit it to finance much of its own requirements at present. Eventually it is the hope of CEA to do so as a result of its own activities from the services sold overseas, especially enrichment and reprocessing; this situation does not obtain at present – the State has to provide much of the capital requirement. This is a function which the CEA has yet to master. Its commercial activities in association with private industry have been financed by loans from consortia of banks.

Although omnipresent in the nuclear industry the control is not as great as the organization would like; but it is still consolidating its position. For example, when Westinghouse was forced to part with part of its original 45% holding in Framatome, the CEA wanted to acquire a 'blocking minority – 34%. Creusot-Loire objected; the dispute was arbitrated by the *Ministre de l'Industrie* in favour of the private firm. When Novatome was formed exactly the same problem arose. The first intention was to allocate the capital as Alsthom (30%), the CEA (30%), and Creusot-Loire (40%). The CEA again wanted a blocking minority and Creusot-Loire objected. The solution finally reached in November 1977 was a compromise; the CEA was given the blocking minority, but Creusot-Loire obtained an absolute majority in its own right. The arbitration favoured the CEA.

Similarly, Pechiney-Ugine-Kuhlmann (PUK) was persuaded in March 1978 to concede some of its holdings to Cogema. PUK, directly or indirectly, was a partner with the CEA in at least 12 companies involved in the mining and treatment of uranium and the manufacture of plant. The new agreement covers five of these companies.[30]

These territorial advances are interesting. They suggest that when private capital has done its job the CEA will move in to take over control. It is too soon to say, but the immediate future should be revealing.

The objectives of the oil companies can be discussed in similar terms. It is less striking because control of their environment has long been a principle guilding the actions of multinationals. The most significant structural change in the French oil industry during the period under discussion was the fusion of ELF-ERAP and SNPA, the purpose of which was to procure funds for ERAP. For a long time the *Président-Directeur Général* of the two companies was the same man: M. Pierre Guillaumat. Many of their operations were closely linked, but legal barriers prevented transfer of funds between the groups. However, ELF-ERAP possessed extensive prospecting rights for oil and gas all over the world and too little money to finance the programme it desired. The State, the only shareholder in ERAP, would not furnish the additional funds. SNPA, on the other hand, had a healthy cash flow from its industrial diversification, undertaken to compensate for the depletion of the Lacq gas fields. To direct this flow of funds into prospecting, the two companies were fused to form the *Société Nationale Elf-Aquitaine* (SNEA). The operation was contested by the French Left because the financial nature of the operation was such as to reduce the participation of the State. From the SNPA (54% state capital) and ELF-ERAP (100% state capital) was created a company 51% state owned, the remaining state share being sold to private shareholders, again this provided funds to finance further activity.

The CFP has tried to acquire new technology in coal and uranium mining and in solar energy. It is a partner in Sofretes with the CEA and when Renault withdrew, it was a competitor for that holding. It operates with the CEA in uranium prospection. The *Ministère des Finances* through their representatives on the *Conseil d'Administration* tried hard to discourage these new activities and is still trying, so far without success.

The attempts by EDF to control its environment achieve their most perfect expression in the relationship of the enterprise to its markets. In order to attain its objective of a rapidly growing electricity market, EDF has entered into associations with French private industry that all, in their various ways, have the aim of influencing the choice of consumer or of developing new final uses for electricity. These subsidiaries include:[2]

Société Francaise d'Etude Electrique (SFEE)
Société d'Etude de Réalisation et d'Exploitation du Tout Electrique (Soretel)
Société Electricité Isolation (Elise)
Société Maître d'Oeuvre pour la Réalisation d'Immeubles Tout Electrique (Somoritel)
Compagnie pour la Promotion du Transport du Vehicule Electrique (Cotravel)
Société Auxiliaire de Matériaux pour les Equipements Electriques
Société pour le Financement de la Protection de la Nature et la Lutte contre la Pollution

By means of these societies EDF is able to influence the choice of those determining the installation of energy using equipment and to create new markets. It has also, as we have observed, launched an aggressive commercial campaign on which it had been working for many years. EDF also publish a splendid magazine, expensively produced in full colour which is distributed to those whose choice can affect electricity markets and wherein the virtues of electricity are extolled, particularly as a source of heat for homes, commerce, industry, agriculture, swimming pools, etc.

The influence and autonomy that EDF can hope to acquire is limited by its inability to extend its principal sales outside France. But it has built up an extensive international consulting service through the company Sofrelec. Measured in terms of their contribution to the turnover of EDF the activities of Sofrelec would not deserve much space, but they do provide a fascinating insight into the dynamism and attitudes of the enterprise. EDF has professional training centres all over Central and Southern America, the Middle East, French Africa, parts of the Far East and several European countries (Spain, Portugal, Greece and Poland). It is directly involved in construction work in Africa and the Middle East and other consultancy work elsewhere. Its specifications naturally reflect its own traditions and make it easier for French firms to tender for contracts. A similar company, Sofratome, has been set up by EDF in conjunction with the CEA to sell French nuclear plant and services abroad. It has made preliminary contacts in 35 countries.

EDF has always been the architect for its own plant, be it hydraulic, fossil-fuelled or nuclear. This practice has prevented its suppliers competing as well as they might for export rates, because they could not offer 'turnkey' construction. Conscious of this problem, the solution offered by EDF is not to delegate its architecture to Framatome but to accept to play the role of architect for export orders.

The control of its own finance is the other principal aim of EDF's activity; the nuclear programme is, and will be, extremely demanding of capital; for this reason EDF would like to be able to raise electricity prices, at present kept down for the higher purposes of the Barre plan, but that is not without dangers because higher electricity prices would slow down the rate of penetration into heating markets; however, the present rate of penetration is regarded as satisfactory and higher prices are seen to be more urgent. The requirements for finance can also be reduced by keeping down the cost of stations. EDF has a reputation among suppliers for driving a hard bargain; the prices it claims to be paying for nuclear stations are indeed remarkably low. In part this is probably a result of combined hard bargaining with Framatome and the economies of mass production. So important do EDF regard the latter, that they have refused certain improved safety standards desired by the safety inspectorate on the grounds that this would interfere with these economies.[31] However, keeping down costs is ancillary to the question of controlling the sources of finance. Most of EDF's finance is borrowed from consortia of French banks, almost certainly with high level political encouragement, or from the international markets. EDF has put considerable effort into mastering the financial expertise required for these operations.[32] For example, during the last three years it has made a remarkable entry into the American financial market where it has raised more than $1.9 billion with an original scheme comprising loans denominated in eurodollars at floating interest rates for a period varying from 5 to 10 years, with the facility for the subscriber to enter the American 'commercial paper' market where periods are short and interest rates lower. As this market is unstable, the borrower (EDF) can reimburse at any moment by drawing on its long-term arrangements. With the help of Credit Lyonnais, EDF has developed a mastery of the American commercial paper market unparalleled by any other non-American institution; it was the third largest participant in this market in 1976 after General Motors and Ford. The financial requirements of EDF are nevertheless huge and it is active in seeking new sources. The persistent French pressure for Euratom loans that would enable EDF to borrow on the guarantee of the Community is an example of this continual effort.

If the proposed hypothesis of State enterprises working to control all aspects of their environment is correct, then it should follow that EDF would attempt to infiltrate the companies constructing reactors. It is gratifying to learn that when Westinghouse was obliged to sell the larger part of its holding in Framatome, EDF made representations within the Government that it should be allowed to buy the shares. The dispute with the CEA was arbitrated by M. d'Ornano, the *Ministre de l'Industrie*, against EDF.

There is another, as yet unmentioned, element of their environment that these enterprises will try to influence. They will try to influence government policy. The potential for this is high in France because of the close personal relationships that exist between government and industry, the almost imperceptible boundary and the extensive and almost perpetual planning exercise that brings government and public enterprise continuously together. The fascinating questions are to what extent government imposes its guidelines on public enterprise and to what extent public enterprise manipulates the Government.

The answer to these questions will be postponed to a later chapter. First we will examine in detail the present state of the industries and the nature and operation of government control.

References

1. This chapter has been influenced by the work of Professor J. M. Martin, especially by references 2 and 3.
2. J. M. Martin. 'Les industries de l'énergie en France', *Chronique sociale de France*, April–May 1975.
3. J. M. Martin. 'L'évolution des relations état-entreprise dans le domaine des activités énergétiques en France', Université des Sciences Sociales de Grenoble, October 1973.
4. *Electricité de France; Entreprise nationale, industrielle et commerciale*, La documentation française, Paris, 1976.
5. J. Lepidi, *Le Charbon en France*, La Documentation Française, Paris, April 1976.
6. 'La CFP a cinquante ans,' *Pétrole Informations*, 29 March 1974.
7. Jean Choffel, *Le Problème Pétrolier Français*, La Documentation Française, Paris, 1976.
8. J. Bour, 'La passation des commandes et des marches de l'Electricité de France,' *Revenue Française de l'Energie*, 1959.
9. J. H. McArthur and B. R. Scott, *Industrial Planning in France*, Harvard University Press, 1969.
10. '1939–1945: le purgatoire,' *Pétrole Informations*, 29 March 1974.
11. N. J. D. Lucas, *Energy and the European Communities*, Europa Publications, 1977.
12. F. W. Saab, *France and Oil, A Contemporary Economic Study*, MIT, 1960.
13. *Les Perspectives de développement des centrales nucléaires en France*, Rapport de la Commission consultative pour la production d'électriceé d'origine nucléaire, April 1968.
14. J. Chevrier, *Les Entreprises Publiques dans une Société Libre: Expérience d'Electricité de France*, VIIe Congrès de L'Economie Collective, 1965.
15. G. Lesayer, 'Les Interventions de l'Etat dans la gestion de l'Electricité en France,' *Revue Française de l'Energie*, 1959, pp. 435–46.
16. A. Peyrefitte, *Le Mal Français*, Plon, 1977.
17. J. Chirac, 'La Réforme du Ministère des Finances,' *Le Monde*, 12 May 1977.
18. 'Face à face avec Paul Delouvrier,' *L'Expansion*, October 1977.
19. *Rapport du Groupe de Travail sur les Entreprises Publiques*, April 1968.

20. M. R. Garner, *Relationships of government and public enterprise in France, West Germany and Sweden,* National Economic Development Office, 1976.
21. 'Réorganisation du Commissariat à l'Energie Atomique,' *Energie Nucléaire,* December 1970.
22. 'Entretien avec André Giraud,' *L'Expansion,* January 1976.
23. A. Giraud, *Revue Française de l'Energie,* January 1966.
24. Interview with Pierre Guillaumat, *Nouvel Observateur,* 12 February 1973.
25. A. Francos and J.-P. Sorein, *Un Algérien nommé Boumedienne,* Stock, 1976.
26. 'La France, a-telle une politique industrielle?' *L'Expansion,* December 1970.
27. 'La Nouvelle jeunesse de la loi de 1928,' *Le Monde,* 30 March 1978.
28. Jacques Sornein, 'New Fuel Cycle Company Operates World-Wide', *Nuclear Engineering International,* December 1976.
29. 'Une victime de l'Uranium,' *Le Nouvel Observateur,* 22 April 1974.
30. 'PUK cède à la Cogema plusieurs de ses participations, *Le Monde,* 31 March 1978.
31. *Le Monde,* 16 February 1977.
32. *Le Monde,* 28 June 1977.

III

Review of the Prevailing Preoccupations of the Sectors

A. Oil

1. MATERIAL DETERMINANTS

France is poorly endowed with fuels. In 1974 she produced less than 1% of the oil which she consumed. This proportion is not only small, but has declined steadily from a maximum of 6% reached in 1965. Considerable effort is being put into exploration, particularly offshore, and officially expectations are high.[1] Exploration on French soil declined dramatically from 1960 (350,000 metres of exploratory wells drilled) to 1973 (39,000 metres drilled), but picked up again in 1974 (46,000 metres) and 1975 (77,000 metres). The results obtained have been disappointing.

Natural gas was discovered at Lacq in 1951 and oil at Parentis in 1956. Up to now nothing else of significance has been found. Aquitaine is still considered the most interesting prospect. Offshore licences have been assigned in the Gulf of Gascony, in the Mediterranean, and recently off Brittany. The most attractive areas in the Northern waters are rather close to the French shore, but in a region perturbed by the presence of the Channel Islands and therefore claimed also by the United Kingdom. The dispute has now been settled but no licences have yet been awarded. The national oil companies in France have made considerable efforts to secure interests in producing areas outside France particularly in areas considered politically stable. They have, for example, a 13.27% share of the Ekofisk field and have been supplying France with crude oil from this source since March 1972. The total amount of oil reaching France from the North Sea is currently about one million tonnes, but it is expected to reach three million tonnes by 1980. The French companies have interests in oil-producing regions all over the world and in 1975 they controlled the production of 87 million tonnes of crude oil. This quantity was made up of crude from France (1 million tonnes), Iraq

(19.7 million), Abu Dhabi (16.6 million), Iran (11.4 million), Algeria (11.3 million), other North African states (2.7 million), Gabon (9.7 million), other black African states (3.8 million), Canada (1.8 million), the North Sea (1.2 million), and Spain and Italy (0.3 million). The meaning of the phrase 'control of production' varies considerably from place to place according to the nature of the host government. A substantial part of French diplomacy is directed towards giving the phrase as much meaning as possible.

2. ECONOMIC DETERMINANTS

Most of the present preoccupations of the French oil industry have been formed by the economic forces consequent on two events; in certain matters these forces interact and reinforce. The seminal events were the nationaliza-tion of French oil interests in Algeria in February 1971 and the rapid rise in crude oil prices and other events following the war in the Middle East in October 1973. The first of these events destroyed the continuity of a petroleum policy that had evolved steadily since 1928; the second created an economic environment which has troubled all the European oil companies ever since.

France defined in 1928 a petroleum policy that was extremely clear; before, during and after the war it evolved in the face of considerable difficulties* along the same coherent line of thought. The principles were confirmed by the *Ministre de l'Industrie* in front of the National Assembly in November 1968; according to him French energy policy had three objectives:

to control production equal to the needs of the country;

to permit French companies and international companies to co-exist on the French market in order to stimulate competition;

to penetrate into refining and distribution abroad and to assure a positive commercial balance in its trade of petroleum products.

The discovery of oil in Algeria had provided the means and the temptation to develop this policy still further by shifting the emphasis of imports increasingly on to crude from French controlled territories (known as *brut franc* or even *brut national*). The policy of *pétrole franc* was characteristic of the nationalistic industrial policies of de Gaulle; it was elaborated by M. Pierre Guillaumat, *directeur-général* of ERAP at the time, and M. André Giraud, *directeur-général* of the DICA and a protégé of M. Guillaumat. These two men were equally Gaullist, equally strong, equally brilliant. The idea of the super dirigiste policy which never finally flowered was not to protect the French market entirely, but to diminish and possibly eliminate imports of crude from outside the franc zone. A decree in 1963 permitted the

* Many of these difficulties were created by the United Kingdom and especially the Foreign Office, probably more to restrict the French political presence in the Middle East than to keep France out of the oil industry although the astonishing rivalry which exists between the Foreign Office and the Quai d'Orsay does seem to demand a policy of automatic hindrance [*ceteris paribus*]; this may have been a factor.

French State to impose an obligation on oil companies to refine *brut national* in their refineries with the intention of obliging the majors little by little to eliminate other imports. Coupled with this, the French State tried to reduce the price agreed for crude with Algeria as determined by state-to-state negotiation. For the Algerians this was the last straw in a policy that they probably would not have supported much longer anyway; fruitless negotiations eventually led to nationalization.

The effect of the events in Algeria was substantially to reduce the production capacity in French hands below the needs of the country. In 1969 French companies were producing 80 Mt against a national consumption of 70 Mt; by 1976 they were producing more or less the same amount in comparison with a national consumption that had grown to about 120 Mt. Since then petroleum policy has been confused, the oil companies have been encouraged to seek petrol outside French territories. It is arguable that the policy went too far and contributed to the present penury; this view is found among some competent French observers.

The second principal event determining present problems was the rapid rise in oil prices. The effect of this was to reduce or stabilize the demand for a commodity that had been universally foreseen to grow strongly in future years. New capacity in production, refining, transport and distribution had been planned and commissioned resulting in world-wide overcapacity in all branches of the industry. Fig. 3 compares the refinery capacity in France during the last 10 years with the crude oil actually processed in those years.

Markets in the U.S.A., Canada, New Zealand, Australia and Japan being either protected or inaccessible to competition, the only region where the consequences of overcapacity can develop fully is Europe. Dumping of oil products in Europe has forced prices down to a level below the costs of production of the European companies. Because these companies have relatively few markets outside Europe, the total of their operations is a loss. Both ELF and Total now have a small or even negative balance on current account.

The consequences of these two events reinforce dramatically, because the need to find reserves to replace those lost in Algeria (and declining in Iraq) requires heavy investment in production and exploration which with a small net income must be financed in large part by borrowing. The problem was mitigated for ELF-ERAP by its fusion with SNPA which gave it access to the strong cash flow from the latter group's diverse enterprises. This operation was probably not undertaken for this express purpose; it is a logical evolution of the history of the two groups; it has, however, been extremely helpful in easing ELF's cash flow problems. Total is heavily in debt (total of long and medium term credit in the 1976 balance sheet is about £1.2 billion). The company contemplated augmenting its capital by an increase in share capital and an issue of convertible bonds; the poor performance of the company's shares on the Bourse prevented this operation. Total has found other sectors (coal and uranium) more profitable than hydrocarbons in recent years; it is probable that it will ask for government financial assistance to maintain its effort in exploration for oil and gas.

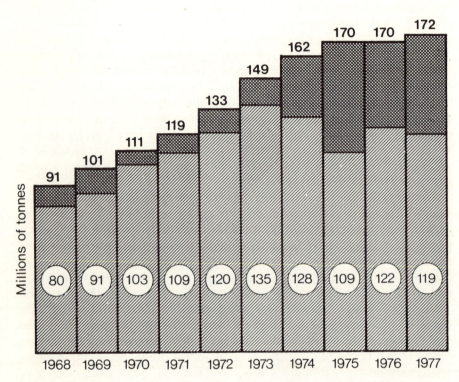

Fig. 3. Refinery capacity and crude oil processed in France, 1968–1977.

The extensive State control of the oil sector has apparently been of little significance in solving the problems of the industry as sketched above. There is a view that State control minimized exploitation by the oil companies in France in the early months of 1974 as the rapid rise in the price of crude worked its way through to refined products. This epoch was marked by strong confrontation of European governments and oil companies; the former attempted to keep prices down, the latter to pass on the increase in costs. It is difficult to see that those countries with an elaborate apparatus of control fared any better than those without. The market was more than usually confused and susceptible to collusion between companies. The oil companies always co-operate to match market demand with refinery output at least cost, by participating in joint ventures, by exchanging refinery capacity and by transferring products; the complex network of relationships built up to sustain this co-operation is a factor in strengthening their solidarity. The extra complication introduced into the problem of matching demand and output of oil products by the licensing system operating in France can only have strengthened concertation between oil companies. In the view of the European Commission 'These arrangements [the licensing system] had the effect of inducing certain concerted practices which went beyond the limits envisaged by the legislators'.[2]

Indeed an investigation by French authorities had already found that a system of distribution quotas had existed in France between 1960 and 1962 and again in 1968 and 1969. Another minor aspect of the State intervention in the oil sector is the obligation to carry a certain percentage of the crude imported into France under the French flag. This has been a heavy burden on companies operating in France because the rates for freight on French ships are much higher than those in other merchant fleets, about twice British rates for example. The policy essentially protects French merchant shipping at the expense of the oil companies.

But the main reason why the apparatus of State control has not worked is the combination of 'stick' and 'carrot' (the constant attraction to the State authorities of keeping oil prices low to encourage industry, minimize the balance of payments deficit and avoid contributing to inflation).

There is a fundamental conflict between the law of 1928 which essentially delegates a monopoly to selected agents and the Treaty of Rome which forbids monopoly practice. After negotiation the Commission conceded the mechanism to France, but on the understanding that the French State would only supervise imports and would not discriminate in favour of its own companies. The Government could in principle prevent the effects of international overcapacity appearing in France by protecting the French market with a tariff barrier for products, but this would infringe the Treaty of Rome. While crude oil can be refined in Rotterdam or elsewhere in the Community and imported into France, there is little use that the French can make of their controls; although they do seem to use them in an occult way to effect certain marginal changes. For example, the oil crisis resulted in a reduction of French imports from Italy; independent French companies had previously contributed to a large extent to these importations. At the behest of the French Government these independents changed their source of supply and started buying from refineries in France. One imagines that their co-operation was encouraged by the idea that otherwise they might have trouble in renewing their A3 licences. A similar marginal effect is the preference in fact given to ELF and Total in the allocation of profitable distribution outlets on the motorways.

The consequences of free trade in Europe are exacerbated by the commitment of the French State to a policy of low-cost oil; this policy did not die with the policy of *pétrole franc* and in certain respects was stimulated by the collapse of the latter concept. Consequently, the State issued A3 licences to small distributors for the import of low cost products from Rotterdam and even recently extended the issue to chemical companies and other large industrial enterprises. Moreover, the prices of petrol and gas oil (and from

1973 to mid-1976 light and heavy fuel oil also) are fixed by the Government in a complex way, but with reference to certain measures of Rotterdam prices. The fact that Rotterdam prices have recently reflected short-run marginal costs, plus the desire of the Government to keep prices low, has led to prices fixed at a level giving little or no margin to the companies. The French companies have only recently managed to convince the Government that this policy was on balance wrong; that the advantages of low cost for the consumer were outweighed by the inadequate profits accruing to French oil companies. The conversion is still only partial, i.e. more marked in the Ministry of Industry and the Quai d'Orsay than in the Ministry of Finance. Nevertheless, France has supported the demands of the European petroleum companies for protection of product prices throughout the Community and for controls over the construction of new refinery capacity. The French view conflicts with the interests of West Germany, which traditionally has adopted a policy of importing refined products bought below long-run marginal cost on the world market. The periods of depression on the market, having in the past been considerably larger than the periods of pressure, this policy has been on balance profitable; certainly West Germany has no interest in protecting French refinery capacity. Similarly the United Kingdom interest in building new capacity to refine North Sea oil conflicts with the French position, and the Dutch must also view protection as a threat to the profitable role enjoyed at present by their refining industry. One should note that historically the French objective of becoming a net exporter of products caused them to build refinery capacity in France that has contributed, along with excess capacity in Italy and Holland, to the problem. Furthermore, there are inconsistencies in the French position; she could protect her oil companies unilaterally by setting minimum prices for oil products in France. It is also true that the French oil companies have not maximized the use of their French refineries; CFP, for example, in 1976 achieved a utilization factor above 99% on its refinery at Vlissingen in the Netherlands compared to utilization factors of less than 70% on its plant in France. Also ELF and CFP, particularly from Vlissingen, are substantial contributors to the Rotterdam market whose effects are apparently so depressing. One should not make too much of these contradictions between policy and practice as they are forced on the companies by prevailing commercial pressures.

Finally, one should note the appearance of national protectionist views. M. Chalandon, President of ELF-Aquitaine, recently declared in a public statement (the baptismal speech of the world's largest oil tanker – christened the *Pierre-Guillaumat*) that 'In the absence of an agreement between the partners of the European Community . . . governments must recover their liberty. . . . We look to the initiatives of the French government to sustain our industry and preserve employment in this area.'[3]

3. FINANCIAL APPRAISAL

An investigation of the financial accounts of the French oil companies is extremely illuminating; it makes clear the financial consequences of the economic problems sketched above. Total is the most straightforward case; firstly, because it is primarily an integrated oil company which has retained the same financial structure for many years and therefore it is not necessary to sort out from the consolidated accounts the contributions of related and unrelated activities and the effects of changes in company structure and, secondly, because it published particularly lucid and detailed accounts. Table 4 lists the main operating and financial ratios for 5 years.

Table 4. Operating and financial ratios for the Total Group, 1972–1976.

Group Operating Ratios (before income allocation)	1972	1973	1974	1975	1976
$\dfrac{\text{Cash flow} \times 100}{\text{Shareholders' equity} + \text{Minority interests}}$	24.8	34.0	48.5	23.1	28.1
$\dfrac{\text{Cash flow} \times 100}{\text{Sales (net of taxes)}}$	12.8	14.7	9.5	5.6	6.1
$\dfrac{\text{Net income} \times 100}{\text{Sales (net of taxes)}}$	4.6	6.0	4.1	1.8	0.3
$\dfrac{\text{Net income (CFP share)} \times 100}{\text{Shareholders' equity}}$	10.0	14.1	21.1	9.7	−0.1
$\dfrac{(\text{Net income} + \text{Financial cost of long-term debt}) \times 100}{\text{Capital employed}}$	7.8	10.6	14.0	6.9	5.0
Group Financial Ratios (after income allocation)	1972	1973	1974	1975	1976
$\dfrac{\text{Long-term debt}}{\text{Capital employed}}$	0.33	0.33	0.34	0.41	0.46
$\dfrac{\text{Inventories and other current assets}}{\text{Current liabilities}}$	1.18	1.20	1.17	1.21	1.15

The first row of entries demonstrates the health of the market up to 1974 as sales and/or operating margins improved. After 1975 this ratio deteriorates. The second row suggests that a principal contribution to this decline was a fall in operating margins which was indeed detectable at an earlier stage in 1974. The third row shows the drastic effect of this decline on profits and the fourth row the even worse effect on CFP's interest. The last of the operating ratios is a measure of the profits before interest relative to capital employed; it removes that element of the fall in profitability which was caused by the rise in interest rates; it shows even more clearly the effects of the specific economic problems of the oil industry without the further problems arising from high prevailing interest rates.

The latter of the two financial ratios has been maintained at a satisfactory value over the past five years, but the ratio of long-term debt to capital employed is most revealing. Conventional wisdom in the United Kingdom would regard a value greater than 0.5 as suggesting a disturbing exposure to interest rate fluctuations; the value in 1976 of 0.46 is not good, but in isolation is not unduly worrying. The trend in this ratio since 1972 is, however, most disturbing; the climb from 1974 to 1976 is very rapid and the consequences of this rising total of debt must have been reinforced by the contemporary rise in interest rates with the result that a high proportion of operating profit went to pay off debts. Operating profits have probably declined further in 1977; CFP would have been unable to compensate for this further decline by short-term debt without decreasing the ratio of current assets over current liabilities to an unacceptable level; it will therefore have been obliged to increase the long-term debt although that also is already uncomfortably high. One would expect a company in this position to cut down on its investments to avoid incurring further long-term debt. For these reasons CFP would like to increase its share capital; such a move was authorized by the Extraordinary General Meeting of April 1976, but the poor performance of CFP's shares on the stock market prevented this operation. The Government could assist with public finance, and CFP have suggested this in the Annual Report, but the Government seems reluctant. It is difficult, however, to see from the accounts, and the belief that the oil industry will remain relatively depressed for some time, how CFP can undertake the scale of exploration and development of production that is politically desirable unless it can get government aid.

All this is reinforced by the fact that oil production is an extractive industry. As a company loses access to production because of depletion or political intervention, so it must replace it to stay where it is. A high gearing ratio that would be acceptable in a company with prospects of rapid growth is unacceptable if it is incurred for the purposes of replacing lost production. Unless some other factor intervenes this can only lead to continuously increasing indebtedness.

It is not possible to distinguish so clear a trend from the accounts of the ELF-Aquitaine group because of the frequent changes in company structure, the recent merger with SNEA, the extensive non-oil interests and the relatively opaque accounts.

4. RELATIONSHIP TO FOREIGN POLICY

Another aim of French policy in the early months of 1974 was to establish bilateral agreements by diplomatic negotiation with producing countries. These agreements arranged for supplies of oil to be paid for by export of manufactured goods. These bilateral agreements have not been a great success. The main agreements were with Algeria and Iran. Algeria has bought considerable quantities of French manufactured goods, but there has been little oil trade; France has bought much oil from Iran but has had difficulty in selling commensurate quantities of manufactured goods. Agreements of this nature are not viewed well in the French oil companies, for two reasons. Firstly, bilateral relationships are commercially intrinsically less attractive than multilateral relationships because they are less flexible in all respects. Secondly, they often run counter to the realities of the international oil industries. Algeria can obtain a higher price for its crude in the U.S.A. than in France because of its low gravity and low sulphur content; moreover the French system of licensing tends to discriminate against imports of light crudes because crude import licences are expressed in terms of the quantity of crude required to make a specified amount of gasoline; the other products from the refining can then be sold freely; refining of light crude uses up too much of the import licence. The French oil companies have an obligation to provide the lowest cost supply and this conflicts with bilateral agreements. There is considerable reluctance to take responsibility for the policy of bilateral arrangements; the oil companies are unlikely ever to have viewed them with approval even in the difficult days of 1974. The initiative was almost certainly diplomatic; it is now commonly attributed to the other partner, the supplier, but this does conflict with the impression obtained at the time of an aggressive and even anxious French diplomatic assault on producing countries at the beginning of 1974.

In somewhat similar style, the aim often expressed of diversifying sources of supply also conflicted with the provision of a least-cost supply. As it turned out, it was the economic factors which determined events; the origins of French crude imports are now, if anything, slightly more concentrated than they were in 1972/73.

The other traditional aims of French energy policy were to preserve competition at home and expand abroad. The first of these is no longer a concern, competition is perceived as excessive. The second has never been achieved with any permanence. In 1976 the percentage of crude oil processed by Total outside France was about 40% of the total processed by the group; the percentage refined outside Europe was less than 10%. Over 50% of its sales of finished products were made outside France but only about 13% were made outside Western Europe. It is fair to say that Total has successfully extended its activities throughout Europe, but has made little impact further afield. ELF-Aquitaine is even more home based; over 80% of its crude processing in 1976 was done in France; 75% of its sales of products were in France; it does little refining or marketing outside Western Europe.

B. Gas

Gaz de France appears a relatively timid organization compared to its United Kingdom counterpart; in its relationships with EDF it is usually defensive; this again contrasts with the relationships characterizing the gas and electricity industries in the United Kingdom. The difference is explicable in terms of the profitability of the industries in the two countries and their access to supplies. British Gas had access to low-cost supplies of natural gas, which as monopoly buyer it was able to purchase at a low price; this fortunate circumstance allied to the vast volumes of gas available, permitted the industry to penetrate many markets rapidly and easily in order to finance the necessary infrastructure of supply; moreover the financial freedom which the industry enjoyed permitted it to adopt aggressive and non-commercial marketing policies in other markets to the discomfort of its competitors. In contrast the resources available to GDF built up more slowly and, with the exception of the deposits at Aquitaine, under less favourable circumstances. Supplies from Algeria and Holland were higher cost or subject to the normal commercial market forces. As a result GDF has had three main pre-occupations: its precarious finances, to secure supplies from outside France and to find markets.

1. FINANCIAL PROBLEMS

The difficult birth of natural gas in France was partly a natural result of material difficulties, but it was reinforced by the policy of low-cost oil and price controls as a measure against inflation. The weak cash flow would not finance the heavy investments. As a result, by 1969 GDF was greatly in debt; the total of medium- and long-term debt far exceeded its own capital resources. The period from 1969 to 1973 was characterized by a rapid increase in sales (25% per annum on average) and higher profits, particularly after 1970-1971 when the price of oil began to rise. But the poor financial state of GDF did restrict its growth in those years; in real terms the investments during the period 1969–1973 were no more than in 1963–1968. Emphasis was placed on financial recovery. In this the enterprise was partly successful; the proportion in which investments are auto financed has risen considerably, from 19% in 1968 to 51% in 1974, 73% in 1975, 95% in 1976. This result was achieved partly by the increasing profitability of the organization; from 1968 to 1973 the operating deficit decreased regularly from 198 million FF to 12 million FF (i.e. from 9.8% to 0.3% of revenue). In 1974, for various reasons which we shall come to, the organization suffered a massive operating deficit of 221 million FF, but in 1975, after 12 years of loss it made a profit of 91 million FF; 1976 confirmed this profitable turning. The net income is still, however, extremely small as a percentage of sales:

$\dfrac{Net\ Income}{Sales}$	1968	1973	1974	1975	1976
	−9.3%	−0.3%	−5.0%	+1.2%	+0.2%

The second contribution to the favourable evolution of the proportion of investment self financed has been the fall in the importance of investment. This is best shown by expressing investment as a proportion of sales:

	1968	1969	1973	1974	1975	1976
$\dfrac{Investment \times 100}{Sales}$	35.6	39.1	28.6	24.3	27.3	18.3
$\dfrac{Cash\ Flow \times 100}{Sales}$	6.5	9.5	16.3	12.4	20.0	17.3

The improvement of the proportion in which investments are self-financed has been accompanied by a reduction in the proportion of medium- and long-term debt in the capital employed, but this ratio still remains high (0.63 in 1974 and 1975, 0.61 in 1976). In summary, therefore, a reduction in the amount of investment, plus an improvement in the operating balance, has permitted investment to be nearly matched to depreciation plus State contribution (*fonds de dotation*); but the amount of long-term debt is still high and the operating benefit is low. One would expect a company in this position to continue the strategy it has apparently adopted in recent years, that is, to reduce its rate of investment in order to reduce its long-term debts. The financial recovery of GDF has been brought about at the expense of investment; this will presumably affect its potential contribution to French energy supplies in the long term.

The emphasis on financial recovery to the detriment of investment and future supplies has been particularly strong since the late 1960s. An understanding of the tensions existing between the different parties involved can be gleaned from the reports of the various Commissions and Committees of the Sixth Plan. The relatively low level *Comité du Gaz*, containing a large proportion of specialists in its membership and in which the industry was well represented, argued for substantial growth and investment to match the efforts being made in other Western European countries. But the higher level *Commission de l'Energie* with a strong representation from the *Ministère des Finances* argued that financial stability came first. The poor financial performance of GDF in the mid-1960s was partly the result of the legacy of debt from the days of coal gasification that plagued all the gas industries of Western Europe and partly the result of the policy of cheap oil. The debts of GDF were not written off by the Government as happened in the United Kingdom; the financial problems were reinforced by the strong competition from heavy fuel oil. The weakness of GDF is undoubtedly one of the deleterious results of the policy of cheap oil.

2. SUPPLIES

Since 1966 the evolution of the European gas market has been characterized by substantial international collaboration in the construction of a European transmission network and in the organization and exchange of supplies. Gaz de France, as a consequence of the attitude and problems described earlier, has played a smaller part, has taken the initiative less often and has been less successful than one might have expected.

The original sources of supply for the French natural gas network were Groningen, Algeria and Aquitaine. By 1975 the structure of supplies bought by GDF was:

Aquitaine	Netherlands	Algeria
19%	62%	18%

The contracts with the Netherlands extend to 1988. The deposits at Aquitaine are in decline (production in 1976 was half the level of 1974). The

51

principal areas of future interest for France, and indeed all continental European gas companies, are the northern basins of the North Sea, the U.S.S.R., Algeria and Iran. For France, delivery of gas from all these areas is most easily achieved in participation with third countries; most negotiation and contracts therefore involve international consortia. By 1974 GDF had contracted to buy 2.5×10^9 cubic metres per year of gas from the U.S.S.R. by 1980 and 2.0×10^9 cubic metres per year from Ekofisk after 1976. The first contract involved exchange of gas with West Germany, the second was negotiated by a consortium animated by the West German company Ruhrgas, but of which GDF was a part.

In February 1975 the *Conseil Central de Planification* set targets for the gas industry of 15.5% of total primary energy supply by 1985, equivalent to 370 billion therms a year. At the same time, indeed a little earlier, GDF began vigorous negotiations in several areas to secure further supplies. The amount of the contract with the U.S.S.R. was increased from 2.5 to 4.0 billion cubic metres per year from 1980 in December 1974. In April 1975 a new contract was signed between the Ekofisk producers and the consortium of European companies which had bought the output; the contract concerned the gas from the Eldfisk field and neighbouring deposits; it increased the GDF's supply from the Norwegian sector of the North Sea by 1×10^9 cubic metres per year after 1978. The gas is to be transported by a submarine pipeline to Emden along with the Ekofisk gas and carried by pipeline across Belgium to the region of Paris; the transport across Belgium is the responsibility of an international company in which GDF has a 20% holding.

GDF has an interest in several projects concerning gas from Iran that would be undertaken in concert with other European companies. Some projects propose the transport of gas by pipeline, others foresee transport as LNG in cryogenic tankers, others require Iranian gas to be supplied to the U.S.S.R. in exchange for deliveries of U.S.S.R. gas into Western Europe. In November 1975 a consortium comprising GDF, Ruhrgas and an Austrian company signed an agreement providing for the purchase of 13 billion cubic metres a year of gas at the border of the U.S.S.R. and Iran. Two billion cubic metres a year will be left in the U.S.S.R. as payment for the right of passage. GDF will be entitled to a third of the gas delivered at the border between West Germany and Czechoslovakia. Transport across Western Germany will be the responsibility of two joint subsidiaries of Ruhrgas and GDF, in both of which Ruhrgas has 51%. The Mitteleuropäische Gasleitung (Megal) and the Mitteleuropäische Gasleitung Finanzierungsgesellschaft (Medal-Finco) are charged respectively with responsibility for the construction and operation, and financing of a pipeline across Western Germany. The pipeline will have a capacity of 15 billion cubic metres a year and will cost some £300 million. It will pick up the 11 billion cubic metres of Iranian gas at the German-Czech border. The 4 billion cubic metres of Soviet gas purchased by France will be delivered to the border of Austria and Czechoslovakia, these deliveries will be taken across Austria to the German border and eventually into the Megal pipeline. This operation is the responsibility of another joint subsidiary of GDF, Ruhrgas and an Austrian company.

The North Sea has a particular interest for GDF because of the existing supply structure in North East Europe undertaken for the Groningen and Ekofisk gas. The company has therefore joined a consortium of Belgian, German and Dutch companies with the purpose of attempting to arrange massive purchases through a gas-gathering line linking various fields in the North Sea.

The most attractive prospect of all for GDF remains the supply of Algerian gas by a pipeline which would provide a permanent link between the French markets and Algerian centres of production via a cross country line through Spain. The Segamo (*Société d'étude du gazoduc de la Méditerranée Occidentale*) constituted between the Algerian State Oil Company, Sonatrach (50%), GDF (25%), and the Spanish company Enagaz (25%), has been studying the project for several years now. The line could conceivably supply an additional 40 billion cubic metres a year by 1984. France has tried hard to convert the project from a study to a reality and has expended considerable diplomatic effort to that end, including negotiations in 1974 during the course of the visit by Giscard d'Estaing in Algeria when the two Presidents announced in a joint communiqué that they had decided to construct the pipeline. There is no sign of negotiations coming to fruition. In contrast Sonatrach has signed a contract with the Italian oil company ENI to supply 12 billion cubic metres a year by a trans-Mediterranean pipeline. This successful agreement has caused some resentment amongst French diplomats and representatives of GDF.

Finally, GDF has made some purchases on the natural gas spot market which is developing in the Middle East as a consequence of investments that have been made in LNG plant without adequate prior arrangements for markets. Although the transport cost is three times that of LNG from Algeria, the low purchase price compensates for this and the costs at the French terminal in Fos are roughly equivalent. There is said to be a difference of opinion between GDF and the *Délégation Générale de l'Energie* as to the potential prospects of LNG from the Middle East. The purchases may be a small sign of a more independent attitude in GDF.

The first gas to cross the French border in exchange for Soviet gas did so on the date agreed – 1 January 1976. Until the Megal system is complete the Soviet gas deliveries are provided by an exchange with Italy. The supplies from the North Sea through the terminal at Emden in Germany were by contrast two years late, arriving in October 1977. Providing that the contracts already arranged are executed without delays, then GDF has already assured itself of a supply of about 320 billion therms by 1985, out of the target of 370 billion in 1985. The supplies so far arranged break down roughly as.

56.5 billion therms from Arzew (Algeria)

35.0 billion therms from Skikda (Algeria)

35 billion therms from Iran

40 billion therms from the U.S.S.R.

30 billion therms from Ekofisk/Eldfisk

40 billion therms from Aquitaine

90 billion therms from the Netherlands.

The structure of supplies of natural gas in the past and of contracts so far arranged for the future is shown in Fig. 4.

GDF is investigating the possibility of providing the remainder either from Algeria, Nigeria or the Middle East. There is little doubt it will achieve its target.

France is well placed, geographically, to receive supplies from North Africa, the Middle East, the U.S.S.R., the North Sea and West Africa. Large quantities of gas associated with oil are still flared off in the Middle East (about 1,000 billion therms, or nearly three times the requirements of France by 1985). The potential production from OPEC is several times greater and, as noted above, many of the members with large gas reserves are conveniently situated.

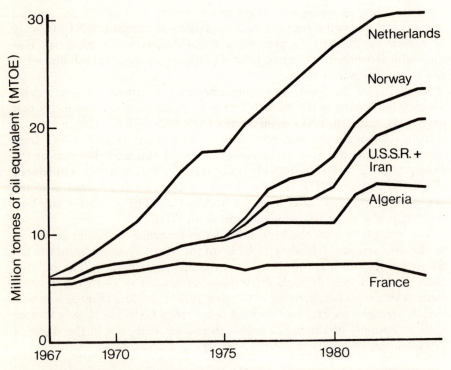

Fig. 4 The structure of supplies of natural gas in the past and contracts so far arranged for the future, expressed as millions of tonnes of oil equivalent.

The period of restraint of GDF in the 1960s and early 1970s must have restricted the rate at which France could take advantage of these factors.

GDF is also hampered in its supply policy by its lack of authority to explore for gas. To the oil companies, gas is less attractive than oil, all other things being equal, because the price obtainable for the commodity is lower, the difficulties of exploitation are greater, there is less flexibility for disposal and it is generally a less profitable venture than oil. Oil companies therefore tend to find the marginal gas fields either by accident or if they are in conjunction with oil. GDF has apparently no plans to try to obtain this authority which would require an alteration in the law of nationalization and would entrain formidable legislatory difficulties. One cannot help but speculate that EDF faced with a similar obstacle to its interests would have no hesitation in attempting the change.

3. MARKETS

The arrival of gas from Groningen in 1967 was the cause of a rapid growth in sales. The rate of growth corrected for climatic effects in the following years were:

Years	'67/68	'68/69	'69/70	'70/71	'71/72	'72/73	'73/74	'74/75	'75/76
%	13.0	15.6	19.6	27.2	32.9	25.0	13.4	6.2	13.6

This rapid growth was associated with a redistribution of sales among final markets:

Sector	1970	1973	1974	1975	1976
Domestic	56.6	37.2	33.4	33.3	31.1
Commercial	23.4	24.0	19.2	21.1	21.2
Industrial	20.0	38.8	44.8	43.4	44.8

A redefinition of sectors between 1973 and 1974 has slightly exaggerated the trend, but it is nevertheless true that sales have shifted strongly away from the domestic sector to the industrial sector. Sales to all sectors have continued to grow, but at different rates; since 1974 a certain stability has been achieved.

The reasons for the increased proportion of sales to industry are firstly that gas was an expensive fuel (especially by United Kingdom standards) and not attractive to the domestic consumer in comparison with competing fuels. Secondly, the gas distribution system had suffered from lack of investment and it was easier to dispose of gas rapidly by sales in bulk to large customers located near the transmission mains.

Even after the October War the price of gas to the domestic consumer relative to the price of domestic fuel oil was too high to permit rapid expansion of the domestic market. Moreover, the low capital cost of electric space heating equipment reinforced by a vigorous advertising campaign in favour of electric space heating, stimulated considerable sales of electricity for space heating. The competition first from fuel oil and later from electricity has restricted natural gas to a modest share of the market. In 1965 it had about a 10% share of the domestic market, by 1970 this had risen to about 15% where it has stayed ever since, apart from random fluctuations. The relatively poor performance of gas in this market was reinforced by a serious rupture of supplies in 1973/74. At a most unfortunate moment, in December 1973, just after the October War, all three lines of the liquefaction plant at Skikda broke down; one was restored in May 1974, the other two only began to function properly again in late 1975. As a result GDF could not meet demand, gas had to be rationed and the calorific value reduced. The effect on consumer confidence was dramatic, especially in the domestic sector, and the sales of heating appliances fell off sharply. Its poor performance in the domestic sector is a serious worry to GDF.

C. Electricity

The main commercial concerns of EDF are the financing of its programme of investment, the assurance of markets and the provision of adequate quantities of plant.

1. FINANCE

Electricity generation is always a capital-intensive industry and this has been, and is, especially true of France where the emphasis was put on hydroelectric plant after the war and is put on nuclear plant now; both forms of generation have a higher capital cost than fossil fuelled plant. Table 5 (facing) reviews the evolution since 1956 of the investments made by EDF and their financing.

Between 1968 and 1971 the level of investment was almost static which corresponded to a fall in real terms. As a percentage of sales the investments fell almost continuously from 1960. A slight increase in 1972 because of the initiation of the nuclear programme was reinforced in 1974; nevertheless, in constant francs and as a percentage of sales, the investments of 1976 were well below those of 1956.

The means of finance of the investments have developed in three relatively distinct phases. From the formation of EDF in 1946 up to about 1968 the dominating preoccupation of the *Ministère des Finances* was to keep the price of electricity as low as possible. As a consequence EDF had the greatest difficulty in balancing its accounts and in generating sufficient revenue to finance an appreciable part of its investments. A large proportion of investment had to be financed from outside the company and because of the heavy indebtedness of EDF the possibilities on the financial market were also restricted, consequently a substantial part, about half, of the investments were financed by the State. The large proportion of investment financed by loans, reinforced by the inability to generate any substantial internal cash flow led inevitably to a vicious circle, in which the need to service a growing volume of debt detracted ever more strongly from already small operating margins, reduced still further the possibilities of self-financing and obliged recourse to further loans.

Table 5.   Sources of finance for investments of EDF.

Investments	1956	1960	1964	1968	1970	1971	1972	1973	1974	1975	1976
n FF 10^6	1,557	2,857	3,966	5,166	5,127	5,242	5,956	6,333	7,491	9,968	11,931
as a % of sales	49.4	54.2	49.5	44.3	34.5	31.3	31.7	29.9	29.3	32.1	37.6
Finance											
% from own resources	17.3	36.7	21.0	37.0	50.8	40.7	60.6	65.6	22.5	36.9	31.7
% from outside	82.7	63.3	79.0	63.0	49.2	59.3	39.4	34.4	77.5	63.1	68.3
% from state	48.7	40.8	49.4	38.0	22.4	17.2	14.9	0	6.7	10.0	22.8

57

Initially, the State contributions were made exclusively in the form of loans from the FDES (*Fonds de Développement Economique et Social*), but to rectify the vicious circle of increasing indebtedness the State several times converted the old loans from the FDES into allocations of capital (3,150 MF in 1957, 5,800 MF in 1963, 944 MF in 1972). Moreover, after 1965 a part of the State's contribution to investment has regularly taken the form of an allocation of capital.

After 1968, and particularly after the signing of the *Contrat de Programme*, the participation of the State in the financing of the investments of EDF was reduced by the simple expedient of permitting increases in tariffs. As this period of increased cash flow corresponded with the period of static investment already noted, the financial stability of EDF improved rapidly; the most successful year was 1973 when the proportion of investment auto-financed rose to 65.6% and the contribution of the State fell to zero; the cumulative volume of long-term debt began slowly to fall.

The financial recovery of EDF was considerably assisted by inflation. The more an organization finances its operations by loans at fixed interest the more it benefits from inflation.

But the financial recovery was checked by the rise in fuel oil prices in 1974 which was not compensated by permission to make a corresponding increase in tariffs; it was not until 1 March 1976, following the permission to increase tariffs by a further 15%, that it was possible to remove the principal anomalies remaining in the tariffs as a result of the large change in fuel oil prices in 1974. Hardly had EDF managed to obtain permission for this increase in tariffs when they were struck by a natural calamity. The finances from year to year of any electricity supply system with a large hydroelectric component are subject to large and unpredictable variations depending on the rainfall. Having installed hydroelectric plant the output is essentially free; the amount of electricity that can be generated from this source in a given year therefore strongly influences the balance sheet. Nineteen seventy-six was the driest year since EDF was formed; the shortfall of hydroelectric power had to be generated from expensive oil (and less expensive coal) at a supplementary cost of some 800 MF. With an average rainfall the deficit of 620 MF would have been converted to a benefit of 180 MF.

Aggravating as these factors have been they should not distract from the difficult underlying problem, to finance an ambitious capital-intensive nuclear programme out of a modest cash flow. Inevitably the proportion of investment that is self-financed has dropped sharply.

Assistance from the State has again become an important part of EDF's financial life. The allocations of capital were nearly tripled between 1975 (700 MF) and 1976 (1,865 MF), and loans from FDES increased from 255 MF to 860 MF, but this is still only a relatively small fraction (22.8%) of a growing need.

Up to 1973 loans from abroad were only of marginal importance to EDF, but the conjunction of circumstances in 1974 led EDF to take out very large loans abroad, especially in the U.S.A. The total long-term debt of EDF is now 64.5% of its permanent capital worth 51 billion FF. The proportion of long-term debt in the permanent capital is growing steadily:

1972	1973	1974	1975	1976
53.4	53.1	56.3	60.3	64.5

The cash flow is acceptable (15% of sales in 1976), but is made up mainly of depreciation; EDF actually made a loss on current account in 1976. The financial demands of EDF will increase substantially in the near future and it is interesting to consider the options open to the company to meet these demands.

The present programme of EDF roughly comprises 10 GW(e) of stations begun in 1974/75 plus 12 GW(e) in 1976/77 and similar, but as yet unsanctioned, installation rates in later years. Five GW(e) of plant represents an investment of 15.5 billion F at a unit capital cost of 2,600 F/kW, including interest under construction. Those 15.5 billion F are spread out over the five or six years of construction, but after 1978/79 there will be, if the present plans are adopted, some six annual programmes in course. The total annual financial requirement of EDF by that time will therefore be roughly 15.5 billion F of which 4.5 billion correspond to interest during construction. The remaining 11 billion F for new investment is large compared to similar figures for recent years, i.e.:

1974	1975	1976
2,000 MF	3,780 MF	5,780 MF

Faced with an inadequate cash flow and a formidable accumulation of debt EDF has two, not exclusive, options:

To reduce its investments either in the nuclear programme or for hydro-electric schemes, transport and distribution;

To lobby the *Ministère des Finances* for a substantial increase in tariffs that would increase cash flow.

The adoption of one or both of these options seems inevitable.

2. TARIFFS

EDF, most especially since the appointment of M. Boiteux to the position of Director-General, has practised a policy of relating tariffs to marginal costs. EDF maintains that a properly constructed tariff should not only aim at ensuring the commercial, economic and financial health of the enterprise but, in the case of a public enterprise, should aim at directing activity towards an economic optimum for the community. There is a large body of economic writing – to which in the 1950s and early 1960s M. Boiteux was a most distinguished contributor – which suggests that in some sense prices set at long-run marginal costs will have the desired effect and will neither encourage waste nor discourage economic application of electricity. Naturally this requirement also excludes the possibility of cross subsidy between sectors or classes of consumers.

The requirement to translate the marginal costs for a specific consumer, which will be complex and a function of other variables, into tariffs which are relatively simple and of wide application leads inevitably to compromise and generally to a formula whereby the customer pays partly according to his maximum demand (in kW) and partly according to the number of units taken (in kWh).

The greatest controversy is centred around the tariffs designed to encourage electric space heating in the home and in commerce, the so-called tariffs *tout électrique*. These are described by the capacity of the supply, i.e. as 12 kW, 18 kW, 24, 30 or 36 kW.[4] They comprise a payment to cover the fixed costs of the installation which is roughly proportional to the installed capacity and unit costs for electricity taken during the day and at night. The fixed costs (in March 1976) were between 55 F and 65 F/kW per year according to the tariff; the unit costs were 17.3 c/kWh. The cost of a new kW of nuclear plant would be 2,600 F/kW and would generate electricity at a unit cost of 3–4 c/kWh. Clearly the tariffs require a larger payment for units and a smaller payment for capacity than EDF incurs in buying and operating a nuclear station. If a consumer installs electric heating and EDF meets that increment in load by installing a new slice of nuclear plant, then it appears at first sight as if the costs incurred by EDF bear no relation to those recovered from the consumer by the tariff and that therefore the tariff is a long way from reflecting true costs.

In fact in a certain mathematical sense it is true that the tariff is a rough measure of marginal costs; this arises because each consumer is not supplied by a dedicated piece of plant, but by an integrated system. Therefore the subscription of a new consumer or the commissioning of a new piece of plant alters the operation of the entire system. A new increment of nuclear plant will be operated preferentially because of its low operating cost; it will therefore cause a steady operating saving even without a new increment of load. These steady operating savings discounted back to the commissioning date are equivalent to an alleviation of the high capital cost of the nuclear plant; the effective capital cost of an increment of nuclear plant to meet an increment of demand is in this sense low. Similarly the cost of the units to satisfy the incremental increase in demand will be the generating cost from the relatively expensive plant which has to be brought into the system to meet the demand; this generating cost is, of course, much higher than the generating cost of the nuclear station originally installed to meet the incremental demand. These ideas can be given mathematical form and it does transpire that the marginal cost of meeting a new load by an incremental slice of nuclear plant has something like the form of the tariffs in EDF's *tout électrique* policy. But this is only true to the extent that a stream of future benefits can be replaced by an equivalent present value; this notion is the basis of discounted cash flow appraisal of investment and is not to be disputed in mathematical terms. In financial practice it means that EDF investments in capital intensive plant are covered by future payments from its customers extending 20 years ahead.

In other words, although its tariffs mathematically cover its costs, they do so only in the sense that the enterprise's present, and growing, indebtedness is covered by a stream of future benefits. But this does not guarantee a sound financial structure in the conventional sense and indeed EDF is not in a sound financial state as a result. There is a movement in France away from an excessive reverence towards pricing at long-run marginal costs; this movement may be encouraged by aspects of this sort.

In order to reduce, for reasons of its own, the rate of growth of electric heating, the *Agence pour les Economies d'Energie* proposed to the Council of Ministers that an advance payment should be made by the constructor to EDF for any building that depended on electricity for one-half or more of its heating power. The payments of 3,500 F for a house and 2,500 F for an apartment are intended to go some way towards representing the capital cost of the new necessary generating capacity. Half the payment is reimbursed after five years, the other half after 10 years.

The measure was resisted by EDF as a serious impediment to their domestic marketing, but was supported by the other fuel industries, especially gas, by the *Ministère des Finances*, the *Agence pour les Economies de l'Energie* and reluctantly by the *Délégation Générale de l'Energie*.

It may even be that EDF were a little taken aback by the rate of penetration of electricity and that they did not contest the measure as strongly as they would otherwise have done.

The measure may have a serious effect on the market for electric space heating, but the market is flourishing and may survive the attack; it is too soon to say.

3. MARKETS

EDF has made no secret of its view over the last 10 years that continual rapid expansion of the electricity supply industry depended on selling electricity for heat, especially for domestic and commercial space heating where the low initial cost, ease of control and cleanliness were most likely to compensate for the high running cost.

By means of a vigorous advertising campaign (later banned by the intervention of the *Agences des Economies de l'Energie*) reinforced by aggressive marketing and the perpetual attraction to constructors of a low first cost, EDF successfully captured a large proportion of the space heating market for new buildings. This market was the subject of vigorous conflict during the course of construction of the Seventh Plan, of which more later. This success was achieved despite the higher cost of electric heating. The consumers' magazine *50 millions de consommateurs* made an independent study of heating costs with systems using fuel oil, gas, electricity and propane in four different styles of house. The annual operating cost for the electric heating was 30% higher than for fuel oil or gas; even after amortization of equipment and insulation, the electrical systems were more expensive. (Fuel oil had the smallest operating cost and gas the smallest total cost including amortization.)

Nevertheless, electricity continues to have extraordinary success, and at the present rate will exceed by an additional million the objective of two million lodgings assigned it for 1985.

Officials of EDF might be expected to see a dilemma between the need for low prices to encourage market penetration and high prices to finance the nuclear programme. In fact the financial burden is so onerous and marketing is so successful that they are exclusively interested in obtaining tariff increases.

4. PROVISION OF GENERATING CAPACITY

Increasing the part of electricity in the French energy balance requires simultaneously increasing generating capacity and markets. It is not possible to achieve exact coincidence. Generating capacity comes in large units with a long lead time, the capture of markets has a shorter lead time but cannot be made as quickly as the commissioning of new capacity. Consequently the markets must, and do, appear before the generating capacity. This has two consequences during the period in which the nuclear stations are under construction; firstly, it requires more fossil fuel to be burnt than would otherwise be the case; secondly, it makes substantial demands on the existing fossil fuel capacity which, until the nuclear stations come on stream, must meet a higher maximum demand than foreseen. The former point is well illustrated in Table 6 and Fig. 5.

Table 6. Fuels burnt by EDF.

Fuel (Mtoe)	1960	1969	1971	1973	1975	1976
Coal	2.7	7.8	5.8	3.4	4.8	7.8
Lignite and blast furnace gas	0.2	0.3	0.3	0.4	0.6	0.7
Heavy fuel oil	0.5	3.5	8.1	14.1	10.8	13.9
Natural gas	1.0	1.6	1.9	2.5	3.1	2.6
Total	4.4	13.2	16.1	20.4	19.3	25.0

It can be seen that in 1976 EDF burnt more fossil fuel than ever before; this was exaggerated by the drought but the general tendency is likely to persist for some years yet. Fig. 5 shows the fossil fuel burn increasing until 1980; this is a relatively optimistic forecast.

The pressure on generating capacity in 1976 was also aggravated by damage to the heat exchangers at Saint-Laurent and Phénix, plus repairs to the primary circuits at Chinon. The outlook for the immediate future is not much better. Much of the coal burnt was imported (7.5 Mt or 5.0 Mtoe), and was found to be more abrasive than usual, causing rapid wear of the pulverizing mills; the high sulphur fuel oil bought cheaply by EDF has caused corrosion problems; finally maintenance was reduced in 1975 for budgetary reasons and postponed in 1976 because of the poor rainfall; a lower availability of plant is therefore foreseen for the following years.

The effects of the rapid growth of markets, plus the contingent problems of the hydroelectric and fossil fuelled plant, have been reinforced by delays in the nuclear programme. Fessenheim I was 20 months late coming on stream, and the subsequent five sets have also been delayed by several months during construction. More serious delays are likely in the second pluriannual programme. These arise from:

the inability of the constructors to keep up the pace;

a spacing out of orders for financial reasons;

strengthening of security standards which demand time-consuming changes;

public opposition, which translates itself into longer delays than were expected in obtaining permission to exploit sites.

The technical problems are susceptible to technical progress and likely to become less significant. The financial and political problems represent greater uncertainty; EDF seeks help from the State in overcoming these more intractable problems.

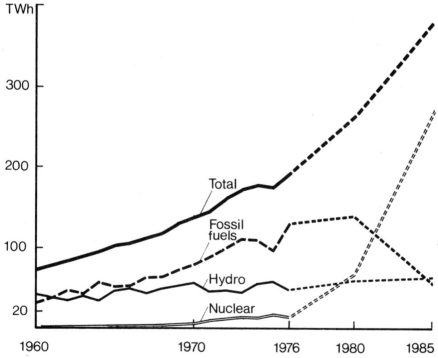

Fig. 5. The historical balance of sources of electricity generated by EDF and a possible future evolution.

The present state of the French nuclear programme is summarized in Table 7; Fig. 6 indicates the geographical distribution of sites. Fig. 7 indicates the nuclear generating capacity operating in France in the past and shows several future projections. The heavy line ending in 1978 shows historical fact. The line of medium thickness which continues the heavy line shows

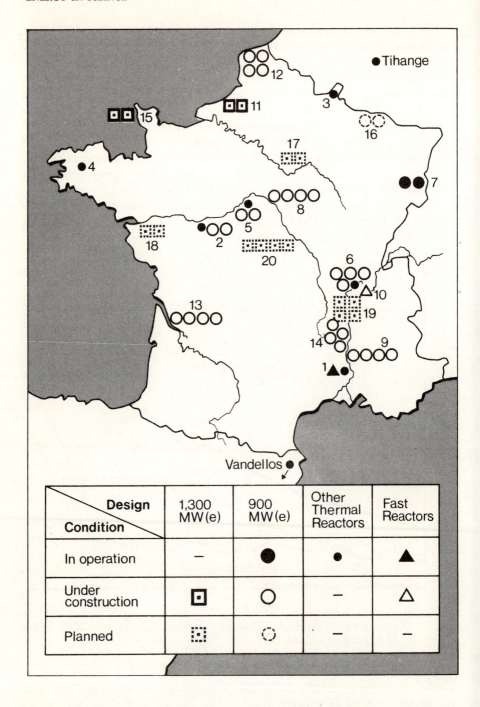

Design / Condition	1,300 MW(e)	900 MW(e)	Other Thermal Reactors	Fast Reactors
In operation	–	●	•	▲
Under construction	▣	○	–	△
Planned	▦	⦿	–	–

Fig. 6. The sites of the nuclear stations in France: operating, under construction, and planned. Numbers on map refer to Table (page 66).

EDF's present official prognostication (April 1978). The thin solid line shows an early EDF hypothesis (1974). It will be seen that the official EDF forecast sees installed capacity rapidly recovering from production delays and achieving in 1980 almost what was forecast in 1974. Thereafter, the more recent forecasts fall steadily away from the earlier more optimistic targets. The argument behind this is that, as manufacturing delays are brought under control, so lost time will be made up and the capacity intended for 1980, which is determined by orders placed in 1974, will be achieved. After 1980 the past and present forecasts part company because the orders in 1975 and later were not made at the rhythm on which the earlier forecasts were based. The argument is not impregnable. Even if manufacturing delays are recovered, which is unlikely, new sources of delay are likely to arise as a result of having six or more plants to commission in a year. If these factors are taken into account, along with the likely sources of delay in the second pluriannual programme listed earlier, then the volume of installed capacity in the future is likely to be still less than the present official forecasts. The thin dashed line in Fig. 7 is a personal estimate of the likely outcome.

The conjunction of circumstances is such that EDF is unlikely to be able to meet with its nuclear programme the markets which it has, and is, creating. It is likely that it will have to construct additional fossil fuel stations to meet

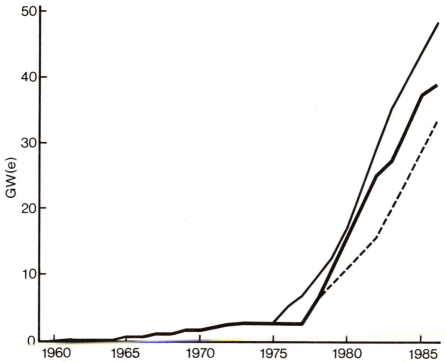

Fig. 7. The growth of nuclear generating capacity in France in the past and some possible future developments.

Table 7. French nuclear power stations, in operation, under construction and planned.

Name Number on Map	Numbering of the Sets	Type	Electric Power Output MW(e)	Year of Ordering	Year of Operational Service	Observations
Marcoule (Gard) (1)	G2	Gas-graphite	40	1955	1959	Prototypes
	G3	Gas-graphite	40	1955	1960	
		Breeder	250	1967	1973	CEA/EDF
Chinon (Indre-et-Loire) (2)	1	Gas-graphite	70	1956	1963	Chinon 1
	2	Gas-graphite	210	1957	1965	taken out
	3	Gas-graphite	480	1959	1967	service in 1973
	B1	PWR	925	1976	1982	
	B2	PWR	925	1977	1982	
Chooz (Ardennes) (3)		PWR	280	1960	1967	50% EDF 50% SENA (Belgium)
Brennilis (Finistère) (4)		Heavy water	70	1961	1967	CEA/EDF
St-Laurent-des-Eaux (Loir-et-Cher) (5)	1	Gas-graphite	480	1963	1969	
	2	Gas-graphite	515	1966	1971	
	B1	PWR	925	1976	1981	
	B2	PWR	925	1976	1981	

Name Number on Map	Numbering of the Sets	Type	Electric Power Output MW(e)	Year of Ordering	Year of Operational Service	Observations
Bugey (Ain) (6)	1	Gas-graphite	540	1965	1972	Bugey 2, 3 went critical 1978
	2	PWR	925	1971	1978	
	3	PWR	925	1972	1978	
	4	PWR	905	1973	1979	
	5	PWR	905	1974	1979	
Fessenheim (Haut-Rhin) (7)	1	PWR	890	1970	1978	In operation
	2	PWR	890	1972	1978	
Dampierre (Loiret) (8)	1	PWR	4×925	1974	1979	
	2			1975	1980	
	3			1975	1980	
	4			1976	1981	
Tricastin (Vaucluse) (9)	1	PWR	4×925	1974	1979	
	2			1974	1979	
	3			1975	1980	
	4			1975	1981	
Creys-Mal ville (Isère) (10)		Breeder	1,200	1976	after 1984	Station constructed in collaboration with Germany (RWE) and Italy (ENEL)

continued on page 68

67

continued from page 67

Name Number on Map	Numbering of the Sets	Type	Electric Power Output MW(e)	Year of Ordering	Year of Operational Service	Observations
Paluel (Seine-Maritime) (11)	1 2 3 4	PWR	2×1,300	1976 1977 1978 1979	1983 1984 1984 1985	The first 1,300 MW sets in France
Gravelines (Nord) (12)	1 2 3 4	PWR	4×925	1974 1974 1975 1976	1979 1980 1980 1981	
Le Blayais (Gironde) (13)	1 2 3 4	PWR	4×905	1975 1976 1977 1978	1981 1981 1982 1983	
Cruas (Ardèche) (14)	1 2 3 4	PWR	4×905	1978 1978 1979 1979	1984 1984 1985 1985	

Name Number on Map	Numbering of the Sets	Type	Electric Power Output MW(e)	Year of Ordering	Year of Operational Service	Observations
Flamanville (Manche) (15)	1 2	PWR	2×1,300	1979 1980	1985 1986	
Cattenom (Moselle) (16)		PWR	2×905	after 1980	after 1986	Planning application made
Nogent s/Seine (Aube) (17)		PWR	2×1,300	after 1980	after 1986	Planning application made
Le Pellerin (Loire-Atl.) (18)		PWR	2×1,300	after 1980	after 1986	Planning application made
St. Maurice–St. Alban (Isère) (19)		PWR	4×1,300	after 1980	after 1986	Planning application made
Belleville (Cher) (20)		PWR	4×1,300	after 1980	after 1986	Planning application made

69

the demand in the early 1980s when the markets are there but the nuclear plant is not. The classical stations will most probably be fuelled by imported coal available more cheaply on the world market than is heavy fuel oil.

Nineteen seventy-six was also marked by a serious fault in transmission. Brittany produces little electricity and is only feebly linked to the main producing areas; it is difficult therefore to maintain a stable supply; consumers were cut off several times during the winter and at one particular time, after a tempest had destroyed transmission lines, power was only restored after a considerable delay. It could be that investment in distribution and transmission has been neglected for the nuclear programme, which may mean that such incidents will become more frequent. More serious, but less obvious and detectable, it may be that nuclear stations may be concentrated near industry so obviating the need for additional investment to strengthen the transmission system, but exacerbating regional problems.

D. Coal

At the beginning of the century coal made up more than 90% of the energy supply to France. The entry of petroleum in massive quantities on to European markets in the 1950s plus the recession at the end of the decade had the same effect on the French industry as it had elsewhere. The extent to which European governments protected their industries depended on several factors; in France little protection was offered. French coal was relatively high cost and the great lines of French industrial policy at the time were to reform French manufacturing industry. This was not facilitated either by diverting new investment to coal mines or by accepting to pay higher prices for coal than the market price for oil. As a result national production fell from 58 million tonnes in 1960 to 28.4 million tonnes in 1973.

The forecasts of the Sixth Plan made before the October War provided for only about 13 Mt by 1980. In January 1974 the *Charbonnages de France* (CDF) was asked by the Government to re-evaluate the potential of the French coal reserves given the new prevailing economic conditions. The result of this re-evaluation was not dramatic. It is shown in Table 8 below:[5]

The astonishing thing about this table is that the new economic conditions, determined by a price for fuel oil nearly three times the previous price, had apparently not affected the economically recoverable reserves of coal to any considerable extent. The immediate reason for this is that the actual cost level used to determine the economically recoverable resources did not much change; previously cost had been way above selling price because of subsidy. The increase in fuel oil prices simply made the same production roughly profitable without subsidy. The annual level of production sustainable by these reserves and competitive with fuel oil would be some 20–21 million tonnes by 1980[6] and would decline therafter.

The fundamental reason why the increase in fuel oil prices has not permitted an increase of much consequence in the quantities of coal that are

Table 8.   French Coal Reserves (MTCE).

| Field | Evaluation on 1 January 1974 | | New evaluation |
	Technically Exploitable	Economically Recoverable	Economically Recoverable
Nord-Pas-de-Calais	460	67	80–120
Lorraine	801	331	350–355
Centre-Midi	112	62	70–90
Total	1,373	460	500–565

considered economically recoverable should be sought in the history of investment in French coal mining. This is shown in Fig. 8, and investments are expressed in francs of the year; in constant francs the decline is still more dramatic. The war devastated the French mines; after the war considerable investment was allocated in the First and Second Plans to the coal mining industry, but the aim was to produce as much coal as possible as quickly as

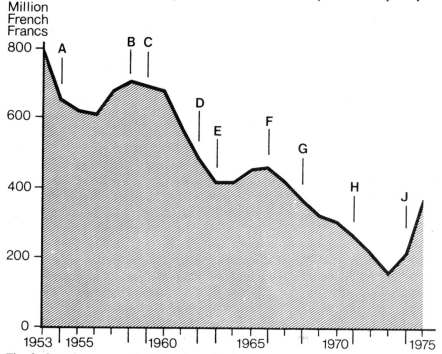

Fig. 8. Past investment in French coal mines, expressed in millions of French
    francs. The events shown are:

A. Second Plan
B. Third Plan
C. Plan Jeanneney
D. Fourth Plan
E. Plan de la Table Ronde

F. Fifth Plan
G. Plan Bettencourt
H. Sixth Plan
J. Nouveau Programme

possible rather than to expand the industry profitably and securely. The Third Plan, which proposed a further expansion, was scarcely a few months old when in 1958 came the turning point for West European energy supplies. The French introduced the Jeanneney Plan to reduce output; this was applied strictly as were subsequent plans for regression, *le Plan de la Table Ronde* and *le Plan Bettencourt*. As a result the industry was starved of investment for 16 years until 1974. But coal mining is an extractive industry and cannot suffer such a regime without serious damage. Accessible reserves are in the nature of things removed and unless new pits are sunk and access provided to new reserves then the productivity inevitably falls, output falls, costs rise, finance of new investment becomes increasingly difficult, the vicious circle is closed, mines are closed, whole coal mining regions disappear and mining communities are destroyed. Moreover the brutal regression and redundancies, following a period of rapid growth and recruitment, completely shattered the confidence of miners in their employers, contributing again to the difficulties of reversing contraction.

Another related factor assisting the catastrophic decline in French coal mining was the perpetual pressure on prices. The price of heavy fuel oil relative to that of coal is shown in Fig. 9. It can be seen that between 1947 and 1958 the price of fuel oil was a much larger multiple of the price of coal than could be justified by its greater convenience in use. The discrepancy arose because CDF was obliged by the Government to set prices at a level which just permitted the enterprise to break even. In the prevailing context of a scarcity of energy, this meant that price levels were well below those at which coal might have been sold and at which fuel oil was sold. Between 1958 and 1962 the price of coal remained steady; the changes in the graph are the result exclusively of the steady decline in fuel oil prices. After 1963 a combination of government control and, to a persistently increasing extent, the competitiveness of fuel oil kept coal prices low. By 1969 the pressure of fuel oil prices was the dominating feature and it was not until 1974 that this was temporarily removed.

It is evident that the average cost pricing policy imposed on CDF between 1958 and 1962 denied it revenue which it could have expended in new investment that would have better prepared it for the advent of low cost oil. The precarious state in which the industry was left was exacerbated by the later policy of low cost oil. When government has such control over the finances of an industry there is little the industry can do either to resist or to prepare for a withdrawal of government support. Enormous power is put into the hands of government and the administration.

Estimates of the loss suffered by CDF because of their obligation to sell below market prices during the period 1946–1957 have been made.[7] They amount to 20,000 MF when expressed in 1974 francs. By comparison the cumulative operating deficit from 1964 to 1974 was less than 11,000 MF. It appears then that the loss imposed on CDF in those years far exceeds the deficits which the community has subsequently been obliged to make up.

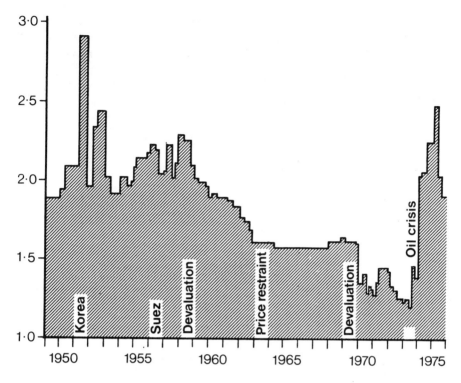

Fig. 9. The price of fuel oil by weight, as a multiple of the price of coal by weight, since 1949. The indicators are the ex-refinery price of No. 2 fuel oil, and ex-mine price of coal in Lorraine; they are not comparable to the indicators in Fig. 2. Note that the calorific value of fuel oil is typically 40% higher than that of coal.

The finances of CDF since 1949 can be resumed as follows:

Table 9.   Finances of CDF since 1949.

Period	Gross profit (MF at 1974 levels)		Subsidy (MF at 1974 levels)	
	Accumulative	Average	Accumulative	Average
1949–1959	7,650	695	0	0
1960–1964	418	84	3,420	684
1964–1969	−6,580	−1,097	10,550	1,760
1970–1974	−4,316	−863	12,255	2,450

The acknowledged difficulty and relative paucity of French coal reserves, reinforced by the savage financial handling in the past, do not give grounds for expecting any expansion in the future. As a result of estimating the future markets for coal, the *Conseil Central de Planification* recommended that the part of coal in the national supplies of energy should be stabilized at 45 Mt until 1985, compared to the 25 Mt previously proposed. For the French industry this means a temporary halt to the plans for retraction, in order to provide an extra 50 million tons during the period. Especially this will provide the gap between electricity demand and supply until the nuclear programme begins to take effect. The effect is only temporary as can be seen from the forecasts of future production:[6]

Table 10.   Future production of coal in France (MTCE).

	1974	1980	1985
Nord-Pas-de-Calais	9.0	4.8	0.7/0.8
Lorraine	9.1	10.5/11.0	9.0/10.5
Centre-Midi	6.4	5.1	2.7/3.6
Others	2.3	2.2	0.5
Total	26.8	22.6/23.1	12.9/15.4

Indigenous production is planned to fall even in this period. The remaining requirements for coal will be made up from imports.

A large autonomy has been given to CDF in achieving these targets. This can probably be cynically interpreted as showing the administration's lack of interest in whether CDF succeeds or not. CDF can choose where and how it mines coal providing that it is produced below a specified cost level (72 c/GJ in constant francs of 1 January 1974). In fact the Seventh Plan does not allocate a great deal more investment to the coal industry than did the Sixth Plan.

In January 1978 CDF signed a *contrat de programme* with the Government. The provisions of the contract permit CDF to recover some commercial freedom in pricing; they also provide for the State to make a subsidy of about 82 FF/tonne and to pay costs not linked directly to production, for example pensions. These provisions will not prevent the decline in indigenous production; in some quarters the *contrat de programme* is seen as a means by which the Government is washing its hands of the coal industry, by leaving it to its own devices at a critical period. CDF is investing in producing capacity abroad, notably in Australia.

E. Nuclear

The whole nuclear industry in France is controlled by the *Commissariat à l'Energie Atomique*. Its non-commercial activities, namely research and development, military applications and safety are financed by a direct allocation in the Budget of the *Ministère de l'Industrie* or indirectly through a budgetary allocation to defence which is used to purchase services from the CEA.

The whole of the CEA's activities relating to the fuel cycle have been, with effect from 1 January 1976, the responsibility of a private subsidiary known as *Compagnie Générale des Matières Nucléaires* (Cogema). Though 100% owned by the CEA, Cogema has a private legal status which is intended to help joint ventures with private enterprise and foreign partners. Cogema's objective is to provide full support for the French reactor programme and to sell where possible fuel and fuel cycle services abroad.

The CEA's involvement in the reactor industry is expressed by holdings in joint subsidiaries with private industry, including Framatome, Novatome and Tecnicatome. Framatome is concerned with the construction of existing reactor designs, the involvement of CEA in the management is said to be, and appears to be, small. In the other companies where technology is less well established it is probable that the CEA plays a more active part; they are not at present of the same commercial significance.

As a guide to the objectives of Cogema in the various activities of the fuel cycle it is helpful to list the amounts of different services which the nuclear programme is likely to require in future years:

	Uranium oxide (tonnes)	Enrichment (million SWU)	Reprocessing (tonnes)
1977	3,300	0.45	11
1980	6,400	2.4	140
1985	7,500	5.3	780

The problems and opportunities which these developments are likely to offer Cogema are conveniently classified under the operations concerned.

1. MINING

On her own territory France has an estimated 60,000 te of low grade, but economically recoverable uranium. At present output from French soil is 2,200 tonnes of metal; it could be 4,000 tonnes by the 1980s. France also has been prospecting, through a wide variety of subscribers, with foreign partners and French capitalism, in many parts of the world, but especially in her old colonies. Reserves so far discovered and the prospecting programme underway encourage Cogema to think that it will be able to market 5,500 te of ore by 1980 and 10,000 te by 1985. The company sold some 4,000 te in 1975.

The CEA had claimed from the moment of its constitution the right to prospect for uranium. It was granted despite opposition from CDF who regarded digging the ground as their prerogative. Exploration and exploitation at home and abroad exceeded the demands of the French nuclear programme and looked like continuing to do so for some time to come. In October 1970 the CEA set up, in conjunction with private industry, a group known as

Uranex with the purpose of marketing the surplus. The private partners were Pechiney-Ugine-Kuhlmann and the *Compagnie Française des Minerais d'Uranium* (CFMU). Uranex sold at low cost and doubtless contributed to the problems of uranium suppliers in that period. Subsequently it played an active part in the sellers' cartel; it is said that the secretariat to the cartel was provided by the CEA on the grounds that that was the location where a group with no obvious purpose would arouse the least interest.

As it turned out the surplus available to the CEA did not last for long; French controlled supplies are unlikely to be enough by 1980, but will be more than enough by 1985. To fill the gap France has arranged contracts with, for example, South Africa. She no doubt expects that her own production, which these contracts will cause to be released on the world market by 1985, will be saleable at a price above the contract price then prevailing.

The CEA's happiest hunting ground has been Niger, where it has been prospecting since 1955. Eleven years later it discovered economically exploitable deposits of uranium at Arlit to the north of Agadez. In 1968 the company Somair (*Société des Mines de l'Air*) was constituted and in 1971 commercial exploitation of the deposits began with a production of 410 tonnes of uranium metal. Production has grown steadily since; it will be 1,800 tonnes in 1978 and will exceed 2,000 tonnes by 1980. The main partners in Somair are Cogema and the organization of the State of Niger known as Onarem (*Office National des Resources Minières*). The capital is distributed as follows:

Onarem	33.0%
Cogema	27.0%
Compagnie Française des Minerais d'Uranium (CFMU)	11.8%
Société Minière Pechiney Mokta (SMPM)	7.6%
Minatome	7.6%
Urangesellschaft (West Germany)	6.5%
Agip Nucleare (Italy)	6.5%

18 billion FCFA ($80 million) has been spent by the company of which 10 billion has been financed by loans.

At the time of writing (May 1978), the commercial exploitation of a new mine at Akouta is getting underway. The mine will be worked by a company Cominak, made up of:

Cogema	34.0%
Onarem	31.0%
Overseas Uranium Resources Development (Japan)	25.0%
Empresa Nacional del Uranio (Spain)	10.0%

43.3% of this mine's output will be supplied to Japan over the next 20 years. The necessary finance, 43 billion FCFA, has been supplied mainly by loans, 33 billion FCFA. The uranium deposits presently being exploited in Niger are mortgaged well into the 1980s.

A decision to open a third mine at Imouraren was scheduled for 1977/78. The signs are that agreement has now been reached. Finance for the third mine has been difficult to arrange because although the ore body is large, it is of poor quality and the prospects are marginal; the mine will never be a money spinner. The operating company is constructed:

Cogema	35.0%
Conoco	35.0%
Onarem	30.0%

The projected production from these three mines is:

	1978	1980	1985
Cominak	—	1,800	2,000 tonnes U/year
Somair	1,800	1,800	2,500 tonnes U/year
Imouraren	—	—	2,000 tonnes U/year

A fourth mine at Arni could be on stream by 1982, worked 50/50 by Cogema and Onarem, producing 1,500–2,000 tonnes U/year. There are also other significant prospects; total annual production could be 9–10,000 tonnes of metal by 1985.[9] The countries mainly involved are France and Japan, with West Germany, Italy, Iran and the United Kingdom also in the running.

Despite the considerable success of these ventures, there are still problems. The conditions of operation are extremely arduous; the area of Arlit in which all four prospects are situated is totally deserted and the temperature regularly reaches 45°C. The area is 250 km from the nearest town and 2,000 km from the sea. Recruitment and communications are difficult. There are few indigenous skilled miners; training is necessary. Training staff and operators from foreman upwards have to be Europeans. The turnover in the work force is high. To improve communications much of the State revenue from the mining is directed to the development of an internal road network and its connection to maritime states. The principal project is the *route de l'uranium*, which for 700 km will help to connect the mining regions to the south of the country. The project will cost 40 billion FCFA and will be financed by the mining countries.

All this is just to show that finding the uranium is only the beginning. None of the above problems is insuperable, but they require sustained effort. More serious is the doubt that must always exist about the political security of the host countries. The Niger has always been an easy country for the operating companies, not only the French. But there has been one attempt at nationalization of the uranium deposits (see Chapter II). It is probably only a matter of time before uranium producers begin to extend their control over their resources, but it could still be a long time, and to prolong the period is important for France. But this observation takes us away from the CEA and into the arms of the Quai d'Orsay.

2. ENRICHMENT

The main sources of enrichment open to Cogema before 1979 are provided by long-term contracts for services from ERDA (Energy Research and Development Agency) in the U.S.A. and Techsnabexport in the U.S.S.R. These will decrease in steps in 1979, 1984 and finish in 1990. The enrichment plant at Pierrelatte, now no longer fully occupied by the military programme, supplements these sources. But the principal projects are the enrichment plants generally known as Eurodif and Coredif.

At the beginning of 1972 a study group with the name Eurodif was constituted by companies from the United Kingdom, West Germany, Belgium, France, Italy, the Netherlands, Spain and Sweden. France was not prepared to consider any other process for enrichment than the diffusion process perfected in France by the CEA over the preceding 30 years. The West German, British and Dutch partners considered that this technology had been superseded by centrifugation and withdrew from the consortium. In November 1973 the remaining partners agreed to a factory operating on the diffusion principle. The study group was dissolved and a company of the same name was created with the task of constructing and operating the factory and selling the services. Initially the capital was distributed as follows:

Country	Company	%
Sweden	AB Atomenergi	10.00
Italy	Agip Nucleare	11.25
Italy	Comitato Nazionale per l'Energia Nucleare	11.25
Spain	Empresa Nacional del Uranio SA	10.00
Belgium	Société Belge pour l'Enrichissement de l'Uranium	10.00
France	Société d'Etudes et de Recherche d'Uranium	47.50

Sweden withdrew in 1974 and her participation was shared among the remaining members; other augmentations of capital have somewhat changed the distribution. The most important change came in 1975 when the Iranian Atomic Energy Organization took a 10% stake by means of a joint subsidiary with the CEA. The present capital distribution is given in Chapter II.

The plant is sited at Tricastin in the Rhône Valley. Production is intended to start in 1979 at the level of 2.3 million SWUs. The output will be lifted in stages to 6.3 million in 1980, 8.4 million in 1981 and to the full capacity of 10.8 million by 1982. Cogema, which after the various capital reconstructions at the moment holds 42.8% of the capital, will avail itself of 4.5 million SWU by 1982 onwards, a proportion of output roughly proportional to its capital holding. The Eurodif company during the course of 1974 successfully negotiated long-term contracts for the period 1979–1990 which covered 95% of the capacity for the period; 89.5% of the contracts were with the shareholders, 10.5% with third parties, from West Germany, Japan and Switzerland. The total cost of the plant at January 1974 prices is estimated at 9.55 billion F; there appears to be little overrun on the budgeted cost as yet. The finance of the project is progressing well. The shareholders increased the share capital to 1 billion F in March 1977, considered to be the final figure. The total of liabilities at the end of 1976 was 5 billion F made up mainly of advances from customers, back loans (mostly French) and a long-term loan from the CEA of 1.6 billion F. Up to December 1976 France also supplied some 350 million F in various subsidies.

Such was the success of Eurodif that a subsidiary company Coredif was formed with the task of launching a second uranium enrichment plant on the same principle. It was planned that the Coredif plant will reach a production of about 5 million SWU per annum by 1985 and that this would be increased to 10 million a year as demand justifies it. Cogema, which holds 50.8% of Coredif shares, would take 1.5 million SWUs from 1985 and possibly 2.7 million SWUs from 1988. Delays in the French nuclear programme have postponed the original schedule to the 1990s, but the intention is still there.

The total enrichment capacity available to Cogema will therefore be about 6.0 million SWUs by 1980 and some 7.2 million by 1990. This enrichment capacity will be used in the first place to supply EDF including a one- to two-year stock pile of enriched uranium. The remainder is intended to permit Cogema to meet other requirements, in particular for the fuel for reactors exported by France to countries that are not shareholders.

This is an impressive story. It is interesting to consider what the real value is to Cogema and to France. The economic viability of the Eurodif plant is apparently ensured up to 1990. The companies who have contracted to take the output have agreed severe default clauses so, in the event of their not requiring the output, Eurodif will not itself suffer unduly. It avails France as a whole little that Eurodif does not suffer if it is EDF that pays the default, but the reactor capacity at present under construction should be sufficient to absorb the output which Cogema is committed to take. An alternative threat is that the producing countries will insist on enriching their own uranium so that, contract or no contract, the Eurodif plant will not be used. This is unlikely to happen much before 1990 and anyway, as we have seen, Cogema controls substantial uranium mining capacity in France and old French colonial territories. The success of Eurodif certainly seems assured. At the end of the day France will not strictly have exported enrichment because it has bought no more output than its capital share entitled it to. The other shareholders have supplied their own capital for a project which happened to be in France. France has, however, like the others, benefited from low-unit costs by combining resources in a single large plant. Against this must be set the fact that she has provided, through the CEA, a large long-term loan at low interest plus various subsidies; she is therefore to some extent financing the other partners to whom will go the rent from the low interest rate and also that which will arise from the inevitable inflation. Successful though it is in certain terms, the Eurodif project is not such a money spinner as it looks at first sight.

But the real benefit comes from the stranglehold that France is developing over the European market. The debate about whether the diffusion principle or the centrifugation principle is lower in cost can only be an academic diversion while France is prepared to invest persistently ahead of demand. Providing that she ensures a permanent slight degree of over-capacity, she can effectively prevent the West German/Dutch/British technique from being built in commercial quantities. She has done that with Eurodif and threatens to do so even more markedly with Coredif. Such a procedure carries certain economic penalties, but it can lead to a powerful market position.

3. REPROCESSING

France has two reprocessing plants, at Marcoule and at La Hague. They were originally built and operated by the CEA, but have now passed to Cogema. The larger and newer plant is at La Hague; it was originally intended to reprocess irradiated fuel from the gas graphite reactors operating on natural uranium, but has recently been equipped with facilities to handle the irradiated fuel from light water reactors burning enriched uranium. Future developments will be concentrated at La Hague and the reprocessing of spent fuel from the gas graphite reactors will be transferred to Marcoule.

The reprocessing operation is undoubtedly the least satisfactory aspect of the French nuclear programme. The factory at La Hague was originally conceived for the purpose of reprocessing natural uranium fuel; in this capacity it was the object of detailed and vigorous criticisms from the union representing the largest part of the workforce. The plant has now been equipped with a new unit known as the HAO (*haute activité oxyde* – high activity oxide) for the stripping and dissolution of (irradiated) fuel elements from reactors operating on enriched uranium. This unit, in the view of the union, posed such serious health problems to the workforce that they struck in September 1976 a few months after it had come on stream.

The union has published a seemingly careful and detailed account of the operation of the reprocessing plant.[10] Their allegations (which I am in no position to check) are as follows:

The union claims that there have been many dangerous events at La Hague in recent years arising from the following sources:

deteriorating equipment, hastily repaired and strongly contaminated;

additions poorly engineered and badly designed;

increasing drive for profitability and technical performance at the expense of safety;

a dramatic shortage of qualified personnel, to the point where the newly engaged staff are set to work without training.

Processing at La Hague is at present carried out in an industrial agglomeration known as UP2 (UP1 is at Marcoule). The centre covers an area of about 2.2 km² at the extremity of the peninsula of Cotentin. The site was chosen because of the proximity of a strong current of tidal origin that carries away the radioactive effluent.

The amounts of fuel treated in UP2 in recent years have been, in tonnes:

1966	1967	1968	1969	1970	1971	1972	1973	1974	1975
50	100	190	230	140	160	250	210	365	425

they came from the gas-graphite reactors in France and Spain.

In the past the workforce were trained for a month at Marcoule under conditions which permitted the job to be learnt without the imperative need for production. Now, apparently, new workers are given a course of a single day and sometimes no prior instruction at all. The new workers are largely unused to working with radioactive materials and are enticed into the work by payments at a salary level greater than normal. The presence of the members of the SPR (*Service des Protections contre les Radiations*) at the work place is diminishing.

Many parts of the factory that were originally designed for normal access have become contaminated and now any intervention requires special clothing that isolates the entire body as well as respiratory equipment. This is apparently particularly grave in the areas of 'average plutonium activity'. Here the average annual radioactive exposure of a worker was 650 mrem in 1974/75 compared to the maximum admissible dose of 5,000 mrem. This is serious enough in itself because the average will include a proportion of doses higher than the mean, but what especially worries the union at La Hague is that the enriched oxide fuel is roughly 10 times as radioactive and that if the factory must treat the same volume of fuel at 10 times the radioactivity then the doses received by the workforce would be, even on average, well above the maximum admissible dose.

It is the operation involved in stripping the fuel elements which causes the most incidents involving contamination. The average exposure in this area is about 3,000 mrems a year.

In the plant as a whole for 1975 there were 572 incidents involving contamination by radioactive substances, in 205 of which the victims were contaminated internally. In 41 cases the internal contamination was caused by plutonium and in 16 cases the quantity inhaled exceeded 10% of the maximum permissible dose. Of course it is argued that the maximum admissible dose is already set very low, although this can also be contested, but nevertheless the impression given is quite definitely that of a seriously mismanaged operation.

The number of incidents is apparently increasing regularly because of the age of the installation and the growing emphasis on production, throughput and profitability. This change of attitude is associated in the minds of the union with the transfer of responsibility for the operation to a private company – Cogema. However, Cogema, though in law a private company, is in fact completely owned by the CEA and should not necessarily be capitalistic in outlook. In its own study, the union dates the change of attitude to 1970, six years before the management was handed to Cogema. Nineteen seventy was the time of the great reorganization of the CEA and the shift of purpose from research and development to commercial operation. It is logical that if there is a conflict between secure operation and a commercial outlook that it should have surfaced at that time. The transfer to Cogema may have aggravated the process because of changes of senior management, but it is unnecessarily emotive to describe the company as private enterprise.

The discharges to the environment have also increased; they are resumed in Table 11 below.

Table 11.   Discharges of radioactivity to the environment from La Hague.

Year	Weight of Fuel Treated (Tonnes)	α activity (Cu)	β, γ activity (Cu)	α activity per tonne (Cu/tonne) ×10³	β, γ activity per tonne (Cu/tonne)
1967	100	0.5	2,300	5	2.3
1968	190	1.0	3,300	5	1.7
1969	230	0.5	2,200	2	0.9
1970	140	0.8	10,600	5	7.6
1971	160	4.0	20,000	35	12.5
1972	250	3.1	14,000	12	5.6
1973	210	3.6	17,000	15	8.1
1974	635	27.0	33,000	42	5.2

These figures should be compared with the authorized rejects for one year which are 90 Cu of α emitters and 45,000 Cu of β, γ emitters. As well as the increase in activity resulting from increased throughput it is disturbing to see an apparent trend towards greater activity released per tonne as time goes by. This is in contrast to the situation in the United Kingdom where, on the whole, techniques have systematically improved with time. The figures, of course, are for natural uranium fuel; enriched fuel being 10 times as active will presumably cause larger discharges of radioactivity. There are apparently no plans to improve the effluent treatment plant, but it is intended to apply for permission to increase the amounts that may be discharged.

It is difficult to know what weight to put on these charges, which might be expected from people practically involved but relatively ill-informed on a theoretical level. It is impossible in a short account to reproduce the extremely worrying detail of the union study or of the evident concern. One quotation may give some feeling for the latter aspect:

What is most striking is the complicity of the management who permit the working conditions to deteriorate and who talk only of production, statistics, productive work hours without understanding the state we are getting into. It is criminal to allow into the active zones agents who have no knowledge of the risks, with the sole aim of repairing as quickly as possible.

One should perhaps add that the union in question, the CFDT, is essentially socialist, generally reasonable as unions go and in no sense committed to the universal overthrow of capitalism.

Several studies have been made by government bodies, but, the union alleges, nothing has come of them. The most recent was made by the *comité d'hygiene et de sécurité élargi*, a body internal to the plant. The report was published in June 1977; in a way it is the most worrying aspect of all, because it appears to accept the bulk of criticism whilst recommending relatively minor changes to the organization and modifications to the plant and has every look, to an outsider, of dissimulation.

The problems experienced with UP2 have caused the union to take a strong line on the commissioning of the HAO. The latter unit was planned to start operation in September 1975. The storage facilities at the site received the first consignment in January 1975. The plant was late coming into operation and by February 1976 the storage facilities were full with 130 tonnes of irradiated uranium, mostly from outside France – the largest part from West Germany. The first few months of 1976 saw rapid modifications, described as 'frantic' and 'disorganized', by the CFDT. The plant came on stream in May 1976 and handled 17 tonnes of fuel before the factory was shut in September 1976 by a strike. The strike took the form of a 'bottleneck strike' involving the smallest effort necessary to paralyse production, thereby minimizing the loss of salaries. One hundred and forty workers struck, preventing several thousand from working, but according to the union the majority supported the action. In November the management attempted to get the HAO unit started by their own efforts, but failed. It should be borne in mind that so far no factory has been shown capable of reprocessing irradiated enriched uranium fuel as a commercial proposition, although it has been done for military purposes. This is not to say that it cannot be done, but it would suggest that it is incompatible with haste and improvisation.

Nevertheless, the official plans remain to bring the throughput in the HAO up to 400 tonnes by 1978 and 800 tonnes by 1980. This is far in excess of national requirements and it is clear that the CEA intends to capture much, if not all, of the world reprocessing market. Indeed it is the intention to construct a third plant UP3. This process plant will have two similar reprocessing lines of 800 tonne/year each, functioning in parallel. The two lines are planned to come on stream at two-year intervals, the schedule at present being in 1984/85 for the first and 1986/87 for the second, giving France a capacity of some 2,400 tonne/year compared to a national requirement estimated at less than 1,000 tonne. Cogema is seeking long-term contracts for reprocessing and storage all over the world to justify this capacity, and hopes to benefit from the delays and problems dogging reprocessing elsewhere.

So far its initiatives have been extremely successful, particularly as it has enjoyed a world-wide monopoly of reprocessing services and as some of its clients were obliged by their governments to find an acceptable means of disposing of irradiated fuel before being authorized to proceed with the construction of nuclear power stations. Cogema has used its powerful negotiating position to impose severe conditions on its clients. The client companies will in effect finance the extension of La Hague through a condition in the contracts which obliges them to pay the principal part of the costs before the first deliveries of irradiated fuel. The contracts already signed (3,925 tonnes) represent a contribution of about 12 billion FF to the finance of UP3. Moreover the final price for the reprocessing service (presently around 3,000 F/kg fuel) is not fixed in advance, but will be notified to the customer after the operation, thereby removing from Cogema the financial risks associated with unforeseen operational difficulties.

The export contracts so far signed by Cogema are: with Japan in autumn 1977, worth 3 billion FF; with a Swedish company in March 1978, worth 2 billion FF; with a West German company in April 1978, worth 5.6 billion francs. An Austrian contract was also agreed in March 1978 for 310 million FF, but has not yet been finally signed. Cogema is also negotiating with Belgium, Switzerland, Finland and the Netherlands.

Work has begun on the construction of UP2 to the accompaniment of extensive local protest. The CFDT has gone to some trouble to inform the populace of the region of its point of view and this has doubtless contributed to the disquiet. The Government has been laconic, not to say abrupt, in its treatment of the local elected representatives. When M. Louis Darrot, député (PS) and Maire of Cherbourg, questioned the *Ministère de l'Industrie* on the importance of the contract with Japan for reprocessing irradiated fuel, the latter replied so briefly that the local council issued, unanimously, the following text:

> Without building permission, without a declaration of public utility, the CEA has begun to construct on the site at La Hague a second reprocessing plant. . . . The local population has never been informed; it is the duty of its elected representatives to do so and categorically to oppose such a construction.

The text goes on to claim that the reprocessing plant is not required for French fuel, but is to cope with the reprocessing of foreign fuel, thereby converting Cotentin to 'the atomic dustbin of the entire world'. The council states its resolve to oppose the construction by all the means in its power. It should be noted that the local council is drawn exclusively from the opposition parties (34 socialists, 11 communists and 5 non-aligned), so no doubt they were not displeased at being able to chastise the Government. But there have also been many popular demonstrations against the extension in the region.

It would not be possible or correct to judge this conflict of opinion; what is clear is the lack of effort put by the authorities into convincing the motley opposition. There has been no official reply to the claims of the unions about plant performance and where the management, or their union, have entered into debate in the press it has always been with a most patronizing attitude.

The CEA have begun construction of a sensitive plant without a clear demonstration of having satisfied the necessary procedures. Again we cannot judge who is legally correct, but in such a case it would seem only sensible to wait for the declaration of public utility. The *Ministère de l'Industrie*, when approached by the local elected representatives of the people, was apparently not prepared to discuss the subject. Here, as elsewhere in the nuclear programme, the polarization of public opinion has been encouraged, deliberately or otherwise, by the State.

4. REACTOR CONSTRUCTION

Construction of nuclear steam supply systems (NSSS) in France is a *de facto* monopoly of Framatome. To produce an NSSS requires four factors:

a reliable and competitive design;

a strong team of engineers;

an efficient and advanced electromechanical industry;

certain specific investments for the larger and heavier components.

Framatome was originally owned by Creusot-Loire (38%), Jeumont-Schneider (30%) and other companies of the group Empain-Schneider (10%). The company acquired the licence for the PWR from Westinghouse in 1958, which met the first of the four requirements. In 1960 it won, in co-operation with Belgian industry, the order for the NSSS for the light water reactor at Chooz in the Ardennes; this was almost certainly a loss leader, obtained in the face of fierce competition from CGE, who were preferred by EDF, only by quoting a price near, or below, cost. Chooz went on stream in 1967. No further order came until 1968 when Framatome was given the task of constructing the first European 900 MW(e) PWR station at Tihange in Belgium, and again the work was done in co-operation with Belgian industry. In 1970, after many years' debate, France decided to concentrate on the LWR line of development. In September the order for Fessenheim I was given jointly to Creusot-Loire and Framatome. The order was only obtained after severe technical and commercial competition with CGE. Framatome and Creusot-Loire immediately began a rapid expansion of the engineering facilities and personnel associated with reactor construction. By 1971 Creusot-Loire was able to begin an important extension to its heavy mechanical engineering factories at Creusot to permit the fabrication in series of pressure vessels and steam turbines.

At the same time it prepared at Chalon-sur-Saône an investment programme aimed at providing the matching manufacturing capacity for steam generators. Framatome, at that time essentially an engineering office, increased its staff by 50%. By 1972 the new factories were nearly completed; they had been designed to permit the construction of 5 to 6 NSSSs each year. In 1972 the capital of Framatome was augmented from 1.5 MF to 12 MF. As part of its increased capital share Creusot-Loire brought to Framatome the two new factories at Creusot and Chalon. The new capital structure was:

Creusot-Loire	51%
Westinghouse	45%
Jeumont-Schneider and others	4%

The reconstruction was agreed in November 1972 with retroactive effect to 1 July 1972. Framatome could now be said to have acquired control of the four factors identified earlier as being essential to the construction of nuclear steam supply systems. The engineering division of Framatome contained at that time about 250 professional scientists and engineers and the number was rapidly increasing. The company had also established an effective working relationship with the manufacturers of the other components, almost exclusively within the Creusot-Loire group; e.g. Creusot-Loire for the reactor internals, which were made in their conventional workshops, Jeumont-Schneider for the coolant pumps. Framatome had risked substantial investments in people and plant, apparently largely on its own initiative. The CGE refused to make similar commitments until after the orders had been passed. Eventually EDF were to choose exclusively PWRs and Framatome became the monopoly supplier; the principal determinant of that outcome was probably Framatome's initiative between 1970 and 1972. The motivator in the nuclear policy in all other respects seems to have been EDF, but in the choice of reactor manufacturer, Framatome, by taking risks was able to outmanoeuvre the favourites.

In a way Framatome was lucky because it was only after the oil crisis that the orders from EDF began to match the manufacturing capacity of their new plant. The company was capable of six units a year. In 1970 it received one order; in 1971 it received three; in 1972 it received none at all; in 1973 it received two orders from EDF and two orders for the pressure vessels alone from Westinghouse. Nevertheless Framatome continued to increase the number of design engineers employed and to make studies of still larger nuclear boilers containing four steam generators instead of the three current at the time. The report of the PEON Commission in April 1973 recommended a programme of between 8,000 MW(e) and 13,000 MW(e) for the period 1973 to 1977, which would have meant an average two to three orders a year for Framatome. It is unlikely that the revenue from these orders would even have paid the interest on Framatome's debt. How relieved the company must have been at the oil crisis and the programme 'Messmer' for 13 units in 1974–1975. Framatome's efforts to export were also crowned with success in 1974. Two NSSS were ordered by Belgium (Doel III and Tihange II) and Framatome received a letter of intent from Iran for two stations. In response to this considerable development Framatome decided that it was necessary to construct a new factory at Chalon and to extend the facilities at Creusot in order to increase the capacity for making pressure vessels to eight units per year and for making steam generators to 24 per year. This is the output necessary for eight complete boilers of the three loop system actually on order by EDF. The plant came into service in 1976. The necessary investment was only 350 MF. Framatome anticipates that after 1979 it will only manufacture 1,350 MW(e) systems. The existing production equipment is largely adequate for this step; the principal additional investment is a 9,500 tonne press to forge the shell courses for the larger reactor pressure vessels, and this has already been bought. The capacity of the industrial ensemble to produce systems of 1,350 MW(e) will be less, measured in complete units, than the eight 925 MW(e) systems; it will probably be about six. Measured in MW(e) the change represents a slight increase in capacity from 7,400 MW(e) to 8,100 MW(e).

The total investment by Framatome and its affiliates, which is specific to the production of reactors, is valued at 1,000 MF. If this is amortized at 20% over 10 years and distributed equally over the output capacity it amounts to some 50 F/kW. This may be compared to the estimated cost of a finished station of 2,650 F/kW. This calculation is a personal estimate and bears no resemblance to any accounting process in operation at Framatome. Another largely fixed cost to Framatome is the cost of its staff, in particular of the trained engineers assembled over many years. The total staff is 2,800, of which perhaps 500 are professional engineers and perhaps as many again are highly skilled technicians. At a rough estimate the cost of keeping this staff represents some 75 F/kW contribution to the output. The total cost of the NSSS is probably about 25% of the total cost of the complete station, i.e. about 600 F/kW. Framatome's fixed costs, though by no means overwhelming, are a substantial fraction of the total. This means that there will be considerable economies to be gained by ensuring as high a throughput as possible; indeed the economies will be greater than this rough estimate suggests because the costs of the supplies of components to Framatome will tend to have a similar structure with similar economies and consequently Framatome can negotiate lower prices for components if it can place orders for large quantities at a steady rate. A high throughput is not the same as a high load factor on the plant. If a great variety of reactors are being produced, although the factory may be operating continuously at a high level of activity, it will be producing less than if the units were similar. At each step along the production process machines have to be set up differently for the different reactors. Framatome estimate that the production work for a new reactor design could take 80 months but for a duplicate might take 60 months (the times are illustrative, but the ratio is more reliable than the absolute values).

Not only does mass production reduce the setting up time for machines but it also intervenes by its effects on the learning curve for operators.

Similarly the production of a duplicate obviates the need for new design studies and revised procedures of quality control, both for Framatome and its suppliers.

In short the economies of series act directly and indirectly – directly on Framatome's own substantial, but not dominating, fixed costs and indirectly through the analogous effects on the suppliers of steel, materials and components which make up the principal costs. In order to help ensure that the suppliers recognize and are confident of these economies of series, Framatome have confined their purchases almost exclusively to the Creusot home group. Their contracts with suppliers extend no further into the future than their own contracts but there is a *modus vivendi* and understanding which is preserved from order to order. These close relationships also help ensure high standards of quality control, of which we have said little, but which is a technical preoccupation of Framatome of the highest priority. Steel for the pressure vessels and other components manufactured by Framatome comes, of course, from Creusot-Loire.

The commercial preoccupations of Framatome consequent on these economies of series must be, firstly, to remove all obstacles to the rapid and steady production of reactors and, secondly, to ensure a full order book for reactors of design as nearly identical as possible.

The principal obstacles to steady and rapid production have, alleges Framatome, been mainly found in the supplies of components; it has been difficult to organize the supply of components such as valves, fittings and pipework. Many hundreds of suppliers and subcontractors were drawn into a complex system of quality control requiring standards which not all were willing or able to achieve. The difficulty of establishing this network of suppliers was exacerbated by the suddenness of the demand from EDF. These sources of delay are being systematically eradicated.

The necessity for Framatome to have some guarantee of future orders is recognized by EDF. That is to say, it was conceded by EDF and the *Ministère de l'Industrie* as being a necessary condition for Framatome to undertake the new investments of 1974–1976. There are three distinct levels of commitment by the State to buy reactors. They are the general sketch of developments provided in the Five-Year Plan, the multiannual contracts, and specific orders. The status of the plan briefly is of a moral commitment or *obligation ardente*. There is no financial compensation to the suppliers if the obligation is not met. The Seventh Five-Year Plan (1976–1980) does not actually specify an installed nuclear capacity for 1985, but its proposals for the quantity of electricity generated are consistent with orders of about 30,000 MW(e) during the period.

The multiannual contracts are even more ardent obligations backed by default clauses if EDF should change its mind. The first multiannual contract was signed in April 1974 after the Council of Ministers had authorized EDF to place the order. The contract covered 16 identical units of which 12 were firm orders and four were options, and the start-up dates were spread from 1974 to 1976. The second multiannual contract was signed in February 1976, covering 10 identical units differing in only a few respects from those in the preceding order. Construction was to begin in early 1977. The third multiannual contract was in fact concluded before the second, in January 1976; it covers eight 1,350 MW(e) units with production dates beginning from mid-1977. After, or sometimes within, the multiannual programme come the firm orders. By this means Framatome has sufficient security to benefit from the economies of series. In a rather more nebulous sense, Creusot-Loire is present in the PEON Commission whose deliberations largely determine the size of the multiannual contracts still to come; the mechanism therefore provides Framatome with some idea of what domestic requirements might be up to four or five years ahead.

The final question to be asked is what profit Framatome is making from the programme. It is impossible to assess this from the annual reports and accounts, because Framatome has not yet been paid for most of the work it has undertaken; it will only be possible to judge how profitable the business has been at a much later time. The senior management of Framatome profess not to know what profit, if any, they are making because of this impossibility of assessing financial results in the short term. Of course, this is the response one would expect from people in this position, but it is also inherently plausible. In the early years the costs of design studies, assembly of personnel, investment were almost certainly not recuperated; these losses have accumulated over the years and subsequent heavy investments have also had to be financed. The question is when, if ever, will the operating profit pay off these debts. Traditionally in France the heavy electrical and mechanical engineering industries have been tied closely to one customer – the State. This customer has, the industry maintains, forced, by negotiation backed by a thorough investigation of costs, prices down to a level which just permitted the industry to keep offices and factories turning over, but without permitting more than a modest return on capital employed. Certainly the CEA and EDF, the former by its participation in Framatome, the second in its role of monopoly buyer, are in a strong position to assess costs and squeeze the price down. The low cost of French PWRs compared to the figures quoted in West Germany and the U.S.A. again suggests that Framatome's margin is small. A plausible summary of Framatome's strategy is that the domestic orders will just permit Framatome to cover its costs including the amortization of investment, but that large profits, if they are to be made, will come from export sales of products built with amortized plant.

A reduction of domestic orders is already in sight; the *Parti Socialiste* (PS) has proposed a moratorium on nuclear investment extending from 18 months to three years depending on the spokesman. There is considerable doubt as to whether the PS could, or would, go through with this idea if it came to power in the legislative elections; the proposal is widely seen as a manoeuvre to capture the ecological vote. But, moratorium or not, the orders from EDF will definitely fall off as it re-established an optimum structure of generating capacity. Framatome is therefore engaged in a powerful export drive. There are relatively few possibilities in Europe. The proposals by General Electrical Company to build PWRs in the United Kingdom include the notion of buying the pressure vessels from Framatome, but this would be a small, irregular, limited and uncertain market. It is said that French diplomats have let it be known to Portugal that they would look more favourably on a Portuguese application to join the EEC if the Portuguese were to manufacture Renault cars, buy the Secam colour television system and purchase Framatome built PWRs. Again the market must be small. Future large markets are likely to lie outside Europe; there will be fierce competition between reactor suppliers, most of whom already have excess producing capacity. The outcome will depend on factors that are difficult to assess: the evolution of oil prices, the attitude of the United States Government to exports, the success of the suppliers in sharing out the market without debilitating competition. The high prices obtained for reactor systems in Iran by both Framatome and KWU suggest that these companies may have established a fragile understanding, taking advantage of the absence of Westinghouse and General Electric in the export market, as a result of prevailing American doubts about proliferation.

The conclusion is that the rent from nuclear-generated electricity, if any, is not to be found at Framatome; the financial success of Framatome will depend very much on exports and is uncertain. There will almost certainly be frantic competition for export markets beginning in about 1980.

F. Unconventional Energy Sources

Serious interest in new energy sources in France has mostly developed since the October War. The initiative has come from both the State and private capital; in both cases the potential for exports of hardware and services has been a significant incentive. The State established the *Délégation aux Energies Nouvelles* (DEN) headed by M. Jean-Claude Colli in April 1975. The function of this body is not to research but to promote the idea of renewable sources and to help in the definition of objectives for industrialists whom the idea pleases. The institutional structure of the sector is still changing rapidly.

1. SOLAR ENERGY

The State has recently created a *Commissariat à l'Energie Solaire* (CES) which will undoubtedly become the most important actor in solar energy, but up until now the main role has been taken by the *Centre National de la Recherche Scientifique* (CNRS).

The CNRS owes much of its prestige in solar energy to the dedicated work of Professor Félix Trombe who has been working there for 20 years during a period when the subject was not encouraged. Trombe was an exception, but even he was allocated few resources.

The main work was on solar ovens, the greatest of which, at Odeillo, was begun in 1968; work was also done on the technology of heating buildings. After the energy crisis all the laboratories of CNRS began to look to see what they could do on solar energy.

The CNRS, after considering all the changes that the crisis had brought about, decided not to construct a single new laboratory for the study of solar energy, but to design a co-ordinated programme of research using the facilities of the existing laboratories. The CNRS became, *de facto*, the centre for the co-ordination of national research on solar energy.

The CEA has also shown a marked interest in mastering the technology which at some distant date might threaten it and which in the meantime permits it to employ the numerous scientists and engineers released by reallocation of, and changes in, the responsibility for nuclear research. It is engaged mainly in fundamental research on the properties of materials for use in photovoltaic devices and flat-plate collectors. It has recently become the principal shareholder in Sofretes, a private company for the development of solar-powered pumps for use in developing countries.

The history of Sofretes is interesting; its capital was originally divided: CEA, 20%; CFP, 20%; Pompes Mangin, 51%; Renault, 5%; and others, 4%. Renault also had 35% of Pompes Mangin and an option to become the majority shareholder in Sofretes. The company has been technically extremely successful and innovative; it has built and installed the first water pumping stations to be operated from solar energy and the first electricity generating station to work from flat-plate solar generators. The plant operates on Rankine cycles using butane or freon as the working fluid. In addition to its technical success the company is the first to have mastered 'turn key' capability in solar energy; design, construction, commercialization. Plant has been installed in several countries in Africa, in the Persian Gulf, Central and South America and in Asia. In spite of these contracts the company is losing money; in part the losses have arisen because the costs of construction in these countries have been higher than expected, but above all there is no domestic market to support a distribution network for exports. The company considers that it might be possible to build up a domestic market for installations using industrial process heat as the source if the devices could be made more efficient by increasing the operating temperature. Alternatively photovoltaic devices might be what is required. It is estimated that it would require 30 MF over five years to make the company profitable. Renault decided not to go on and offered its participation for sale. Two Arab groups were interested but the DEN wanted to see control in French hands. The CFP has an overseas network capable of arranging distribution; it also believes that the ability to offer solar energy technology will help in its negotiations with developing countries over licences for exploration for oil and uranium, but the CEA won and became the main shareholder in Sofretes. The negotiations lasted several months; they came to a speedy end when it became known that the CES was in the offing. Presumably the CEA wanted to pre-empt its new, and more plausible, colleague.

It comes as no surprise to find that EDF has a stake in the new technology. The main venture of the enterprise is the construction of central solar heat engines in collaboration with the CNRS, and a group of industrialists comprising Renault, St. Gobain, Heurtey and Babcock. There are two projects, one of 2 MW(e) and one of 100 MW(e). Both are designed principally for export, although EDF does profess a not very credible interest in the bigger version. These two projects take most of the research funds for solar energy. Partisans of decentralized solar energy technology deeply resent the success of EDF in diverting funds for the exploitation of a diffuse energy source into the development of central production units instead of decentralized units. It is also claimed that one of the reasons CNRS is putting so much effort into these high technology routes is a sense of chagrin, hung over from the 1960s, when the responsibility of much advanced technology of commercial promise was taken over from it and attributed to special State bodies with a commercial vocation: e.g. CNEXO for marine technology, Liria for computing and information, CNES for space research. If this reading is correct then the creation of the CES cannot have pleased the CNRS.

EDF is also involved in studying solar heating in houses outside Paris. Again it is interesting, but not surprising, to find the enterprise forcing the technology to its own requirement. Its aim is to design a solar heating system which will provide the peak heating requirements for an electrical heating system, rather than the straightforward aim of supplementing a solar heating system with a fuel burner for the peak demand.

There are other French activities directed to providing commercial outlets for solar energy systems; they are in the main directed at developing countries.

The creation of the CES was announced by M. Giscard d'Estaing in an interview with *Le Monde*.[12] He reasoned:

> In this domain [new energy sources] France is among the world leaders. In particular solar energy is going to become a very important business. That is why I consider a *Commissariat à l Energie Solaire* to be necessary, to co-ordinate efforts, as was done in 1945 with the CEA.

It is probable that the decision was advanced, and possibly even determined, by the Presidential desire to recuperate the ecological vote at the legislative elections; only 2% but important in the context. There was no question of the CES being given new resources; its role was essentially to co-ordinate existing activities. It appears that parts of the administration are not convinced that the new body will make better use of resources. The DEN will be threatened by the new institution; already it is suggested that it may in time disappear. The operation shows every sign of having been carried through quickly under Presidential pressure.

2. GEOTHERMAL ENERGY

France possesses deep reserves of hot water in the Parisian Basin, the Basin of Aquitaine, in Alsace and the Massif Central. Already 12,000 homes are heated by geothermal energy and another 12,000 are ready. But the development of this form of energy has been hindered up until now by the existing heating contracts in old buildings.

The Seventh Plan provides for 500,000 homes to be heated from geothermal energy by 1985. The figure more usually suggested now is 300,000 and it is unlikely that they will materialize.

The Government has created a new public company, *Géo-chaleur*, to help the marketing, technical development and finance of geothermal energy. Its capital is divided between *l'Union de HLM* (a body responsible for State housing), certain State banks and CDF.

Wind, waves, tides, thermal gradients and biomass are not receiving the same interest as solar energy and geothermal. There is some laboratory work and non-commercial development.[13,14]

References
1. Jean Choffel, *Le Problème Pétrolier Français*, La Documentation Française, Paris, 1976.
2. Report by the Commission on the Behaviour of the Oil Companies in the Community during the period from October 1973 to March 1974. COM(75)675, Brussels, 1975.
3. *Le Monde*, 11 October 1977.
4. *Electricité de France*, La Documentation Française, 1976.
5. *Le Charbon de France*, La Documentation Française, 1976.
6. *L'Avenir du Charbon*, Ministère de l'Industrie, Paris, 1976.
7. M. Toromanoff. *Le drame des Houillères*, Seui., Paris, 1969.
8. 'Les CDF vont retrouver une certaine liberté commerciale,' *Le Monde*, 14 January, 1978.
9. *Uranium: Resources, Production and Demand*, OECD/International Atomic Energy Agency, December 1977.
10. *L'usine de la Hague: situation industrielle, conditions de travail, sécurité*, CFDT, July 1976.
11. 'La France retraitera 1700 tonnes de combustibles nucléaires ouest-allemand,' *Le Monde*, 13 April 1978.
12. 'Un entretien avec M. Giscard d'Estaing,' *Le Monde*, 26 January 1978.
13. M. Magnien, 'Utilizing alternative energy sources in France,' *International Journal of Energy Research* (1), 1977.
14. D. Probert, 'Development of small-scale benign sources of energy in France,' *Applied Energy* (4), 1978.

IV

Nature and Operation of Government Control

A. Controlling Institutions

Powers to investigate the affairs of public enterprise are vested to a greater or lesser extent in the *Assemblée Nationale*, the Ministries and in the *Commission de Vérification des Comptes des Entreprises Publiques* attached to the *Cour des Comptes*. The *Assemblée Nationale* can constitute commissions of inquiry into a variety of matters including the policy and management of public enterprises. Their powers are somewhat less than those of a United Kingdom Select Committee and their reports are generally even less influential. The *Assemblée Nationale* has no power akin to those of United Kingdom members of parliament to question ministers on specific topics; the significance of this idiosyncracy in the United Kingdom has certainly been exaggerated; it is doubtful if it is of any real effect, but no such device at all exists in France. The *Commission de Vérification des Comptes des Entreprises Publiques* was created in 1948 following the nationalizations introduced after the Liberation. Its functions are to audit the accounts of the public enterprises placed under its jurisdiction and to report on the efficiency with which they are managed. These functions can be extended to companies in which public enterprise has a majority participation. The Commission plays to some extent the same role with respect to public enterprise as the *Cour des Comptes* plays with respect to the administration. The Commission is divided into five sections, each investigating a particular branch of industry, one of which is energy. The members of the Commission are drawn mainly from the *Cour des Comptes* (whose members are recruited exclusively and directly from the *Ecole Nationale d'Administration* and whose appointments cannot be revoked) and partly from the *Ministère des Finances*. Detailed auditing is done by personnel recruited from a variety of sources under the supervision of a member of the Commission.

The Commission establishes a report at certain intervals on the enterprises under its jurisdiction, which is discussed in draft with the technical and financial tutelles, i.e. the *Ministère de l'Industrie* and the *Ministère des Finances*. The final reports are not published but are sent to the Ministries who transmit them to the enterprise; the report is sent also to the Parliament. The role of the Commission in devising and operating policy is definitely to frustrate. This is not a criticism of the work of the Commission but simply a result of its relatively narrow interest. As public enterprise is increasingly required to incorporate political guidelines into its decision making, for example to reduce unemployment, to conserve foreign exchange and a host of other considerations, so its activities open themselves to criticisms from the Commission. The Commission's responsibilities for control conflict with controls imposed by other institutions. Apart from this secondary factor, the controls exercised by the Commission are not important for this study; they are designed to ensure good management and may or may not succeed in that aim; they are not designed in any way to facilitate the evolution or operation of policy.

For the purpose of policy the most important controls are those exercised by the Ministries. Public enterprise is generally said to have two tutelles or sponsor ministries; one is a technical tutelle, the other the financial tutelle. In the case of the energy industries the former is the *Ministère de l'Industrie*, the second is the *Ministère des Finances*. Generally the technical tutelle is responsible for the elaboration of sectorial policies and the financial tutelle for ensuring that the activities of the enterprise conform to whatever principles are guiding the economy as a whole.

B. Means of Control

The means of control are classified as *a priori* and *a posteriori*; they are further subdivided by Garner as follows:[1]

a priori
(a) powers of appointment;
(b) the presence of civil servants at many levels of the organization of the enterprise;
(c) the provision or authorization of finance;
(d) the power to approve investments and other decisions;

a posteriori
(a) revocation of appointments;
(b) monitoring of results;
(c) the reports of the *Commission de Vérification des Comptes des Entreprises Publiques*.

For the purpose of policy making the *a priori* controls are evidently the most important, indeed it probably is true that in this contect the *a posteriori* controls are of negligible significance.

C. Civil Servants in the Organization

The organizational structure of most of the public enterprises in France operating in the energy field is built around the *Conseil d'Administration* and the *direction*. The *Conseil d'Administration* is in principle responsible for matters of policy; it has at its head a President. The direction is responsible for management; it is led by the *Directeur-Général*. The relationship between these bodies varies from enterprise to enterprise. The main variable is the extent to which the *Conseil d'Administration* modifies the proposals of the *direction*, in other words the extent to which it imposes government policy or, alternatively, filters the initiatives of the *direction* before they are put to the appropriate Ministry. These variations arise in turn from the variety of forms for public enterprise in France; those used in the industrial sector of the economy can be categorized as:

(a) *établissements publics de caractère industriel et commercial;*

(b) *sociétés nationales* (companies in which the State is the only shareholder);

(c) *sociétés d'économie mixte.*

Class (a) includes electricity, gas, coal, ERAP and *Régie Autonome des Transports Parisiens* (RATP). Class (b) includes the *Société Nationale des Chemins de Fer Français* (SNCF) and the *Société Nationale des Entreprises de Presse.* Class (c) includes the *Compagnie Française des Pétroles* and *Elf-Aquitaine*; (a) and (b) are largely indistinguishable in matters of government control.

It is worth looking in detail at an example of the composition, responsibilities and powers of the *Conseil d'Administration* in an organization with no private participation. *Electricité de France* is administered by a Council of 15 members, nominated by decree on the recommendation of the *Ministre de l'Industrie* for a period of five years. The origins of these 15 members are required to be distributed as:

five representatives of the State; two proposed by the *Ministre de l'Industrie*, two proposed by the *Ministre des Finances*, one proposed by the *Ministre de l'Agriculture*.

five are people designated because of their personal competence in industrial and financial matters, at least two of whom should be representatives of the few local gas and electricity distribution companies which still exist (publicly owned). At present the other three are André Giraud (the *Administrateur Général du Commissariat à l'Energie Atomique*), the President of St. Gobain and a *Maire*.

five representatives of the personnel proposed by the unions which are most representative of the personnel. At present there are two representatives from the CGT, one from the CGT-FO, one from the CFDT and one from the UNCM (a management union).

The five representatives of the State comprise the *Chef de Service à la Direction du Trésor* and the *Directeur du Budget* from the *Ministère des*

Finances. *Les Finances* has made the most of its two seats, by appointing two of its top men. The *Ministère de l'Industrie* has other ways of exerting its influence and is content to appoint two men not actually on its staff, M. Paul Delouvrier (an *Inspecteur général des Finances*) and an *Ingénieur général des Mines*.

The President is named by a decree from the Council of Ministers or the proposal of the *Conseil d'Administration* and the advice of the *Ministère de l'Industrie*. In practice the *Conseil d'Administration* has only a formal role in this appointment. The President is almost invariably a senior civil servant from one of the *grands corps* – at present it is M. Paul Delouvrier, *Inspecteur général des Finances*, one time *préfet*.

Although the law has fixed in considerable detail the composition of the Council it has not, surprisingly, defined its powers and these have been determined by usage.

On the basis of the reports submitted to it by the *Directeur-Général* (who participates at the meetings of the Council with a consultative voice) the Council defines the general policy of the organization taking into account the guidelines given by the public authorities. They approve the Annual Report of the organization, approve the accounts and balance sheet of the past year and the proposed budget for the following year, presented to it by the *Directeur-Général*. The Council has also certain specific powers which it has assigned to itself; it sanctions long-term borrowing when the amount exceeds a predetermined sum fixed by the Council itself; it sanctions investment, acquisitions and certain sales when these exceed predetermined limits set by the Council. With rare exceptions the Council meets only 10 times a year, once a month save July and August. Two commissions prepare the work for the Council; one of these commissions deals with matters involving investment, for example the planning and financing of plant; the other handles matters of operation, i.e. production, transport, distribution of electricity. The *Directeur-Général* can be questioned at these meetings on any matters concerning the enterprise.

Despite this impressive list of duties, the practical role of the *Conseil d'Administration* is extremely limited. The decisions which are approved by the Council are almost invariably those for which the enterprise requires approval from one or other of the Ministries; the negotiations preceding the formulation of proposals invariably take place directly between the officers of the Ministry and the Direction. The *Conseil d'Administration*, despite appearances, acts very little as a filter.

Recognition of this limited significance of the *Conseil d'Administration* has caused many English-speaking people to wonder at the 'weakness of the boards'. This confusion is encouraged by the insistence on translating *Conseil d'Administration* by 'board'. In fact the original idea of the *Conseil d'Administration* was that it provided a vehicle by which all the different parties, interested by the activities of a great industrial enterprise in public ownership, should be able to give their opinions and have the actions of the enterprise

97

explained. The Council was essentially a means of informing and receiving the views of a wide spectrum of outside interests; at that time the participation of the State in the Council, both directly and indirectly, was less than now. Then, as now, it was not a convenient forum for the Ministries to express their ill (or good) humour. In time, the outside interests were squeezed out and replaced by the State and the unions. The Council still plays the role of a receiver and emitter of information (mostly the latter) but to a more restricted audience. The principal function now is to instruct the civil service members in the course of affairs and the nature of opinion in the industrial and commercial world. This is considered to be valuable. There are other channels by which the Ministries can obtain information; if the *Conseil d'Administration* is of special value, it is presumably in that it provides a personal experience to some of the top men who otherwise would rely on reports of their agents in the enterprise. It is difficult to see how this is likely to be any more effective than the same material forcefully presented by the enterprise to the same man around a table in the Ministry. One concludes that although the device of the *Conseil d'Administration* may work, and may even work well, as an information centre it is just one out of many possible ways of doing the same thing; it is not a special and unique piece of apparatus.

If one wishes to find an analogy to the United Kingdom Board, which is an exercise of limited use, then a better candidate is the *Direction*, or more properly the *Direction Générale*. The *Direction Générale* assumes the responsibility for the technical, administrative and financial management of EDF. As for the President, the *Directeur-Général* is named on the proposal of the *Conseil d'Administration* on the advice of the *Ministre de l'Industrie* by a decree of the Council of Ministers. Like the President, the *Directeur-Général* will usually have at some time been a civil servant and belong to one of the *grand corps*; he is more likely than the President to come, in his immediate past, from the industry. The powers of management are delegated to the *Directeur-Général* by the President. At EDF the *Directeur-Général* is assisted by a *Directeur-Général Délégué*, a *Directeur-Général Adjoint*, a *Délégué Général* for the elaboration of long-term policy guidelines, and by 11 directors who each have responsibility for one of the fundamental functions of the *Direction Générale*, or for one of the activities of the enterprise, e.g. General Economic Studies, Public Relations, Finance, Personnel, etc. These Directeurs have responsibilities similar to those of departmental managers in a United Kingdom structure, but they act in many ways like a board in that they meet frequently and act as the motor and source of initiative of the enterprise.

The only member of the *Conseil d'Administration* who has any real influence on the enterprise is the President. (The men who are government appointees will exercise a real influence in their Ministerial capacities from their offices in the Ministry, but not as members of the Council.) The relationship between the President and the *Directeur-Général* is important. The *Directeur-Général* controls the staff and thereby the information, he is not completely dependent on the President for resources because he can approach the Ministries directly, which bodies can then intervêne with the President. On the whole the *Directeur-Général* is in the stronger position, but evidently the organization will operate more smoothly if there is close agreement between the two men. The extent to which the President will actively intervene in the affairs of the enterprise will depend on the personality of the man and his conception of the job. M. Delouvrier is an active President of the EDF who apparently enjoys a harmonious relationship with M. Boiteux, the *Directeur-Général*, and shares a common conception of the aims of EDF.

Another State presence in EDF is the *Commissaire du Gouvernement*. The occupant of this post is specified to be the *Directeur du Gaz, de l'Electricité et du Charbon*, i.e. it is the man directly responsible within the Ministry for the sector into which EDF fits. He now has an adjoint, the *Directeur des Industries Métalliques, Méchaniques et Electriques*, also from the *Ministère de l'Industrie*. This innovation is a recognition of the enormous significance of EDF for the heavy mechanical and electrical engineering companies. The *Commissaire* and his adjoint can attend the meetings of the *Conseil d'Administration*; they can speak, but not vote. There is no obvious reason why these representatives should not be members of the Council like the senior civil servants from the *Ministère des Finances*; it is presumably to avoid an undue predominance of departmental representatives. (The *Ministère de l'Industrie* is also in a slightly different relationship to the enterprise than the *Ministère des Finances*; it is the former that is the sponsor or 'protector' of the enterprise.)

Finally there are the *Contrôleurs d'Etat*. They are appointed by the *Ministère des Finances*. Their function is continuously to monitor the progress of the industry. They can establish themselves on the premises of the enterprise and can examine any of its documents and records; they report to the *Ministère des Finances* on the financial state of the enterprise and provide an opinion on any matters which the Ministry may feel it wishes better to comprehend. The head of the mission has the right to attend meetings of the *Conseil d'Administration*, to speak but not to vote, except that he may veto certain decisions until they have been considered by the *Ministre des Finances*. The principle is essentially that of a ubiquitous watchdog. The *Contrôleurs d'Etat* also play a constructive role in indicating to the enterprise the likely attitude of the *Ministère des Finances* towards certain activities that may be in mind. They constitute a special corps drawn from the *grands corps*, usually the *Inspection des Finances* and the *Cour des Comptes*.

The system described for EDF applies with little change to GDF and CDF. CDF does not have a *Commissaire du Gouvernement* and it is my impression that in neither GDF nor CDF is the President so active in helping to put the affairs of the enterprise across to civil servants and the public at large.

ERAP was also set up as a *établissement public à caractère industriél et commercial* under the *tutelle* of the *Ministre de l'Industrie* when it was formed in 1965. The formal structure of ERAP is designed in a similar way to that of EDF. It is administered by a council named for six years, composed of

12 members comprising a senior civil servant as President (in the case of ERAP the decrees specify this), two representatives of the *Ministre de l'Industrie*, two representatives of the *Ministre des Finances*, one representative of the *Ministre des Affaires Etrangères*, and six people of French nationality chosen for their competence. The last group are named on the recommendation of the *Ministre des Finances* and of the *Ministre de l'Industrie*. The *Directeur des Carburants* assumes the functions of the *Commissaire du Gouvernement* (he is the head of the section responsible for oil policy in the *Ministère de l'Industry* and the equivalent of the *Directeur du Gaz, de l'Electricité et du Charbon* for oil). The *Conseil d'Administration* is in this case charged with specified duties, notably to concern itself with the programmes of activity and investment, budget, marketing forecasts, financial accounts, loans and many other specified particulars. In the case of ERAP the *Ministère des Finances* is able to exercise greater influence over the appointments to the Council than in the case of EDF/GDF/CDF. There are also, of course, the *Contrôleurs d'Etat* appointed by the *Ministre des Finances*.

ERAP is obliged to draw up each year a forecast of expenditure and receipts and to present it in a form tightly specified by the *Ministre des Finances*. Forecasts relating to capital transactions may be required to cover several years. These forecasts must be approved by the *Ministre de l'Industrie* and the *Ministre des Finances*. In addition to the forecasts the accounts for the past year have to be approved by the Ministries.

The posts of President and *Directeur-Général* were combined in one man – M. Pierre Guillaumat; thereby avoiding any conflict between the heads of these two crucial elements of the organization. The President is nominated by the Council of Ministers on the recommendation of the *Ministre de l'Industrie*.

ERAP has now been merged with the *Société Nationale des Pétroles d'Aquitaine* to form the *Société Nationale Elf Aquitaine* and the centre of government control has become the latter company. A form of organization was constructed which closely resembles that of the *Compagnie Française des Pétroles* (CFP).

The CFP is administered by a Council composed of not less than six and not more than 12 members. The State has a number of seats proportional to its participation in the capital. The other members of the Council are chosen from among the shareholders and nominated by the general meeting of shareholders. The State, of course, has 45% of the votes in the general meeting and invariably this is enough to determine the vote; the members are effectively chosen by the State, it is not uncommon for the State to wish to put members on to the Council who have no shares and they therefore purchase a nominal holding. The Council is not in practice in any sense representative of minority shareholders, but appointments are used by the Government for the same ends as on the *Conseil d'Administration* of completely State-owned companies. The Council as a vehicle for information is used to instruct a wider audience than in other enterprises. At present the Council includes the *Président-Directeur Général* (PDG) of *Pechiney-Ugine-*

Kuhlmann (20 shares), the PDG of the *Compagnie Auxiliaire de Navigation* (200 shares), and the *Président* of *Crédit Nord* (220 shares). Indeed only one of the 'non-State' representatives has other than a symbolic holding, that is, M. Desmarais who was closely associated with the early history of the company.

This effective control of the Council by the State has developed over time. At the origin the State had only two *Commissaires du Gouvernement*, one of whom had the right of veto, but they had no powers of direction or creative role; they could simply ensure that the company kept to certain points laid down in the statutes under which the company was formed. This in itself was quite bizarre because the company was completely private and the State had no financial interest. Later the State became a shareholder and established a more reasonable legal basis, but did not increase the number of commissaires. Ambiguities remained because the State's shares were held by the *Trésor Public* which was a wing of the *Ministère des Finances* charged also with the duty of watching over the CFP; the Ministry was both shareholder and public watchdog and had a dual obligation to see that the company acted in the way most favourable to its shareholders, but also that the company's actions were in accordance with the State's political objectives. After the October War the State mounted a new offensive on the *Conseil d'Administration*, partly because the Government administration and the Parliament were convinced that the CFP had too much independence – this was the time of the Schwarz Report. The reinforcement of State control took the form of statutory changes and a tightening of existing practices. The State took the right to put four representatives on the Council in addition to the *Commissaires du Gouvernement*.

In the past only the Commissaire representing the *Ministre de l'Industrie* had a veto, the Commissaire representing the *Ministre des Finances* had only the right to make observations. The former was also in practice the more important influence and occupied himself from day to day with the affairs of the company. The *Ministère des Finances* has now strengthened its control over the company; it has established a *mission de contrôle des sociéties pétrolières*, the head of whom is the *Commissaire du Gouvernement* representing the *Ministre des Finances*; he now has a power of veto and an office in the headquarters of CFP; his powers have changed little (he can see documents and attend meetings) but they are now fully used and the *Ministère des Finances* has a much heavier presence in CFP than it has ever had before. The reaction of the *Ministère des Finances* was probably less a result of the Schwarz Report than dismay at the diversification of CFP, especially into banking. The Schwarz Report provided a suitable excuse for action. The CFP fought these new measures for a long time and the matter was taken to the *Conseil d'Etat*, but the State prevailed.

The CFP provided in 1959 an interesting example of how the State could use the *Conseil d'Administration* as a vehicle for transmitting information. It was the time when the State was contemplating the construction of an oil company of which it would own 100%. There was an empty place in the

Conseil d'Administration of the CFP. The President of the Council was asked by the Government to name M. Guillaumat to the vacant place. M. Guillaumat was not the *Commissaire du Gouvernement*, nor a shareholder, but he had the support of de Gaulle and he succeeded. The common view of the staff of CFP is that the action was quite scandalous, although no one has ever suggested that Guillaumat, who is always described as a man of great integrity, abused his position. Now there is considerable intermixing of the *Conseils d'Administration* of SNEA and CFP. In addition to M. Guillaumat there were, in 1976, three other common members: M. Blancard, M. Desmarais, M. Granier de Lilliac. The *Commissaires du Gouvernement* are also common to the two companies.

The structure and nature of the *Conseil d'Administration* of SNEA is similar to that which now exists for the CFP. The representatives of the *Ministre des Finances, de l'Industrie* and *des Affaires Etrangères* have given way to representatives of the State including M. Jean Blancard (President of GDF) and M. Robert Hirsch (a *Préfet*). The *Directeur des Carburants* has been joined as a *Commissaire du Gouvernement* by the Head of the *Mission de Contrôle des Sociétés Pétrolières* of the *Ministère des Finances*, with powers analogous to those they exercise in the same capacities on the Council of CFP. It is interesting how the relationships between the State and the two companies, originally conceived so differently, have moved steadily towards a similar model. The CFP, originally an arm's length relationship, has come more under Government control; ERAP has merged with private capital. The State has gained much more ground in CFP than it has conceded in ERAP. Indeed it is arguable that the State has really conceded anything in the Elf group other than a form of private participation. Certainly the *Ministère des Finances* has extended its own powers in that it now possesses a veto instead of being (in principle) one voice in the Council.

In the case of the companies, the enterprises do not have to submit to direct control by the Ministries of their strategies and plans for investment; consequently the most important means of control by the State is the *Conseil d'Administration*. The important sanction is the right of veto, behind that there is the State control of the shareholders' meeting, but that is never required other than formally. There is, of course, a sense in which the State has arranged to have its cake and eat it too. The enterprises are intended to be *auto-suffisants* (self-sufficient) and are not supposed to seek assistance from the State. On the other hand, the State exercises close control over the enterprise through the Conseil d'Administration. It is difficult to see how these three factors are reconciled: independence from the State for resources, large State shareholdings and State control through the *Conseil d'Administration*.

The opportunities for civil servants to find posts in public enterprise are not confined to the *Conseil d'Administration*. There are extensive arrangements for civil servants to be seconded to posts elsewhere in the public sector or even occasionally to the private sector. One class of secondment (*détache-*

ment) permits a civil servant, either on his own initiative or at the initiative of the Administration, to take up an alternative post for almost any period. The mechanism is widely used and provides for a notable penetration of nationalized industry by civil servants. It is also used to permit civil servants to work in international organizations, local authorities and universities. In all cases he retains seniority and pension rights and is entitled to be reintegrated into his *corps* at the end of his period of secondment. A civil servant with 15 years of service and a previous secondment of five years or more can accept a secondment *hors cadre* which permits an even wider choice of post outside the civil service. He still retains his seniority, pension rights and the possibility of eventual reintegration. Secondment of this nature is in principle open to members of any *corps* of the civil service. But membership of the *grands corps de l'Etat* (*Conseil d'Etat*, the *Cour des Comptes* and the *Inspection Générale des Finances*), allows for almost unlimited *détachement* to other parts of the public sector. This is intended, and does, ensure that members of these *corps* will be found in key positions inside and outside the civil service. Membership of the more important technical *corps* also allows for extensive *détachement* and although each technical *corps* exists in principle to fill posts in a particular industry (e.g. *Corps des Ingénieurs des Mines* for those in the *Ministère de l'Industrie*) their members are again found in many different jobs throughout the public sector. Civil servants from the *Ministère des Affaires Etrangères* are also to be found in industry whenever the Ministry feels its interests are to be furthered by influence within and information from a given sector; the Ministry devotes considerable effort to infiltration of the French oil companies.

The movement is not one way. Members of the nationalized industries are also frequently seconded to the government departments where they may work on matters that are only peripherally related to the interests of their industry. There is a particularly healthy traffic between EDF and the *Ministère des Finances*.

The system of interchange between nationalized industries and the civil service undoubtedly facilitates mutual understanding in what is plausibly a fruitful and constructive way. It not only helps the Administration to operate its policies more easily, but it provides a channel by which the enterprises can influence the Administration. The persistent control of industry by agents of the Administration must also facilitate mutual understanding, in that the presence of government agents causes and permits a better transfer of information, ideas and attitudes, but this aspect of the presence of the Administration within industry is a chronic irritant.

D. Provision of Finance

A French public enterprise can finance its investments in a variety of ways. It can use its own resources, it can benefit from *dotations en capital* (allocations of capital) from the State, it may receive loans from the State at reduced rates of interest or it may borrow on the national or international market. All means other than autofinance require the sanction of the *Ministère des Finances*.

It is probably as well to begin an account of the means of finance available to nationalized industries by describing the elaboration of the budget. The State Budget, which covers the calendar year, is prepared by the *Ministère des Finances* under the authority of the Prime Minister and requires the approval of the Council of Ministers before it can be submitted to the *Assemblée Nationale*. The Finance Law containing the proposed budget for a particular year must be submitted to the *Assemblée Nationale* by the first Tuesday of the October of the preceding year. The examination of the second part of the Finance Law containing the forecast expenditures for each Ministry constitutes the essential means of control that Parliament exercises on government policy. Parliament has, in principle, the opportunity to verify that the projects adopted in preceding years (*autorisations de programme*) are proceeding satisfactorily and that the sums allocated for projects in the coming year (*crédits de paiement*) are sufficient. The *a priori* control of the coming year's budget permits government policy to be defined by the elected members of Parliament; the *a posteriori* control ensures that the defined policy has been respected.

In fact the extent of *a priori* control is restricted; the authority of Parliament in amending any proposed Finance Law is limited to making changes that will increase public revenue or decrease public expenditure. Furthermore, Parliament has the power to allocate funds only among certain broad categories. These allocations must be respected by the Government, but it retains the discretion to determine the details of expenditure within these broad categories.

Parliament is assisted in the operation of the *a posteriori* control by the *Cour des Comptes*. At the beginning of the summer the President of the *Cour des Comptes* meets the *Commission des Finances de l'Assemblée Nationale* which comprises members of the *Assemblée Nationale* to whom has been delegated the responsibility of studying a particular section of the budget (rapporteurs). The *Cour des Comptes* assists the rapporteurs in their study of the execution of the budget proposals on the basis of which study the *Assemblée* will decide whether or not to adopt the law submitted by the Government to Parliament in the spring, recapitulating the actual revenues and expenditures of the State for the preceding year. This law is known as the *Loi de Règlement*; its adoption signifies that Parliament is content with the management of the Government and the administration in that year.

The rapporteurs with the responsibility of reporting on a particular industry have the authority to follow the use of the money voted to the department, *sur pièces et sur place*, which permits them to make investigations on the spot and demand to see any documents which may be relevant to the budgetary control of the Ministries or of the public enterprises and mixed economy companies attached to the Ministries. But, the work of the rapporteurs cannot be used for any other purpose than that of verifying the management of the budget allocated.

In the Fourth Republic both chambers of Parliament had a special committee with wide powers to investigate the financial, technical and administrative record of public enterprise; again they enjoyed the authority to investigate *sur pièces et sur place*. These committees are not permitted under the Fifth Republic; the rights of Parliament are now limited to those of the *Commission des Finances*. The work of the rapporteurs is uneven[2] and their attitude varies considerably (depending principally on whether they form part of the opposition or the majority). Some of them do their best to lend their work a political dimension, but on the whole the restricted nature of the task prevents it from having much political consequence.

An excellent example of the practical irrelevance of the activities of the committees of the *Assemblée Nationale* is the report prepared by the *Commission des Finances* on energy policy for the 1978 budget.[3] This report was extremely critical of the present energy programme and the commitment to nuclear energy. Not only did the report have absolutely no effect on the policy, but when I contacted the public relations department of EDF about the report, it became apparent that they had never even heard of it.

The structure of the State Budget is complex, we can only mention a few points directly relevant to energy policy. The budget only reflects the revenues and expenditures of State enterprise to the extent that the State extends loans or subsidies to them or receives from them payments of interest, dividends or loan repayments. State subsidies to meet operating deficits of State enterprises are included under the heading relating to the Government department which oversees the enterprise. Capital contributions of a general nature to State enterprise (such as a *dotation en capital*) are included in the budget of the Ministry of Finances. Capital contributions made by the State to State enterprises for specific investments are included under the heading relating to the government department which oversees the enterprise. All loans and advances made by the State to State enterprises are included in a special section known as the Loan and Advance Budget. Access to these funds requires the authorization of the *Fonds de Développement Economique et Social* (FDES).

The example of the 1978 budget of the *Ministère de l'Industrie* may help to clarify the structure. The proposed *loi des finances* for 1978 allocated to the *Ministère de l'Industrie* a total of 9,921 MF of *crédits de paiement* and 3534 MF of *autorisations de programme*. The *crédits de paiement* (sums allocated for future projects) break down into 6,456 MF for ongoing expenses and 3,466 MF for expenditure on equipment. The most important components of the former class are an operating subsidy of 3,500 MF to CDF and a subsidy of 1,911 MF to the CEA. The largest components of the expenditure on equipment are 956 MF for space research, 612 MF for computing research and 1,155 MF for the CEA.

Within the confines of energy policy the Ministry disposes of the 3,500 MF subsidy to CDF and the 3,066 MF for the CEA as mentioned above but also smaller sums for the *Agence des Economies d'Energie* (69 MF), the *Agence des Energies Nouvelles* (39 MF), for improving hydroelectric installations (55 MF) prospecting for uranium (20 MF). In addition, but not within the budget of the *Ministère de l'Industrie*, there are foreseen expenditures of 1,245 MF in allocations of capital to public enterprises, 1,250 MF in loans from the FDES to State energy enterprises and 245 MF in a fund intended to promote exploration for hydrocarbons, but at the moment used to disguise losses in oil refining – the *fonds de soutien aux hydrocarbures*.

It appears at first sight that the *Ministère de l'Industrie* disposes of a considerable budget – 9,921 MF of which 6,752 MF are dedicated to the energy policy. But in practice 6,566 MF are for the purpose of subsidizing the CDF and the non-commercial activities of the CEA. The CDF is not an actor of major importance in energy policy and the politically significant parts of the CEA are now incorporated in Cogema, a private company wholly owned by CEA. The vast majority of the Ministry's budget is therefore not of a nature that permits it substantially to affect the course of energy policy. The remaining 186 MF that the Ministry has at its disposal are those mentioned for energy conservation, new sources, improvement of hydroelectric installations and uranium prospecting; the credits for the *Agence pour les Economies d'Energie*, although small, have been skilfully deployed by the Director of that particular agency and permitted the Ministry to intervene directly in aspects of energy policy relating to energy conservation.

One should perhaps also stress that although these budgetary allocations have been won from the *Ministère des Finances* and voted by Parliament, when the Ministry comes to draw on its credits it must justify each drawing to the *Direction du Trésor* and demonstrate that the purpose to which the funds will be put fulfils the intentions of government policy. The *Direction du Trésor* at that moment becomes *de facto* the interpreter and guardian of Government policy. It may refuse to permit the drawing in which case the spending Minister can appeal to the Prime Minister, but there is evidently a limit to the number of times he can adopt that procedure. Consequently, even after the budget has been voted the *Ministère des Finances* retains considerable control. And, in any case, as we have noted, in the particular case of the energy policy the sums which the *Ministère de l'Industrie* can spend with any real discretion are derisory.

The bulk of State payments to State enterprise (*dotations en capital* and loans from the FDES) are part of the budget of the *Ministère des Finances*. Even more importantly the *Rue de Rivoli* controls the access by State enterprise to the national and international financial markets.

The *Conseil de Direction du Fonds de Développement Economique et Social* (Board of Directors of the Economic and Social Development Fund), was created by decree in 1955 to replace the *Commission des Investissements*. The *Conseil* has the responsibility of examining the investment programmes of the public administrations and public enterprises and any investment financed by or with the help of the State. It gives its opinion on the priority, the rhythm of execution of the works and the mode of financing which it considers most appropriate. Subsequently it is regularly informed of the progress of investment programmes.

It is generally unwise for a supplicant to ignore the opinion of the Council because it also has the job of advising the *Ministère des Finances* on the management of the *Fonds de Développement Economique et Social* (FDES). The upshot of all this is that the Council exercises great power over the State enterprises; its sanction would be required even if the investment programme were entirely autofinanced and its power increases as the rate of autofinancing of the enterprise falls.

The Council is dominated by the *Rue de Rivoli*; the *Ministère des Finances* presides and the membership includes several members of his Ministry (the *Directeur du Trésor* and the *Directeur du Budget* amongst others). The Ministers from the more important departments sit regularly on the Council, others attend only for matters which concern them directly. It is interesting that the *Délégué Général à l'Energie* is a permanent member although he is not a Minister; apart from the officers of the *Ministère des Finances* and the banks there are few civil servants, the presence of the *Délégué Général à l'Energie* is a measure of the importance of the energy investment programme. The Secretariat of the Council is provided by the *Direction du Trésor*. The work of the Council is preceded by preliminary work in 14 specialist committees, one of which is devoted to energy. In particular the energy committee has the task of approving the investment programmes of CDF, EDF, GDF, CNR, *Gaz du Sud-Ouest*, the *Société Nationale des Pétroles d'Aquitaine* and the CEA.[4] It would be difficult to overestimate the importance of this committee in the life of the State enterprises.

References

1. A background paper prepared by M. M. R. Garner for NEDO, *Relationships of Government and Public Enterprise in France, West Germany and Sweden*, provides a valuable discussion of this topic.
2. 'Les rapporteurs du budget sont-ils les censeurs ou les auxiliares du gouvernement?' *Le Monde*, 20 October 1977.
3. *Rapport fait au nom de la Commission des Finances*. Annexe No. 23. Assemblée Nationale No. 3131, 15 November 1977.
4. *Rapport pour 1976–1977*, Conseil de Direction du Fonds de Développement Economique et Social.

V

Energy in the Plans

The French post-war experience of indicative planning holds a perennial fascination for Anglo-Saxons. Many writers have found in the French notion of indicative planning a 'third way' characterized by the harmonization of State and individual interests and to be distinguished from the equally unattractive extremes of a free market with rules little improved over those of the jungle or of a planned economy and its inevitable restraints on individual freedom. It is not the intention here to grapple with such difficult ideas, but simply to ascertain the influence that *le Plan* has on the formulation and operation of energy policy. There have been many studies of the planning process, assessments of its effects, judgements as to its value in French conditions and claims for what the techniques might achieve elsewhere.[1-6] There has also been an interesting account of how French industry responds to the Plan.[7] There have been few assessments of how the French planning procedures influence policy in the large technical sectors dominated by public enterprise, and none, as far as I know, of energy policy. This gap is all the more surprising because, in the face of the difficulties in energy supply which confront so many countries in the world, there has been a consistent expression of belief that the only salvation lies in rigorous planning; proponents of this view cite the example of the determined prosecution of a large programme of nuclear power in France in support of this proposition. It is useful therefore to try to gauge to what extent the mechanisms and attitudes of *la planification française* have influenced energy policy.

The space of this investigation is severely restricted to matters related to energy policy in the Fourth, Fifth, Sixth, and Seventh Plans, even within this narrow scope there is an emphasis on the later plans. It would be wrong to transfer any of the conclusions to other sectors or to assume they would necessarily hold for earlier plans, especially as the nature of the French planning activity has evolved and mutated over the years.

The discussion which follows is broken down into what is generally expected of the Plan, the process by which it is formulated, the powers for operating it and the effects that can be detected.

108

A. Expectations of Planning

There are many different formulations of expectations from the planning process which depend on the character of the observer and the epoch to which they relate.

A profound and particularly French expectation of the early plans which was rarely, if ever, made explicit was that this was the chosen medium of the State through which the citizen would be indicated the way to recovery from the effects of the Second World War. It was a natural consequence of the French attitude to industry and the tradition of State direction that the individual would look to the central administration for guidance in coping with conditions of unprecedented social, economic and political disruption.

Many observers have argued that the hierarchical administrative system, reflecting the structures of authority in the Catholic Church, deliberately preserved a complex, but static, social system in which there was a place for everyone and, conversely, in which everyone knew his place.[8, 9] The administration tolerated restrictive business practices which inhibited progress but assured stability and security: security for the capitalist that he would not be put out of business, security for the worker that he would not lose his niche in life, security for the establishment that the *status quo* would not be disturbed. A second consequence of the long-established hierarchical structures of authority to which the majority freely acquiesced was that the progress which was made in the relatively static society was initiated in large part by State institutions. An excellent example of this was the role of the State Bank in the French economic life. From its foundation in 1936, the Bank of France was a principal source of support and encouragement for the private financial groups, the heavy electrical and mechanical engineering concerns, the mining companies and the colonial economy. 'All the strongholds of French economic life were in the main built up, not with private capital and at private risk, but on a foundation of State concessions, with capital provided by the State, with guarantees which removed the element of risk, with the aid of public subsidies and with deficits covered from public funds . . . '.[10]

During the Second World War the economy of France became a military instrument; the same was true of the U.S.A., Japan and the other European countries affected by the War and no doubt the effects can be traced to some extent everywhere, but in France the unprecedented powers over industry assigned to the State as a consequence of the War were particularly appropriate to the centralized administrative structure and particularly difficult to reverse. The prevailing conjunction of circumstance reinforced by a long tradition provided a congenial environment for the direct and powerful appropriation of control of industry by planning and nationalization.

Political changes contributed equally. Immediately after the War the Resistance held political power under the supervision of the Allies until general elections in October 1945. Subsequently, a coalition government was formed under de Gaulle, comprising the Communists, Socialists and Christian Democrats. It soon broke up, but in its short life succeeded in imposing much of the programme of the Resistance, including the national planning procedure and the nationalization of the coal mines by the law of 17 May 1946 and of the gas and electricity supply industries by the law of 8 April 1946. Planning was a technique that appealed both to Communists and to de Gaulle; to the Communists because they considered State control of industrial activity indispensable, and to de Gaulle, in part because he shared the view of the State as the most competent source of initiative and in part because he saw a planned economy as a means of reversing past attitudes. This was the indispensable prerequisite to building a competitive industrial economy, in turn the vital base for renewing the international political role which de Gaulle and his colleagues envisaged for France. Planning probably meant different things to the Communists and to de Gaulle, and the parties probably had different aims, but they shared the view that the industrial establishment had disgraced itself by collaboration, that a new economic order was necessary and that a planned economy was the right instrument.

A fascinating account of the conception of *le plan d'équipement et de modernisation* at the end of the War, the expectations of the architects and the political processes by which it was brought about, has been given by M. Jean Monnet.[11]

After the break-up of the Coalition Government there followed a succession of governments and dreadful political engagements in Indo-China, Algeria and Suez, culminating in the revolutionary junta and the return of de Gaulle to political power. De Gaulle inaugurated a new period of stability and a new dedication to industrial growth. It is interesting that among those involved in the planning operations or on whose activities the Plan impinges, there is little consensus as to what was the Golden Age of planning. Most regard the First Plan as something special, and there is widespread agreement that plans are not what they used to be, but apart from those points of concord the field is split. There are those who believe that the Plan served best in the period of instability whilst de Gaulle was in the wilderness because in that chaotic period there was nothing else. And there are those who believe that planning had been most effective when de Gaulle was there to give it authority and direction. It is likely that there is truth in both views and that the Plan changed its character between whiles. Generally the Plans constructed without de Gaulle were modest in their aims, the architects keeping a low profile in an essentially hostile or indifferent political environment, but nevertheless contributing to continuity where it would otherwise have been lacking. The Plans devised while de Gaulle was in power are more ambitious and generally concerned in a wider political context.

The point of this lengthy digression is that the indicative planning was born of particular circumstances and of a long tradition of State initiative in industry. The greatest and least avowed expectation of the Plan was the expectation that the State would tell the people what to do in difficult times. This expectation was undoubtedly fulfilled which explains the great psychological success

110

of the First Plan, but it is in large part peculiar to the combination of the time and the nature of French society. It would not therefore be at all unreasonable to argue that indicative planning, even in France, had served its purpose and had its day.

But there are more general expectations of indicative planning. Perhaps the most modest expression is that of M. Pierre Massé, who was *Commissaire du Plan* from 1959 to 1966; he coined the celebrated description of the Plan as *l'anti-hasard*; that is to say a mechanism for reducing as far as possible the uncertainties inherent in the future.[5] But however modest or grand the expectations might be of the Plan as a whole, within the confines of the energy sector, they revolve essentially around two factors; the extent to which certain conflicts inherent in the formulation of long-term politices are resolved by the planning process and the extent to which the process permits the consensus of men of long sight and disinterest to prevail over contingent short-term considerations.

To elaborate on the first factor: new developments in energy supply require a long period from their conception to the instant at which they begin to function; they generally require a large investment in capital equipment which has no possibility of finding a use other than the purpose for which it was designed; it is essential therefore that the volume and value of investment made in one year corresponds closely to what will be required many years later. Moreover, many of the investments required have a functional relationship; this is especially true of electro-nuclear plant, but it applies to a lesser degree throughout the whole energy sector. Coherent evolution of investment programmes is clearly impossible without knowledge of what is intended by others, without agreement that the ensemble is indeed what is wanted and without confidence that everyone concerned will do his bit. On the other hand, it is impossible to forecast the way in which many critical determinants of future energy supply and demand will move; it is impossible to forecast what people will want in 10 years' time, impossible to forecast precisely what technology will be available, impossible to know what fundamental changes there will be in geo-political relationships throughout the world; impossible in short to describe the future with confidence enough to support a programme of investment constructed to meet the requirements of that future. A long-term policy is therefore both impossible and essential. One expectation that can usefully be investigated is that indicative planning will contribute to the resolution of this paradox.

One does not have to be naïve enough to expect a complete resolution; a more reasonable expectation is that comprehensive planning of all sectors simultaneously will remove some inconsistencies and permit the specification of consistent if uncertain futures. For example if a survey of the market for electricity concludes that the number of units sold should rise from 180 TWh in 1971 to 400 TWh in 1985, it is not because this is the limit of conceivable demand or because the electricity supply industry could not increase its production further, but rather it is because incomes, industrial production, popu-

111

lation, taxation, urbanization and investment in alternative energy supplies and in conservation will have attained a certain level. It can be argued that a particular industrial sector does not generate by itself information on population, incomes, consumption or the effects of urbanization and alternative investments. Viewed in this light a well-conceived national plan is an essential 'public service' in a modern economy. This weaker formulation of the expectations of the contribution of planning to long-term sectorial policy formation is taken almost verbatim from the writings of Pierre Massé, but modified to convert his example of the automobile industry to an energy industry.[12] In the same source Massé gives an example from electricity supply of an institution modifying its corporate planning because of the conclusions of *le Plan*. *Electricité de France* could never have decided in 1946 to choose as its objectives a near doubling of its highest prewar production figure, had it not been provided with a corresponding growth outlook for other sectors of the economy.' Massé is in an especially good position to know, because he was at the time director of investment at EDF.

In a similar vein the senior management of CFP assert that it was thanks to the forecasts of the First Plan that the company was able to convince itself of the necessity to build large refineries benefiting from economies of scale and that it was able to obtain the necessary foreign exchange from the Ministry of Finances.

The second general proposition is that the Plan will prevent the distortion of events by powerful economic or political groups to their own interests; for example, the planning procedure will ensure that the executive, with its notoriously near horizon, will not adopt policies aimed at appeasing their constituents in the short term, but which are insignificant or injurious in the long term. The great enterprises and powerful unions are obliged to meet in the presence of the State, to expose their intentions, to defend them and to agree a consistent set which in turn are coherent with the objectives of other sectors and the requirements of society at large. The parties that have participated in this vigorous regime of confrontation, discussion and arbitration are subsequently obliged to conform to the exigencies of the future as defined by the process. Or, if they are not obliged, they are at any rate severely inhibited from adopting a course of action that runs counter to the consensus achieved in detailed and relatively open discussions.

B. The Process of Planning

'The process of planning is more meaningful than the plan itself'; so claims M. Massé.[12] A fair appraisal should therefore include as much consideration of the process as of the plan.

The plan is prepared by the *Commissariat Général du Plan* (CGP); the responsibilities of this institution are purely administrative; it has no powers of management. The CGP has three functions; it is responsible for the preparation of the future plan; it monitors the execution of the plan actually in application; it is a permanent source of advice and information to the Government on matters of social and industrial development. The *Commissariat* is a relatively small body of *fonctionnaires* with a broad spectrum of backgrounds; they come from outside the institution and leave after a relatively short period; there is no opportunity for making a career in the *Commissariat*. Evidently the lack of real power and small staff obliges the CGP to proceed by a long process of consultation.

Naturally some of the bodies with whom the *Commissariat* consults have more influence than others. It is no surprise to find that the *Direction de la Prévision du Ministère des Finances* is a weighty participant in matters concerning the middle term; their colleagues in the *Direction du Budget du Ministère des Finances* have a similar authority in matters which affect the balancing of the budget in the short and medium term. Another institution on which the *Commissariat* depends heavily for statistical information, technical studies and macroeconomic projections is the *Institut National de la Statistique et des Etudes Economiques* (Insee) attached to the *Ministère des Finances*. The other administrative departments contribute according to their competence to the preparation of the plan, but it is clear that the *Rue de Rivoli* starts off with considerable power to form the context of the whole construction.

We shall return to the relationship between *les Finances* and the CGP a little later. Consultation does not end with *les Finances*. When Monnet set up the mechanism of the First Plan he considered it vital that the unions and industry should be closely associated with the elaboration of the Plan in order that the conclusions should be genuinely a concerted agreement. *Concertation* has always been the principal apparent characteristic of French planning; the means of obtaining this aim has been to name commissions covering in their ensemble the entire domain of activity. Some commissions have a 'vertical' competence comprising either a productive sector (agriculture, industry, energy . . .) or a public service (health, education . . .); other commissions have a horizontal competence extending over a large part, or the whole, of the domain (finance, employment . . .). The work of these commissions is synthesized by a particular commission whose title reflects the prevailing conception of the work – the *Commission de l'Economie Générale et du Financement du VIᵉ Plan* and the *Commission du Développement du VIIᵉ Plan*. Up to the time of the Seventh Plan the work of each commission was further broken down and assigned to committees or working groups. The result was a pyramidical hierarchy which attained the most perfected form for preparation of the Sixth Plan in which some 3,000 people took part, not counting those whose job it is to brief the committee members; inclusion of these contributors would multiply the total many times.

Attached to the Energy Commission during the Seventh Plan were the:
Comité du gaz
Comité du charbon
Comité de l'électricité
Comité du pétrole.

In addition the Commission also constituted five working groups to look at the following particular problems: energy prices; future guidelines; the energy needs of the residential and tertiary sectors; the energy needs of industry; and natural and enriched uranium.

From the *Commission de l'Energie* were suspended therefore a total of nine lower bodies. This was essentially the culmination of a fairly irregular growth in size and complexity of the bodies involved in the planning process; for reasons we shall come to later this was reversed for the preparation of the Seventh Plan. The number of commissions involved in each plan has been:

First: 8   Second: 22   Third: 21
Fourth: 26   Fifth: 25   Sixth: 28   Seventh: 13.

The commissions work in secret and their proceedings are not published; they, and the committees, do publish final reports. The working groups do not publish at all. As distinct from the Plan itself these reports do not engage the Government in any way; being the product of specialist groups with partial responsibilities they are permitted, and expected, to be incompatible with one another. Part of the justification for this process has always been that it provides a rare occasion for dialogue; it has become an increasingly important part of the justification as quantitative recommendations based on the work of the commissions have been steadily suppressed from the final plan. In the Seventh Plan there are no quantitative targets for the energy sector and precious little qualitative discussion. It is even more difficult to grasp the significance of the report of the Energy Commission, which suggests quantitative targets but which carries a prominent disclaimer from the Government inside the front cover that 'the judgements and recommendations contained in the present report engage only the responsibility of the Commission'.

In addition to consultation with the technical and financial sectors the CGP engages in a political dialogue. One partner is Parliament. Up to the Fifth Plan Parliament was presented with a *fait accompli* in the form of a detailed, and apparently coherent and complete, study. To doubt any part of this would be to destroy the financial, economic and social balance arrived at after years of expert dedication and wise debate. Parliament was never presumptuous enough to commit so indelicate an act. To alleviate the constraint, Parliament asked that the Fifth and subsequent Plans should be prepared in two phases so that the deputies and senators could condone the broad lines of the plan before the juggernaut car got going. The Seventh Plan and the two which preceded were prepared in two stages; the contribution of Parliament has not noticeably increased. It is indeed difficult to see how Parliament could be satisfactorily involved without taking over the whole task to which it would be perfectly ill-suited. Parliament can only sensibly participate in the construction of laws of definite scope and reasonably foreseeable consequence. The unsatisfactory relationship between Parliament and the Plan is inherent in the character of the institutions.

Political control of the Plan is exercised in practice by the President and a few of the more powerful Ministers. The CGP was originally attached to the

Office of the Prime Minister in order to facilitate co-ordination and arbitration, subsequently it was placed under the authority of the *Ministre des Finances*, but in 1962 it was returned by de Gaulle to the Prime Minister.

Finally, the CGP was assigned to a new Ministry along with another agency attached to the Prime Minister, known as the *Délégation Générale à l'Aménagement du Territoire*. The new Ministry was called the *Ministère du Plan et de l'Aménagement du Territoire*. The precise method by which the Government controlled the Plan was for a long time informal (or esoteric depending on the outlook of the commentator). Control proceeded through regular reunions of the Prime Minister with his close colleagues; meetings that might include the appropriate member of the Prime Minister's cabinet, other personal advisers, the *Commissaire du Plan* and certain Ministers. In October 1974, on the initiative of the President of the Republic, the *Conseil Central de Planification* was created in order to improve the means available to the Government for intervening in the elaboration of the Plan. The *Conseil Central de Planification* meets at the Elysée. In addition to the President it comprises the Prime Minister, *le Ministre des Finances*, *le Ministre du Travail*, *le Commissaire du Plan* and Ministers competent in the subjects under discussion. The Council meets regularly and rather frequently for such a high level group – about once a month. By this means the President and the Government can determine the guidelines for planning; they can direct and monitor the work and propose modifications. The creation and the determined employment of this Council has greatly deepened political control, shifted the emphasis of control from the Prime Minister to the President and probably weakened the principal original feature of indicative planning which is the process of *concertation*.

Sketched above are the institutions involved in the Plan. We consider now the nature and timing of their interactions.[13]

The preliminary work for the Sixth Plan led to a '*rapport sur les options*' in February 1970 couched in general terms and leaving the Energy Commission almost complete freedom to make recommendations about market shares and investments, specifying only that the growth rate in energy demand would be about 5%. The work of the Energy Commission was divided among specialist committees, the Commission itself serving to synthesize the sectorial reports. If we wish to identify the original additions to thought about energy policy coming from the planning process, then it is logical to follow the development from the specialist committee reports, through the Energy Commission report and into the final Plan. The most noticeable aspect of the reports of the specialist committees is that they consist almost exclusively of material freely available elsewhere and of arguments raging in other quarters. The report of the *Comité de l'Electricité*[14] for example could be constructed from passages from the *contrat de programme* of EDF and from the reports of the *Commission PEON*;[15] the Committee was concerned with the same problems, made the same analysis and proposed the same solutions. This is not entirely surprising because it comprised largely the same people. Similarly the report of the *Comité du Charbon* has precisely the same tone as the contemporary annual

115

reports of CDF – but then the management of CDF and unions made up a large part of the Committee. The report accepts that coal production will fall by around 3 million tonnes per year thereby fixing the output in 1975 at some 25 Mt. But the important thing about this conclusion was that it had already been forced upon CDF by the Government in 1968 as a condition of the *Plan Bettencourt*. So this crucial policy decision had been made outside the planning process by government. The rest of the Committee report puts the case of CDF for continued subsidies, control of imports and other policy objectives one would expect from a coal lobby. The *Comité du Gaz* reported on the poor financial situation of the gas industry and proposed measures to correct it; the material and solutions were again widely available elsewhere. The report of the *Comité du Pétrole* is more interesting in the sense that as oil is not a national monopoly it is rare to find a document purporting to emanate from the oil industry as a whole. But close perusal of the report induces a sense of disbelief that it is a consensus view of the industry; the suggested objectives have the familiar ring of French petroleum policy. For example it is argued that the evolution of prices and taxes should be such as to favour the development of French industry, which means low prices and deductible VAT; it is difficult to imagine a major oil company perceiving low prices as a desirable objective.

The Committee argues that installed refinery capacity in France should be adequate to assure the entire French market with a margin for export – again this is not a plausible oil company view given the regime of control in France and the superior natural advantages of the Netherlands and Italy. The report gives every impression of being largely the creation of the DICA. This impression is supported by assertions from members of the staff of the DICA and the oil companies; it is also highly plausible given the fragmented character of the oil industry, the aversion of the oil companies, especially those of Anglo-Saxon origin, to exposing their true motivations and objectives outside their own house, the close affinity of the DICA to the CGP, and the greater authority of the DICA than the companies in the governmental framework in which the Plan was constructed. The committees therefore essentially had the qualities of lobbies dominated in three cases by public enterprise monopolies and in the fourth case by a government department.

The Commission de l'Energie then drew up the energy balance for the Sixth Plan. This had to be done within severe constraints. The Commission accepted the proposals for coal production in the Bettencourt Plan and it accepted the recommendation of the *Commission PEON* for electricity consumption and nuclear investment; there is little else it could do. The *Commission PEON* is a nuclear lobby and is dominated by EDF, but with its senior members represented on the Energy Commission it was not conceivable that its proposals should not be incorporated entirely. The representatives of the oil committee, drawing on its detailed market survey reinforced by qualified confidence in stable or falling prices, were also able to pre-empt a rapidly growing share of the market. Interestingly, the oil committee explicitly lent its support to a large nuclear programme as a way of increasing security of supply; this apparently admirable disinterest was another result of the dominating presence of the DICA whose objectives were different from those of the companies and which reflected a Gaullist view of national security. The total demand for energy in 1975 having been defined within limits by the anticipated rate of growth in GNP, decided outside the Energy Commission, it followed that the expectations of the powerful actors could only be satisfied by a relatively slow rate of growth in natural gas. The gas industry being in a parlous financial state had little weight within the Commission and little moral authority to propose an ambitious investment programme. The idea of conservation hardly existed at the time and certainly was not to be born within a commission whose members were dedicated in the first instance to the growth of their sector. The energy balance having been decided by a power balance within the Commission and by external constraints, it only remained to find reasons.

The principal aspects to retain from this account are the following:

(a) In terms of the short-term measures by which the State influences policy in practice (e.g. subsidies, tariffs, price control, fiscal regimes), the Energy Commission simply passed on the recommendations of its lobbies without any evident attempt at synthesis or at giving the ensemble of proposals coherent illogical support over and above the plausible, but isolated, sectorial reasoning.

(b) When it came to constructing an energy balance for the future, the Energy Commission did make a synthesis which reflected the balance of power within the Commission and decisions already taken outside. It could not accurately be termed a consensus view, but for the Sixth Plan it could accurately be termed an agreement. All involved (except some trade union members who disputed the coal figures) appear to have felt that the conclusions fell within the bounds of plausibility; they reflected vested interest, but they were plausible.

The essential recommendations of the Energy Commission were afterwards reproduced in an abbreviated form in the Sixth Plan.

It is apparent that in the Sixth Plan an energy balance was agreed after extremely heavy work, involving many hundreds of people, through a process where everyone could give his view after long, if unequal, discussion. In contrast the Seventh Plan began with a detailed energy balance issuing from the *Conseil Central de Planification*. The process was reversed; the objectives came apparently out of the blue and the job of the Commission was to justify them. In fact the objectives were worked out within the DICA and the DGE on the basis of proposals from the industry. Everyone presented the biggest possible programme and EDF came up with an enormous target. After short work within the DGE and the DICA to make up a coherent balance, the proposals were issued on 1 February 1975 as objectives fixed by the *Conseil Central de Planification*; they retained the enormous nuclear component.

Briefly the process can be described as a collusion between EDF and the DGE, which followed logically from real decisions on investment in nuclear manufacturing capacity that had been taken outside the Plan, sanctioned by the *Conseil Central de Planification*. The *Ministre des Finances* is said to have opposed the nuclear target, but within the Council of Ministers he is only one voice and not the most important. Since then the Ministry has sought to wear down the nuclear component.

The role of the Energy Commission was to justify these objectives. The fossil fuel industries organized concerted opposition, supported by the *Ministre des Finances* and the *Agence pour les Economies d'Energie*. The vigorous debate within the working group on the penetration of electricity is described in Chapter V. The result has been a small but continuous erosion of the nuclear component at the expense of the total, and of coal, and to the benefit of oil. The objectives of the *Conseil Central* and the balance appearing in the report of the Energy Commission are shown in Table 12.

Table 12. Comparison of supply objectives for 1985 (MTOE).

	Conseil Central de Planification	Commission de l'Energie
Oil	96	98
Coal	30	25
Gas	37	37
Primary Electricity	74	69
Nuclear	(60)	(55)
Hydraulic	(14)	(14)
New Sources	3	3
Total	240	232

As a result of this procedure, which in comparison with tradition was arbitrary and illogical, there is widespread scepticism among those involved about the targets proposed; there is also resentment that the process of planning (described by Massé as being as important as the Plan) has been jettisoned.

The *Ministère des Finances* caused to be included in the report several references to the difficulties in providing finance, and the problems of raising tariffs; it also caused to be made explicit that these recommendations of the Commission which applied to public enterprise in no way engaged the administration. The necessity to resort to this clearly indicates the weakness of the Ministry to make its view prevail within this forum, despite its great power in practice and despite its close involvement in the planning process.

C. The Relationship of the CGP to the Ministère des Finances

This observation leads us to enquire just how the enormous real power of the *Rue de Rivoli* relates to the great visions of the CGP. Clearly there is considerable overlap in the competence of these two bodies. Specifically the CGP produces descriptions of possible future states, as does the *Direction de la Pré-vision* and Insee; these descriptions have budgetary and financial implications which interest the *Directions du Budget* and *du Trésor*. In the course of this work the bodies share a number of instruments. The essential difference between the bodies, in the gentle language of the theoretician, is the balance of emphasis on the short and long term. Acceptance of this proposition should not detract from the more sordid observation that the *Ministère des Finances* controls real resources and the CGP does not. Nothing in France gets done without the consent, even if grudging, of *les Finances*; M. Monnet recognized this and knew that it was necessary to involve the Ministry as much as possible. The first principle of any institution responsible for the financial health of an organization is always to avoid long-term commitments especially those involving heavy and long-maturing investment; the second principle is to preserve its own strategies and intentions in utmost secrecy. The objectives of the CGP – to instil a sense of moral commitment to certain long-term obligations, and to reveal the ambitions and objectives of all the actors of the economy – are therefore in direct conflict with the principles of management guiding *les Finances*. It is this difference in attitude as to what constitutes wise preparation for the future, much more than any conflict between long and short sight, which characterizes the actions of the two institutions. The directly conflicting objectives, combined with the overlap in competence and the sharing of instruments, ensure an extraordinarily interesting relation between these two bodies.

The instruments of planning can be grouped into two broad categories. There are those instruments used in the preparation and monitoring of the plan, whose object is to observe, to analyse, to forecast and to encourage debate. The second category comprises instruments used to control the execution of the plan and which permit intervention in the economic and social life of the country to modify the forces at work.

The material manifestation of the first group of instruments is a variety of reports and documents prepared principally by the *Ministère des Finances* (especially the *Directions du Budget, du Trésor, de la Prévision* and Insee) but also the CGP. One of the most important documents produced is the *Comptes de la Nation*, which is a quantitative account of the activity of the various participants of the national economy; it covers both the accounts of past years and future provisional budgets. It is used in the preparation of the *rapport économique et financier* which the Government presents to Parliament at the same time as the initial proposal of the *loi de finances* and which supports and justifies the proposed budget. As would be expected, the superior strength of *les Finances* and its real power over the allocation of resources permits it to dominate these secret negotiations and preparations.

Another important instrument is the FDES whose function has already been described. The activity of this body, and the annual report which it makes, covers the problem of how to allocate the resources available for investment and how to finance them. It deals with investment by the private sector, local authority and public enterprise. Numerous other documents and institutions of lesser importance complete the inventory of instruments of the first category. Among them are the *rapport annuel sur l'exécution et la régionalisation* which provides an overall view of economic evolution in a regional perspective and also the periodical economic forecasts of Insee. Evidently, the freedom of thought and manoeuvre permitted to the CGP is considerably circumscribed by the prevailing view of the economic constraints and their likely evolution as laid down with great authority in these studies and documentation, particularly in the triad comprising the *comptes de la nation*, the *rapport économique et financier* and the *rapport annuel du FDES*, which are almost exclusively the work of *les Finances*.

The *Rue de Rivoli* therefore sets the scene for *le Plan* and also determines certain crucial parameters notably the discount rate to be used for investment appraisal; for example, in the preparation of the Seventh Plan the CGP wanted to take 9% as the discount rate, the *Ministère des Finances* wanted 10% and it was *les Finances* who won.

In the work in committees the *Ministère des Finances* is overwhelmed. At the level of the Energy Commission the presence of the CGP is also weak; the work of producing a coherent report falls to the DGE. The responsibility of the CGP is to make a coherent presentation of the reports of the Commission (horizontal and vertical); the synthesis must conform to the broad economic and financial guidelines defined by the instruments of 'category one', but the individual reports have been constructed with a minimum of intervention from *les Finances*, and may not be compatible with the broad framework. In the Seventh Plan this contradiction was reinforced by the fact that objectives had been set, after relatively little study, by the *Conseil Général de Planification*. Evidently there was no reason why they should be coherent with the prevailing view of the evolution of the economy as defined by *les Finances*. In particular, in the case of energy, there were evidently doubts about the ability to finance the enormous nuclear programme. The CGP, being faced with the problem of synthesizing the sectorial reports into a hostile economic framework, tends to suppress the embarrassing quantitative aspects of the sectorial reports. As a consequence the Sixth and especially the Seventh Plans were less quantitative and less indicative than their predecessors.

It is in the process of *concertation* that *les Finances* is most vulnerable. The preliminary work is largely secret and carried out according to rules laid down by *les Finances*; control of the execution of the plan is also largely in their hands, as we shall see. But the *concertation* combines the two things which most distress the *fonctionnaires* of the *Rue de Rivoli* – exposure to the public and long-term commitments. The inherent contradiction of participation in an operation aimed at undermining its basic principles of management has never been resolved by *les Finances*; it caused one official of the Ministry to describe the preparation of the plan as 'a bad time that had to be got through' (*un mauvais moment à passer*). In energy policy the strategy of *les Finances* has been to keep a low profile in the Energy Commission, but at the same time to

make sure its reservations were noted. And then, to dilute the recommendations at the higher levels of synthesis. Another author during the course of a
study of the strategies of the *Ministère des Finances* was led to the conclusion
that:[16]

> Although a macro-actor [in the Plan], the *Ministère des Finances* does not appear
> to have any other strategy, in the process of *concertation*, than to protect the
> interests it has already acquired, that is to say its discretionary power. But, by a
> logic which is that of life itself, preoccupation with keeping one's hands free is to
> develop the power of prevention, not of direction.

After the 'bad moment has passed' there comes the period of execution of
the Plan. This period is characterized by the instruments of the second
category and the renewed domination of the *Rue de Rivoli*. The instruments
at the disposal of the State for directing or encouraging the actions necessary
for the realization of the Plan can themselves be divided into two classes.
There are those instruments that depend on the direct intervention of the
State, for example the allocations of credits in the budget, the sanction of
investment or borrowing in public enterprise and the control of prices. Then
there are instruments which permit the State to create conditions favourable
to the ideas embodied in the Plan, for example the provision of investment
incentives either generally or in specific sectors, by subsidies, by low interest
loans, by fiscal charges, or by any of the enormous range of devices at the disposition of any government in modern times for the modification of the factors
governing the use of labour or capital. It has been established in an earlier
chapter that, almost without exception in the energy sector, the immediate
control of these instruments lies in the hands of the *Ministère des Finances*.
And where, in the past, a part of the sector, notably the oil industry, has in
certain aspects escaped the full rigours of the regime, there *les Finances* is now
consolidating its grip.

D. Effects of the Plan

There are two obvious and quite distinct means by which the effectiveness of
the Plan might be measured. One is to compare the numerical forecasts of past
plans with the eventual outcome; the other is to investigate how a knowledge
of the provisions of the Plan changes the attitudes of those whose actions make
up the economic life of the country.

An assessment by the first criterion of the last three completed Plans
follows. The terms of comparison change because the different Plans used
different conventions and definitions.

There is a discrepancy of about 5% between the forecast for electricity
consumption and the outcome. This is about par for the course as far as predictions of electricity consumptions go throughout the world. But the authors
of the Fourth Plan did note disconsolately that a simple extrapolation would,
in the event, have provided a better estimate than the relatively complex procedure used which took into account the anticipated rate of economic growth.

1. FOURTH PLAN

Table 13. Comparison between forecasts and outcome of the Fourth Plan for 1965.
Primary Energy (MTCE)

	Forecast for 1965	Outcome 1965
Solid fuel	82.0	68.5
Petroleum products	58.4	74.6
Primary sources of gas	9.2	7.7
Hydraulic and imported electricity	17.7	18.8
Nuclear	0.7	0.4
Total	168.0	170.0

Electricity Consumption (TWh)
Forecast of Fourth Plan	109.5
Outcome (1965)	102.0

There are only small discrepancies between predictions and outcome for gas and hydraulic electricity. This is not surprising because the availability of both energy sources at that time was determined principally by the volume of productive capacity, which was easily estimated; the forecasts for hydraulic energy depend to a secondary, but important, extent on the rainfall, forecast of which does not as yet fall within the competence of the Plan. Fortunately 1965 was a year of average rainfall. The discrepancy in nuclear production was a result of delays in the ordering and commissioning of plant; it had no important consequence because the nuclear component was so small. The total consumption of energy was accurately estimated. The glaring discrepancy is in the way in which the bulk fuel market was distributed between coal and oil. The consumption of coal was grossly overestimated, and the consumption of oil products was grossly underestimated. This divergence was the natural consequence of the unforseen competitiveness of oil products and the corresponding penetration of traditional coal markets. But the example poses in the most lucid form the basic questions which hang over this form of planning. They are as follows:

Do these discrepancies mean the Plan has failed?

If yes: was the failure in not foreseeing the penetration of oil or in not preventing it?

If not: then in what respect has the Plan succeeded?

Some light is shed by an analysis of the consumptions of oil and solid fuels by use.[17] as shown in Table 14. (The totals are not comparable with the overall balance listed above because the small end uses are excluded.) Perusal of the Table makes it quite clear that most of the forecasts bear a respectable relationship to the corresponding entries for the outcome and the discrepancy in the overall balance is the result of large discrepancies in a few sectors. The use of coal in the iron and steel industry was overestimated because the production of steel was overestimated and a substantial improvement in the use of fuel was not appreciated. This then was simply an error in judging the future economic environment which is one of the expectations of the Plan. Demand at power stations was overestimated because the demand for electricity was overestimated and the coal burn was reduced in preference to the oil burn. The penetration of oil into industry and the domestic sector was misjudged. It is clear from this analysis that the discrepancies arise from a failure to assess properly the significance of underlying trends which were perceived qualitatively. One of the principal objectives of the Fourth Plan was to modernize industry and to make it competitive in international markets. The energy balance for 1965 was constructed on the basis that cheap energy would be used to encourage modernization and assure competitiveness. The conclusion must be therefore that the Plan simply failed to assess the consequences of this guiding principle. It is an excellent example of the obvious, but overlooked, fact that policy lies in the decisions that are taken, not in forecasts. This conclusion is supported by the reaction of the administration to the events. The fall in sales of indigenous coal caused a violent reaction at the mines and a long strike. Instead of introducing measures calculated to restore coal output to the level foreseen by the Fourth Plan, the administration instituted a 'Round Table' between Government, management and unions and fixed an enormous programme of recesssion set out in the *plan de la table ronde* in 1963. No effort was made to achieve the targets of the Fourth Plan because the targets were not important. It is particularly ironic that the Fourth Plan should have been styled by the *Commissaire Général du Plan* of the time as an *ardente obligation*.

Table 14. Comparison between the forecasts of the Fourth Plan by sector, for solid fuels and oil products, with the outcome for 1965 (Entries in MTCE).

	Solid Fuels		Petroleum Products	
	Forecast	Outcome	Forecast	Outcome
Transport	2.0	1.8	19.5	22.6
Iron and Steel	19.0	15.3	2.2	2.0
Industry	12.9	12.1	12.2	19.6
Domestic	18.6	16.5	11.5	14.6
Power Stations	22.6	18.8	3.1	3.7

Adapted from: *Rapport Général de la Commission de l'Energie Vᵉ Plan, 1966–1970, Documentation Française.*

Was the Plan of any use? It is difficult, within the energy sector, to advance any defence for the Plan. It was accurate in areas where the outcome was already determined but it was seriously inaccurate in other areas. It cannot have been an adequate guide to investment. The oil companies presumably ignored it, or if they took any notice it can only have reduced their investment programme and therefore the penetration of cheap energy – but it is unlikely that they took any notice. The Administration did not stand by the Plan

123

because it was the principles that originated outside the Plan and not the targets that were important. It can be argued that these actions were reasonable, but then the justification for the indicative Plan is hard to grasp.

There are even greater discrepancies of a similar character between the forecasts and outcome of the Third Plan, but the evidence is not given here.

2. FIFTH PLAN

Table 15.   Comparison between forecasts and outcome of the Fifth Plan for 1970.

Primary Energy (*MTCE*)

	Forecasts for 1970	Outcome 1970
Solid fuel	63.0–64.8	57.2
Petroleum products	94.0–99.7	131.0
Primary sources of gas	14.7–15.2	13.9
Hydraulic and imported electricity	20.7	22.6
Nuclear	3.6	1.8
Total	196–204	226.5

Electricity Consumption (*TWh*)

Forecast of the Fifth Plan	147–151
Outcome (1970)	140

It is striking that the discrepancies between the forecasts of the Fifth Plan and the outcome are almost identical in character to those already found for the Fourth Plan. The nuclear component had been underestimated because of delays in orders and commissioning; the sources such as natural gas and electricity which depended on existing production capacity or long-term contracts (gas from Groningen began to enter France during this period) were accurately estimated; the contribution of solid fuel was overestimated, the shortfall being made up by oil. The extent to which consumption of oil exceeded the forecast was exacerbated by a misjudgement of the total consumption of energy, the discrepancy being made up entirely by oil imports. Again, as a technical exercise to forecast the balance of demand in the future consequent on certain actions designed to achieve specified political objectives, the Plan can only be said to have failed. The targets cannot have given any useful guide to investment in the coal industry or the oil industry. In 1968 the coal mining industry was the object of another specific Plan, the *Plan Bettencourt*, which fixed a rhythm of regression of 3 Mt/year. Alternatively if the Plan is to be construed as a moral obligation to achieve the targets then the will or skill of execution is shown to have been lacking.

The Energy Commission of the Fifth Plan acknowledged that the energy industries were characterized by long lead times for investment and believed that as a result the energy balance five years from any date was essentially determined. They therefore suggested targets for 1975. A comparison between these targets and the outcome is shown in Table 16.

Table 16. Comparison between forecasts and outcome of the Fifth Plan for 1975.

Primary Energy (MTCE)

	Forecasts for 1975	Outcome 1975
Solid fuels	56.3– 57.8	41.3
Petroleum products	124.0–136.1	154.3
Primary sources of gas	22.5– 23.9	24.7
Hydraulic and imported electricity	23.2	25.3
Nuclear	10.0	6.6
Total	236–251	252.2

Electricity Consumption (TWh)

Forecasts of the Fifth Plan	210–218
Outcome (1975)	181

The comparison demonstrates exactly the same tendencies as before, but exaggerated by the longer period they have had in which to develop. Over 10 years there was time to influence investment and modify events, but there is no sign of it happening. This suggests a slightly sinister aspect of planning. It is possible that the planning is imposed on certain sectors, which cannot resist because of their financial weakness, and is ignored by others. Specifically, if this hypothesis were correct, the roles would be distributed as follows: the gas industry, timid and in financial deficit had planning imposed upon it; EDF, aggressive, competent and working up to the *contrat de programme* and *le tournant commercial*, had disproportionate influence; the oil industry took minimum notice. It is interesting to note that in the period under consideration France always had a refining capacity in excess of its internal requirements despite the persistent underestimates in the Plan. This is shown in Table 17.

Table 17. Refining capacity, consumption and forecasts.

	Mt/year		
Year	Refining Capacity	Internal Consumption	Forecast of Internal Demand
1965	62	50	39 (Fourth Plan)
1970	105	87	65 (Fifth Plan)
1975	154	103	87 (Fifth Plan)

Even allowing for a margin of capacity for export, there is a striking suggestion that the oil industry was not unprepared for events; it had its own ideas about how things were moving and acted accordingly.

3. SIXTH PLAN

Table 18.   Comparison between forecasts and outcome of the Sixth
Plan for 1975.

Primary Energy (*MTCE*)

	Forecasts for 1975	Outcome 1975
Solid fuel	37–42	41.3
Petroleum products	180–205	154.3
Primary sources of gas	23–27	24.7
Hydraulic and imported electricity	24	25.3
Nuclear	5.5	6.6
Total		252.2

Electricity Consumption (*TWh*)

Forecast of Sixth Plan	192–207
Outcome	181

This is by far the best agreement found to date. The consumption of oil is grossly overstated (for a change), but there are obvious reasons for that. If one overlooks the October War, it can be said that the Plan was a technical success. If one takes the October War into account it can be said that the Plan only woke up to the potential for oil when the party was over.

The findings of this series of comparisons can be stated as follows:

(a) There is no evidence that the state has ever felt obliged to intervene and direct events in such a way as to achieve the energy balance recommended in the Plan.

(b) It follows that the significance of the Plan must be as a *forecast* of the consequences of a combination of decisions in energy policy. This conclusion demonstrates quite clearly the obvious truth that the decisions (which lie outside the competence of the Plan) are more important than the *forecasts* (which are the responsibility of the Plan).

(c) There is no evidence that the Energy Commission has ever helped to detect or demonstrate weaknesses in French energy policy, e.g. the policy of *pétrole franc*, the belief in the permanent availability of cheap oil, the denigration of natural gas.

(d) On the contrary there is evidence that the function of the Energy Commission has often been to reinforce the power of the dominating institutions and to burden the weaker institutions with a new weight of moral weakness as a consequence of having done badly in the share out within the Energy Commission.

A second possible measure of the effectiveness of the Plan is the extent to which the attitudes of those whose actions make up the economic life of the country are influenced by the recommendations of the Plan. This is a subjective assessment which I have only attempted on an anecdotal level.

It is alleged that the Plan definitely provides executives in the energy industries with the confidence to elaborate their own corporate strategy and to act upon them. The examples of EDF and CFP in the years following the Second World War have already been cited. But these examples relate to a specific period with specific problems and specific characteristics: the need to modernize and re-equip an isolated and partially destroyed economy and industries with little resources to spare for their own corporate planning. As industry recovered, and particularly as state enterprises became more aggressive after the mid-1960s, so companies undertook their own corporate planning. Today the resources which any of the great public enterprises can devote to planning exceed the total resources of the CGP. The corporate plans for the companies, especially the oil companies, differ from those of the Plan. Logically one would expect the companies to follow their own ideas, otherwise there is no point in doing the work themselves; interviews with those responsible suggest that on the whole they are logical. The relationship between the corporate plan of an institution and the national plan depends on the character of the institution. The enterprise which tried hardest to make the national plan consistent with its corporate plan was EDF. It did so because its policies were tied closely to hypothetical requirements at a distant date. This position is evidently vulnerable to the representatives of the *Ministère des Finances*, possessing the money and a notoriously near time horizon. The more support that EDF could obtain from the Plan, or the PEON Commission, the stronger its negotiating position with *les Finances*. Consequently EDF has always put considerable effort into its collaboration with the Plan and bemoans more than any other energy industry the contemporary deterioration of the Plan in practice and prestige. Hard as EDF works to incorporate its own objectives in the Plan it does not appear to modify them should it not succeed.

Disillusion with the national plan after the Seventh Plan has never been greater. The following quotations from interviews with representatives of Government and the industries are illustrative:

> EDF is obliged to work with much the same horizon as *le Plan*; we regret the passing of the Plan; all the actors involved should wish for a long-term plan.
>
> Executive of EDF.

> *Le Plan* has been one of my greatest disappointments. Since the VIth Plan we have abandoned quantitative objectives; now they are simply indicative and *le Plan* does not give the means of obtaining these objectives – there is no coherence. It makes a very bad effect not to have a plan.
>
> Civil servant in the *Ministère de l'Industrie*.

> *Le Plan* is the Holy Ghost.
>
> Oil company executive.

> It is not quite a joke.
>
> Oil company executive.

> We make plans because the machine is there. We don't believe it will happen, but we do not know any other way of proceeding. *Les Finances* is the real arbiter.
>
> Executive in Public Enterprise.

Evidently anecdotal evidence of this nature cannot carry a great deal of weight, but it is typical and it is difficult to avoid the conclusion that the process of *concertation* is much less effective now than it has been in the past.

E. Conclusions

The introduction to this discussion of the influence of *le Plan* on French energy policy proposed two reasonable expectations of the planning process: first that it would contribute to the resolution of the apparent paradox that a long-term policy is both essential and desirable, second that it would permit the consensus view of men of wisdom and long sight to prevail over the short-term interests of politicians. In this section we assess to what extent these expectations have been satisfied.

The evidence of the way in which *le Plan* has been formulated and executed in recent years demonstrates conclusively that it has made little original contribution to the specification of the objectives of an energy policy or to the formulation of that policy. The work of *le Plan* has been in practice to forecast the results of decisions taken elsewhere. There is almost no evidence since the Fourth Plan of action being taken to make events conform to the Plan. In the early years it appears that the allocation of investment funds by the *Ministère des Finances* was influenced by *le Plan*, but more recently the Ministry has followed its own ideas or instructions from the highest political levels and has negotiated with the enterprises outside the Plan.

Le Plan has little or no effect on the real decisions which determine energy policy in practice; i.e. prices, investments, taxes, choice of technology, nature and structure of institutions, powers of appointment. Nor has *le Plan* been sucessful in its role as *l'anti-hasard*. Almost every plan has had to be severely modified as a consequence of some unexpected event. The Third Plan (1958–1961) was introduced just as the recession hit France and was out of date as it appeared. A special plan had to be adopted for coal (*le Plan Jeanneney*); a few months after the inauguration of the Fifth Republic a new programme of financial and economic recovery was launched (*le Plan Pinay-Rueff*); finally an entirely new intermediate plan for 1960 and 1961 was drawn up. The Fourth Plan covering the period 1962–1965 was incapable of absorbing the economic consequences of the Algerian War and the repatriation of French colonialists. A supplementary plan of economic recovery was designed by the *Ministère des Finances* in 1963, many of whose provisions contradicted the Fourth Plan. The unforeseen predicament of the coal industry merited *le Plan Bettencourt*. The application of the Fifth Plan (1966–1970) was overtaken by the devaluation of the franc accompanied by a regime of restrictions that ran counter to the Plan. Coal was the object of *le Plan de la Table Ronde*. The Sixth Plan was thrown into disarray by the October War, with particularly severe effects on the energy policy, but with serious consequences for finance, prices and growth, which touched all sectors. Reflection on the difficulty of foreseeing these kinds of events leads one to the conclusion that, even if they could be foreseen, there is little that can be done about them. If the influx of Algerian colonialists had been foreseen, it could not have been publicly pre-dicted and openly prepared for without the risks, firstly, of encouraging the event and, secondly, of disturbing French political life. In short there are clear constraints on what it can be politically acceptable to forecast even if it is foreseen. The rise in oil prices is another excellent example. The authors of *le Plan*, had they foreseen this sudden increase, could hardly have argued the likelihood of the event without increasing the chances of it happening. This consideration seriously impairs the function of *le Plan* as an *anti-hasard*.

Le Plan mostly assembles materials and arguments from other sources of conflict. This is especially true of anything concerned with the relations between industry and the state. There is some new arbitration of conflicts between separate industries. A good example of this is the allocation of shares of the space heating market in the Seventh Plan. But if the DGE is doing its job this arbitration should occur in any case; the conflict is completely internal within the energy sector and there is no need to settle it within a comprehen-sive national plan. This observation does not detract from the fact that in the French cultural and intellectual context the Plan provides a convenient forum, but it is no fundamental justification for the Plan. There is minimal integra-tion of the energy plan into a wider economic context.

It is instructive to compare what goes on in France with practice in the United Kingdom. After years of ironic commentary on French planning techniques the United Kingdom is beginning to produce detailed long-term prognostications for the future of various sectors and most especially for energy. The United Kingdom assessments of possible energy futures are even more detailed than the recent work of the French Energy Commission of the Plan; they are not put into a wider economic context and they do not commit the administration, but then neither is or does the contemporary work within the French national plan. It appears therefore that the United Kingdom is taking up planning whilst professing to disbelieve it and France is abandoning planning whilst still practising the form. Certainly the attitudes of the two countries are converging. This is an interesting observation which justifies a detour into the subject of how the French anticipate that their planning activities will develop. The criticisms made here, and others, have not escaped those responsible in France and have prompted much debate. There is no agreement about how the planning process might evolve but a widespread view is that the centralized *planification* is ill-adapted to assure the evolution of the complex organism which is a modern industrial economy open to inter-national trade. A more flexible solution, it is argued, might be a system of plans.[18] The principal private and public actors of the economy would elaborate their own plans adapted to their own ends; the central planners would estimate a continuous process of iteration and coherence, firstly, between individual plans and their own concept of how the broad economic context evolve and, secondly, among the plans of the individual sectors. The comprehensive, cyclic ritual as practised now would be replaced by continuous dialogue and comparison of ideas. This activity would not be foreign to the style of the United Kingdom administration. The United Kingdom is beginning activities of this quality whilst not admitting that they constitute planning.

The energy industries in the United Kingdom all produce corporate plans; the Central Electricity Generating Board have even published a version of their corporate plan, but they are more usually kept secret. The public enterprises have all increased in recent years the time and effort which they put into corporate planning and there is reason to believe that the oil industries have also done the same. Of course, it is quite unsatisfactory to plan a single energy industry without close association with the others and knowledge of their intentions. In the past the only formal means for inter-industry communication in the United Kingdom was through the Department of Energy or its equivalent. The establishment of the Energy Commission in the United Kingdom, comprising, *inter alia*, the heads of the nationalized industries has gone a little way towards improving lines of communication but it probably meets at too high a level to be really effective; more useful is the Working Group on Energy Strategy drawn from the second and third lines of management of public enterprise which supports the Energy Commission and which in turn has created sub-groups to investigate special topics. The signs are that communication is still not entirely satisfactory – certainly there is no consensus view. The British Gas Corporation for example predicts a 30% increase in the availability of gas between 1978 and the mid-1980s but only about 5% increase in energy demand. This view of the future differs from the Department of Energy view; if the British Gas Corporation are correct the implications for other United Kingdom energy suppliers are serious. No doubt these matters are debated in the Energy Commission and its subsidiaries, but it would be sensible for the United Kingdom to admit explicitly that these efforts represent another step along a path which converges with the path that many French planners would like to take by decomposing their present universal procedure. This admission would assist discussion in the United Kingdom of where these initiatives might or will take us and would help make transparent the significance of the exercises now being undertaken. If the Energy Commission were formally to be given the job of identifying and analysing inconsistencies in the corporate plans of the individual industries and were to do this in an acceptably open way, then United Kingdom energy planning would come close to what French practice in energy planning should be, if it were functioning properly. This attribution would only be a slight extension of the present unacknowledged and, therefore imperfectly performed, activity of the Energy Commission.

If it is accepted as true that the French planning process applied to energy does not differ substantially from the practice of the United Kingdom, but is simply more formal and open, then it follows that the greater precision of French policy and the greater vigour with which it is pursued must lie in some other aspect of the French system. The difference lies not in the Plan,

but in the homogeneous character of the senior administration and the directors of public enterprise. They share a common education (*grandes écoles*), a
common philosophy (technocratic), common political principles (nationalism,
often Gaullist), and considerable *esprit de corps*. Regardless of who controls
whom, the similarities of outlook permit a policy to be agreed and more
importantly to be applied without constantly being questioned. This great
strength of the administration and this acquisition of part of the authority of
the state by public enterprise are not inhibited by the political assemblies
which are weak. In contrast the most senior political positions carry enormous
power and they are occupied almost exclusively by the same type of person
that provides the top men in the administration and public enterprise. The
homogeneity between the political power, administrative power and economic
power is the factor which permits policies in France to be driven through
without perpetual revision and agony. The chief consequence of this is
actually the *speed* with which France can respond to events, e.g. in February
1971 and in March 1974. The response is even impetuous. The reality of
French policy-making conflicts with the received idea that targets are introduced into the Plan after careful and deliberate analysis and then stuck to
through thick and thin. But such is the strength of received ideas.

This presentation of the political, administrative and economic power as a
monolith is, of course, exaggerated. It is done to emphasize that it is the nature
of these relations which characterizes the formulation of French energy policy
and not the existence of *le Plan*. It follows that examination of the tensions
within this small group of people will reveal much about the origins of policy;
this we have attempted in Chapters II and VI. But the identification of the
policy makers also provides a logical transition to the examination of the
second expectation of the planning process – the expectation that it will permit the consensus view of men of wisdom and long sight to prevail over the
short-term interests of politicians. Acknowledgement of the realities of policy-
making obliges the expectation to be translated from this naïve expression to
the more cynical, but accurate, expression as the question – how does the
existence of a national planning process modify the power relationships
among the actors involved in policy formation?

Broadly, the interests of four groups can be distinguished: *les Finances*, the
rest of the administration, the Government and the operating enterprises. *Les
Finances* possesses in daily reality the means of technocratic control within
constraints imposed by various decisions of the *Conseil des Ministres*. Its
objective is not to compromise its discretionary powers; it is weak within the
specialist commissions of the Plan and its strategy is to prevent as many firm
commitments as possible from being introduced into the final form of the
Plan. The operating enterprises are cynical about the real significance of the
Plan, but recognize at the same time that it is inadvisable to concede too much
ground to others. They try to impose their own corporate objectives on the
Plan with varying degrees of pressure and skill. EDF, to whom it is more important than other enterprises, participates with great force and consummate

ability. The objective of a technical ministry is to elaborate a coherent energy policy – the Plan is a sufficient but not necessary mechanism for this purpose. Recent changes in the mechanism by which the highest political levels liaise with the Plan now permit the Government, in collaboration with the DGE, to exercise almost complete control over the outcome. The influences of the Plan on the power relationships which form policy are therefore to embarrass the *Ministère des Finances* to the benefit of the technical ministry and the operating enterprises, to encourage the most aggressive participants among the operating enterprises and recently to extend the opportunities for intervention by the highest political figures.

F. A Comparison with Some Other Studies

It is not practical to compare these conclusions with those of all other studies of the planning process. The conclusions of two studies are reviewed here briefly because they cover complementary ground and because their conclusions match those obtained here: the studies have, in other words, been selected for consistency and are not typical. First is the study made by American authors of the effect of the planning process on the corporate strategy of industry.[7] It was evident to these authors that the national planning process had little direct influence on company and industrial strategies, nor did it strongly influence the relative measures adopted by the state to control individual enterprises. They did detect that an important force shaping corporate and strategic planning was a close relationship between business and the state, comprising a broad range of political offices and organizations of which the Planning Commission was but a small part. Second is the study by the British economist, Vera Lutz,[4] of the general principles and broad experience of *le Plan*. She concluded that at the very moment when planning in the French style began to attract world opinion, the French were abandoning it. She also maintains (perhaps slightly contradictorily) that no form of central planning has really functioned in France, other than a process of partial aid and *ad hoc* intervention in the economic life of the country similar to that used by governments throughout the Western world.

The conclusions of this study of the effects of planning on lengthy policy are broadly consistent with the findings of these other investigations of quite different scope. I should stress, however, that the discovery that the French planning process has not for some time been radically distinct from the means of intervention employed in the United Kingdom, and that the approaches are still converging, should have the effect of inducing in the United Kingdom greater tolerance and understanding of French planning and not, as curiously is the frequent case, of reinforcing hostility and incomprehension.

References
1. Atreize, *La planification française en pratique*, Les Editions Ouvriers, 1971.
2. C. Gruson, *Origine et espoirs de la planification française*, Dunod, 1968.
3. J. and A-M. Hackett, *Economic Planning in France*, Allen and Unwin, 1963.

4. Vera Lutz, *Central Planning in the Market Economy, an analysis of French theory and experience*, Longmans, London, 1969.
5. Pierre Massé, *Le plan ou l'anti-hasard*, Gallimard, 1965.
6. Y. Ullmo, *La planification en France*, Dalloz, 1974.
7. J. McArthur and B. R. Scott, *Industrial Planning in France*, Harvard University Press, 1968.
8. Max Weber, *Die Protestantische Ethik und der Geist des Kapitalismus*, 1904. English translation, Talcott Parsons, *The Protestant Ethic and the Spirit of Capitalism*, Allen and Unwin, London, 1930.
9. Alain Peyrefitte, *Le mal français*, Plon, 1976.
10. Herbert Luethy, *France against herself*, translated by Grie Mosbacher, Meridian Books, New York, 1957.
11. Jean Monnet, *Mémoires*, Fayard, 1977.
12. Pierre Massé in the introduction to *Industrial Planning in France*, op. cit.
13. *La planification française*, Cahiers Français, La Documentation Française, May–June 1977.
14. *Rapports des comités du 6ᵉ Plan, 1971–75 Charbon: gaz: électricité: pétrole*. La Documentation Française, 1971.
15. *Rapports de la Commission PEON*, Les Dossiers de l'Energie, 1, Ministère de l'Industrie.
16. L. Nizard, *Bulletin de l'Institut International d'Administration Publique*, Jan.–Mar. 1976.
17. *Rapport Général de la Commission de l'Energie, Vᵉ Plan, 1966–1970*, La Documentation Française.
18. G. Mignot, M. Voisset, *L'exécution d'un plan*, La Planification Française, Cahiers Français, La Documentation Française, May–June 1977.

VI

The Formulation of Policy

A. Criteria

Before asking who makes policy it is sensible to decide on the criteria by which we will detect the agencies responsible for the making of policy. One set of criteria will serve to identify the sources of power – who has the power to decide on the factors which in practice determine events? There are no doubt many ways of expressing these criteria; a convenient, although not necessarily mutually exclusive or complete, set is provided by the following tests:

Who controls the organizational structure?
Who measures performance?
Who allocates investment capital?
Who fixes prices for the products?

These four tests should identify the agencies which have the best chance of influencing the components of an organization; the organization in this case being the entire energy sector and the components being the operating industries.

But power is not the only factor. Power without direction is not creative. A possible set of tests which will help us determine the sources of direction are:

Who initiated the policy?
By what political processes was it brought about?
Who benefited from the policy?

These seven questions are intended to be a set of objective tests, the answers to which any disinterested observer would take as being relevant to the final question – who makes policy?

B. Who Controls the Organizational Structure?

The people elect the President, but not with energy policy in mind. The President appoints the Prime Minister, and other Ministers on the proposal of the Prime Minister; there is reason to believe that in the Fifth Republic this latter qualification has not been excessively restrictive. Each Minister appoints his *cabinet*; increasingly Ministers have recruited the members of their *cabinet* from their reservoir of technical and administrative skill which the civil service supplies. The members of the *cabinet* normally belong to the *grands corps* and the mechanism used is that of *détachement*; the *cabinet* members are paid by the *grand corps* of origin – which bodies have every reason so to do.

The heads of public enterprise are appointed by the Council of Ministers on the proposal of one Minister or another. These appointments are considered carefully and in many cases they are in practice the choice of the President of the Republic. The crucial choice of M. Guillaumat as *Président-Directeur Général* of ERAP was undoubtedly a personal choice of de Gaulle. When M. Giraud was appointed head of the CEA it was with the definite intention of dramatically changing the character of the enterprise. These appointments permit intervention at the highest level in the manner expected by the most senior politicians and to a large extent the President himself.

The lower (but still senior) echelons of public enterprise are the object of vigorous attempts at colonization by the *grands corps* and, in certain circumstances, the *Quai d'Orsay*. In the areas relevant to energy policy it is the graduates of the *ENA* and the *Polytechnique* who succeed best. The *Quai d'Orsay* has limited success within ERAP and the CFP; it does not seem to have infiltrated the organizations whose business it is to mine uranium. Numerically the *Polytechnique* dominates, especially the *corps des mines*. Because of tradition and the technical character of the sector, it is likely that the energy industries will be one of the areas where the *Polytechniques* resist the encroaching *énarches* most successfully. Nevertheless the influence of the *Finances* related *corps* from the ENA is becoming strong.

C. Who Measures Performance?

The answer to this question is in the preceding text. A variety of bodies measure the performance of the public enterprises which make up the active implements of energy policy; it includes the *Contrôleurs d'Etat*, the *Commission de Vérification des Comptes des Entreprises Publiques*, the *Commissaires du Gouvernement* and the *Conseil de Direction du FDES*. The first are appointed by the *Ministère des Finances*, the second come from the closely related *Cour des Comptes*, the third class are mostly from the sponsoring Ministry but in some cases (CFP and SNPA) include also a representative of the *Rue de Rivoli*. The FDES, as we have seen, is dominated by the *Ministère des Finances*.

D. Who Allocates Investment Capital?

In the cases of CDF, EDF, GDF and CNR the answer is almost exactly – the *Ministère des Finances*. It must sanction the investment programme put to it;

it presides over the allocation of *dotations en capital* and loans from the FDES; and it authorizes borrowing from abroad. The *Ministère de l'Industrie* and its agents have very little discretion in the allocation of real resources.

Les Finances must also sanction the investment programme of the CFP and the SNPA; its permission is also necessary to borrow abroad and it has a veto in the *Conseil d'Administration*. In the days when the oil companies had strong flows of cash they could self-finance a large proportion of their investments. The refining crisis has changed that and driven the companies further into the hands of the *Rue de Rivoli*.

E. Who Fixes Prices for the Products?

This question is of almost equal importance to the question of investment. If the tariffs permitted to an enterprise are low it will fall into a poor financial predicament that will weaken its bargaining power *vis-à-vis* the financial administration; if tariffs are generous, the enterprise will enjoy a relative freedom. Again prices have been controlled almost entirely by the *Ministère des Finances*, helped at times for oil products, but in a largely secondary role, by the *Direction des Carburants*.

It is impossible not to notice the overwhelming representation of the *Ministère des Finances* in the responses to these tests; its power dominates the immediate short term, practical matters.

F. Who Initiates Policy?

Evidently different parts of a comprehensive policy are initiated by different interests. Different interests have dominated at different times. In principle the agency responsible for the elucidation of a coherent energy policy is, and has been for many years, the *Ministère de l'Industrie*. Since 1963, the Ministry has possessed a special agency for energy; in that year a *Secrétariat Général* was established with the task of co-ordinating the work of the various *directions* with responsibilities for energy. It had comparatively little real power; the *directeurs* still reported to the Minister. After the events of October 1973 the agency was given the status of a *Délégation Générale* and acquired some of the authority necessary to adopt an executive role in relationship to the *directions*; the *directeurs* (or their equivalent) of the agencies directly responsible for energy now report to the *Délégué Général à l'Energie* (DGE), not to the Minister. The relevant part of the Organigramme of the *Ministère de l'Industrie* is shown in Fig. 10. The DGE also has responsibility for nuclear energy, which is the crux of French energy policy.

French Ministries do not usually have the equivalent of a permanent secretary and the *directeurs* have, in general, no superior other than the Minister. The DGE has sometimes been quoted as a counter example to this general practice, along with a few other similar posts. In the case of the DGE the analogy is not convincing; the *Délégué Général* in fact has much more the

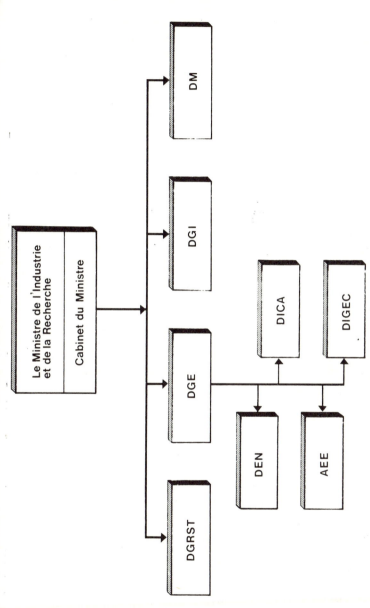

Fig. 10 A part of the organizational structure of the *Ministère de l'Industrie et de la Recherche.* DGRST: *Délégation Générale à la Recherche Scientifique et Technique;* DGE: *Délégation Générale à l'Energie;* DGI: *Délégation Générale de l'Industrie;* DM: *Direction des Mines;* DEN: *Délégation aux Energies Nouvelles;* DICA: *Direction des Carburants;* AEE: *Agence pour les Economies d'Energie;* DIGEC: *Direction du Gaz, de l'Electricité et du Charbon.*

quality of a Minister. He has a small staff, a large proportion of whom make up the *cellule nucléaire* (nuclear cell), that bears more resemblance to a Minister's cabinet than to anything else; he sits on the *Conseil de Direction du FDES* in contrast to many Ministers who are not members; he attends meetings of the *Conseil des Ministres* to present the dossiers relating to energy. Moreover, the present incumbent, M. P. Mentré de Loye, is a political figure close to Giscard d'Estaing and to d'Ornano. Mentré is, in everything else but name, a Minister for Energy; indeed in conversation the management of French public enterprise frequently, and ironically, give him the (non-existent) title. In the past the *Directeur des Cabinets* was similarly baptized the 'Minister for Oil'. The power of this post and of the post of *Directeur* of the other great *Direction*, the *Direction du Gaz, de l'Electricité et du Charbon* (Digec), must have been attenuated by the DGE. It is difficult to believe that the Cabinet of the *Ministre de l'Industrie* do not also feel themselves threatened by the DGE. Certain fundamental principles of human behaviour lead one to suspect that there should be considerable conflict between these bodies. There is, however, no obvious sign of it. It may simply be well disguised or it may be that the existence of members of the *corps des mines* in all these bodies permits a certain *esprit de corps* to overcome potential conflict. It matters little for this purpose – the DGE is certainly the body which synthesizes energy policy and presents it to the political authorities. But its small size must mean that it is dependent for its information on outside sources. Originally its information will come almost exclusively from the great public enterprises involved in generating energy policy – CDF, EDF, GDF, CNR, CFP and SNPA; it may come either directly or indirectly, either through the *directions* or through one of the variety of committees such as the *Commission PEON*. My impression is that the Digec has to a large extent been bypassed in questions of high policy such as investment, pricing and targets; it concerns itself almost exclusively with questions of a technical, administrative and social character.

This short circuit is possible because the administration does genuinely possess in large part the means necessary to determine policy. It is a relatively simple matter to conceive of the desired direction, to let it be known to the State enterprises and then to try to correct discrepancies as they arise.

Construction of petroleum policy is akin to a game of chess. It is necessary to envisage the response of devious and hostile opponents. For this reason the DGE cannot bypass the DICA. With petroleum, the market is open to a variety of national and international competition. There is no monopoly of the State; imports of crude and, to a lesser degree, products are possible across almost any frontier in unpredictable quantities; there are many products, instead of a single product as in electricity; possible supplies, possible refining capacity and possible markets have to be matched in this international environment of free(ish) trade and competition. The making of policy, especially just now, is inextricable from relatively detailed technical considerations.

At this stage it is instructive to look at the origin of some of the ideas in energy policy. Three of the most important components are the nuclear programme, energy conservation and the petroleum strategy.

1. NUCLEAR POLICY

There can be no reasonable doubt that the initiative for almost all aspects of the nuclear programme comes from EDF. This proposition is resisted strongly by the French Administration and curiously by observers from the British Administration – presumably out of administrative solidarity. It is, however, current in the management of French public enterprise; outside the electricity supply industry it is taken as a fact and paraphased as 'EDF is a state within a state'; within EDF it is attributed to the fact that they present their dossiers with greater skill and technical support than do their competitors. Whatever the reason, in the course of interviews with members of CDF, GDF, EDF, the CEA, Framatome and other bodies, the initiative for almost all aspects of electricity supply policy was consistently attributed to EDF. This comprised not only the present nuclear programme but also the reorganization of the heavy electrical and mechanical engineering industries in the late 1960s.

But it is not necessary to rely on hear-say however consistent it may be. A useful way of investigating the extent to which the current ideas of energy policy originated within EDF is to look back at the propositions of the various actors in time past; there is a remarkable similarity between the propositions of EDF in the late 1960s and early 1970s and the basis of the present national energy policy. Out of a wealth of material the most striking is the paper given by M. Marcel Boiteux (the *Directeur Général* of EDF) to the *Académie des Sciences Commerciales* in March 1972. According to M. Boiteux it was in 1970 that EDF defined and adopted what came to be known as the commercial turning-point of EDF (*le tournant commercial d'EDF*). Up to then EDF was seen as a public service obliged to furnish electricity at rigorous technical specifications. Its role with respect to the public was passive; it provided what it was asked for. The principle of the *tournant commercial* was that EDF would actively seek to increase the consumption of electricity beyond that which the market might otherwise require and so progressively to reduce the intolerable dependence on imported hydrocarbons. This new strategy required a new attitude to 'subscribers' henceforth to be 'clients' and to the relevant professionals handling equipment, once thought of as middlemen and almost as parasites, now to be known as 'partners'; it was first and foremost a new spirit which transformed the commercial attitudes of the enterprise.

A principal stimulus to this new strategy had been the inflexion in the growth of sales of electricity; the historic growth rate of electricity sales up to 1966 had been 7%, giving rise to what had been known as the 'ten-year doubling period', i.e. the notion that sales would always double every 10 years. From 1966 to 1970 the growth rate was 6%. The inflection in the rate of growth was attributed to three factors:

(a) in industry, to a slackening of activities in the most energy intensive sectors and to the end of a period of the accelerated phase of mechanization and concentration which preceded the opening of European frontiers according to the regime laid down in the Treaties of Rome;

(b) in the domestic and commercial sectors, the approach of saturation in sales of refrigerators, televisions, lighting and other electricity specific apparatus;

(c) in all sectors the absence of a vigorous challenge to competition from other fuels.

The gloomy analysis of the underlying significance of the inflexion in sales was reinforced by an examination of possible developments in the future. The heating market was solidly held by fossil fuels, and although coal had been forced out of this market its place had been taken almost entirely by fuel oil, to a small extent by gas and virtually not at all by electricity. Fuel oil was still cheap in comparison with other energy sources; it would be difficult to resist its competition in new heating markets let alone dislodge it from the old ones. It was also considered quite feasible at the time that the traditional markets of electricity – lighting and motive power – could be successfully contested by oil and gas through the means of gas turbines and total energy systems (in which a fuel is burnt on site to produce the whole of the requirements of the site for heat and power and electricity).

From this analysis appeared two equally serious risks:

(a) that in the coming 10 to 15 years the electricity supply industry would fail to develop the equipment, services and markets essential to the task of adapting to the inevitable resort to nuclear fuel as the principal primary energy source;

(b) that concurrently the finances of the industry would be compromised because the slackening of sales would reduce the revenue, increase unit costs, reduce the cash flow and lead to a high level of debt and a low level of investment.

The only alternative according to this analysis was a massive commercial exercise to penetrate the space heating market, backed up by a large-scale programme of investment in nuclear energy, making full use of economies of scale and of series. There was no mean way between the strategy of '*tout électrique-tout nucléaire*' and an embarrassing and, in the long term, dangerous weakening of the enterprise.

EDF was wholeheartedly committed to the first option. The analysis was widely shared by the senior management at EDF, but there can be little doubt that the success of the enterprise in eventually impressing their views and solutions on the Government was greatly helped by the character of the

President, M. Paul Delouvrier, and, most of all, of the *Directeur Général*, M. Marcel Boiteux. There appears to be an extremely successful collaboration between these two men that is known and felt throughout the enterprise.

The *contrat de programme*, of which these men were again the motor, was an integral part of this strategy; and the nub of the *contrat de programme* was the phrase assigning to EDF the right and the duty to exercise an effective commercial policy for the promotion of their service. According to M. Delouvrier, EDF struggled for six months to get this clause included in the contract, against the opposition of the *Ministère des Finance* who feared that success in this venture would inevitably stimulate a massive appeal to the State for funds.

The strategy of EDF that would subsequently be sanctioned politically after the October War was therefore well established in the hearts and minds of the enterprise by 1970–1971, and it is difficult to deny EDF the credit for the initiative.

The second question posed at the beginning of this section is: by what processes was the policy brought about? The answer is complex even if the scope of the question is still restricted to the nuclear policy, but an important component has been the skilful work of EDF within the various advisory committees. The most influential of these is the *Commission Consultative pour la Production d'Electricité d'Origine Nucléaire* – known as the *Commission PEON*.

It is interesting to digress to follow the evolution of the membership of this extremely influential committee. The Committee reports to the Prime Minister; the members are drawn from the highest echelons of the Administration, public enterprise and industry; they are appointed by the Government. There are two classes of members, those who are members by right because of the jobs they have and those who are appointed for four years because of their personal expertise. At the 1 April 1968 the members by right were:[1]

l'Administrateur Général Délégué du Gouvernement au Commissariat à l'Energie Atomique (M. Hirsch)

le Haut Commissaire à l'Energie Atomique (M. Perrin)

le Secrétaire Général de l'Energie (M. Jean Couture)

le Commissaire Général du Plan d'Equipement et de la Productivité (M. Montjoie)

le Directeur du Gaz et de l'Electricité (M. Galatoire-Malegarie)

le Directeur des Industries Chimiques (M. Rauline)

le Directeur des Industries Mécaniques, Electriques et Electroniques (M. Colonna)

le Directeur Général d'Electricité de France (M. Boiteux)

le Directeur de l'Equipement d'Electricité de France (M. Cabanius)

le Directeur des Piles Atomiques du Commissariat à l'Energie Atomique (M. Horowitz)

The President at this time was M. Couture. It will be seen that there was a strong technical bias which was continued in the list of members named for four years. It included the *Présidents-Directeurs Généraux* of many of the great industrial firms concerned in nuclear developments: *Hispano-Alsacienne*, Schneider, Alsthom, Pechiney, Babcock and Wilcox, *la Compagnie des Ateliers et Forges de la Loire*; it included also other representatives of EDF and the CEA bringing their total representation to three and four respectively. The *Ministère des Finances* was represented by two members named for four years. This committee was attributed the task of choosing a reactor type. Much blood was spilt, but it came mostly from EDF, the CEA and industry, all of whom were well represented; choice of reactor was not a question of the highest priority for the *Ministère des Finances*. By 1970, when it began to be evident that money was going to be spent, the *Rue de Rivoli* had increased its membership to three representatives for four years. By December 1974 when the financial implications of the nuclear strategy were clear the membership list by right read:

le Délégué Général à l'Energie – Président (M. Blancard)

l'Administrateur Général Délégué du C.E.A. (M. Giraud)

le Haut Commissaire à l'Energie Atomique (M. Yvon)

le Délégué Ministériel pour l'Armement (M. Delpech)

le Commissaire Général du Plan d'Equipement et de la Productivité (M. Ripert)

le Délégué à l'Aménagement du Territoire et à l'Action Régionale (M. Monod)

le Directeur Général de l'Industrie (M. de l'Estoile)

le Directeur des Industries Métallurgiques, Mécaniques et Electriques (M. Engerand)

le Directeur du Budget au Ministère de l'Economie et des Finances (M. Deroche)

le Directeur du Trésor au Ministère de l'Economie et des Finances (M. de la Roziere)

le Directeur de la Prévision au Ministère de l'Economie et des Finances (M. Contesse)

le Directeur de la Prévention des Pollutions et Nuisances (M. Saglio)

le Directeur du Gaz, de l'Electricité et du Charbon (M. Legrand)

le Chef du Service Central de Sûreté des Installations Nucléaires (M. Servant)

le Directeur Général d'Electricité de France (M. Boiteux)

le Directeur de l'Equipement à Electricité de France (M. Hug).

The *Ministère des Finances* now has three permanent representatives: the *Directeur du Budget*, the *Directeur du Trésor* and the *Directeur de la Prévision*;

an extremely weighty trio. Apart from the assault by the *Rue de Rivoli*, it is evident how the membership has ceased to reflect purely technical expertise, and how political interests such as defence, regional policy, pollution and safety are now involved. After the members nominated for four years are added in, the total representation of EDF is four and the CEA is five.

The Commission was first established in 1955, but it was not until 1963 that it began to contribute strongly in the formation of policy; in that year it began to participate in the elaboration of that part of the Fifth Plan concerned with nuclear power. Even then the deliberations of the Commission were directed less to the definition of global nuclear energy programmes than to some of the particular technical problems thrown up by the programmes proposed by the *Commissariat du Plan*. In 1967 the Government asked the Commission to report on the progress made towards the objectives of the Fifth Plan and to recommend the choice of reactor that should be adopted for a slice of nuclear generating capacity that the Fifth Plan had included as an option, subject to later decision. The French nuclear industry at the time was in a shocking state because of the inability of the parties concerned to choose a single design of reactor, compounded by the grave difficulties of showing a clear immediate role for nuclear generation in the face of severe competition from fuel oil burnt in conventional electricity generating plant. The different parties had different interests. EDF strongly desired to build the light water reactors and it made no secret of its views; M. André Decelle, the predecessor of M. Boiteux as Director-General at EDF, had resigned in protest against the will of the Gaullist Government to continue with the installation of the gas-graphite reactors and in particular against the Government-imposed decision, in December 1967, to construct a gas-graphite reactor at Fessenheim. EDF based its case on several points. At that precise moment electricity generated from nuclear fuel was not competitive with that generated from fuel oil. It would nevertheless be shortsighted not to construct nuclear stations, because during the course of the past years France had established teams of nuclear engineers in the CEA, in EDF and above all in industry. EDF recognized that it would be foolish to give up these organizations, painfully acquired, only to reconstruct them in a few years' time, because EDF remained completely convinced that the future for electricity lay in nuclear generation. This concern with the well-being of industry is undoutedly genuine. A corollary to the enormous influence of EDF on policy and its hard bargaining and exploitation of its monopoly position *vis-à-vis* the constructors is its genuine concern to shelter its suppliers from hardship; this enlightened self interest recognizes that they are essential in the long run to EDF's own well-being. EDF wished therefore to undertake a small subsidized programme of reactors in anticipation of the day, soon to come, when it could throw itself into large economic programmes.[2] In this context the priority for EDF was to find a reactor that was reliable, proven and economic. EDF recognized that the LWR was not much better proven at that time then the gas-graphite design, but it argued that whereas some 8 GW(e) of gas-graphite plant was under construction, there was 80 GW(e) of LWR capacity being built. Consequently, when it came to solving the inevitable problems that the nuclear developments would bring, there was reason to believe that the LWR constructors would manage better because of their greater opportunities for collaboration. What EDF really meant was that it did not believe that the CEA would certainly succeed in converting their elegant technology into a reliable commercial tool and EDF felt happier with the enormous support of the American industrial and research expertise. EDF also recognized that the industrialists would find it easier to negotiate the international alliances that formed at the time an integral part of French industrial policy, if they were building LWRs rather than confining themselves to a reactor design that found no interest beyond the frontiers of France. Again it is remarkable how EDF recognizes the demands of wider interests than its own, and again this is probably enlightened self-interest, because it recognized that these strong industrial units would later supply more reliable, cheaper plant than was otherwise likely to be produced by the relatively antiquated French heavy industry. Although the reorganization of the heavy electrical and mechanical engineering industries was certainly consistent with the objectives of the prevailing industrial policy, there is strong reason to believe that EDF again was in a real sense the initiator and motor of this reorganization. Finally, EDF believed that the gas-graphite, although technically successful, produced substantially more expensive electricity than the LWR. The new LWRs it thought might even possibly be competitive with the prevailing price of fuel oil.

The CEA wanted, as one would expect, to continue their own line of development, which they considered a technical success. It is possible that part of the CEA were convinced that the gas-graphite reactor was not economic in relationship to the LWR, but hesitated to abandon the gas-graphite for a reactor design which had suffered from some unfortunate incidents and which required a supply of enriched uranium which France could not provide. The necessary supplies were on offer from the U.S.A. at a 'dumping price'. The CEA consequently made serious study of the Canadian Candu design which ran on natural uranium; it even looked at Euratom's Orgel reactor.

Most of industry also wanted to build the light water reactors; the insistence of the CEA in designing the commercial plant themselves down to the minutest detail had prevented French industry from obtaining the design experience necessary to compete for export contracts; they hoped to escape from the suffocating clutch of the CEA. The CEA had the support of de Gaulle who refused to contemplate the construction of an American reactor; it is ironic that co-operation between France and the United Kingdom (never exactly vigorous) on the gas-cooled reactor line had been destroyed completely by de Gaulle on the grounds that France had nothing to learn from the United Kingdom (the decision was to help drive the French into still worse hands).

An influential part of the French Administration had been convinced by EDF of the merits of the light water designs; there are stories of M. Delouvrier and M. Guillaumat imploring de Gaulle to agree, but in vain. These then were the alliances between whom the battle was fought. The result was for a long time stalemate; the ultimate political authority of de Gaulle was countered by a strategy of passive resistance at EDF. Although the decision to construct a gas-graphite reactor had been taken in December 1967, no allocation of funds for the project appeared in the budget for 1968. In July 1968 EDF succeeded in having the decision suspended on the grounds that the riots of May 1968 and the subsequent increases in labour costs had significantly affected the relative costs of the two reactor designs. EDF probably benefited, in reversing this decision, from the decreasing grip of de Gaulle on the affairs of France. But it is the use of the PEON Commission which is of principal interest. The operation of the Commission at that time was marked by a pluralism of power; the calculations relating to the integration into the electricity supply network of reactors with specified capital and operating costs, and technical characteristics, were made by EDF; the fuel cycle calculations were made by CEA and the calculations of reactor cost and the effect of economies of series were done by the representatives of industry. The normal tendency for each group to exaggerate the expectations of its own favourite line was compounded by the fact that most of the information on the Light Water Reactors came indirectly from the United States. The French did have experience of LWR design and construction, but not as recent or as detailed as Westinghouse and General Electric. The influence of these firms on EDF was considerable, and it was applied largely through EDF's American office; the adventure of Westinghouse Europe was not influential. The great American firms were suffering from one of the periodic bouts of overcapacity which afflict the construction industry and were willing to offer reactors below long-run marginal cost. It was the time of Oyster Creek, sold at $50/kW. They were also anxious as a long-term prospect to enter the European market and this would, even in the absence of overcapacity, have encouraged them to underestimate costs. In view of all the uncertainties and the unreliability of much of the data, it is difficult to understand how the quantitative results of the Commission carried much conviction; they included estimates, to an accuracy of 1%, of the costs of various planting programmes up to the Eighth Plan (1981–1985).

The recommendations of the Commission were cautious and ambiguous. The last phrase of the report reads, 'it seems likely that it will not be possible to choose a single reactor line for the VIth Plan and that to keep options open one should, at least initially, accept the coexistence of two designs'. The report is not clear about what two designs were in the minds of the Commission, but the President has revealed that they were thinking of the LWE and a heavy water reactor.[3]

But EDF had achieved its main objective. The gas-cooled line was finally damned with faint praise, although the body of the report faithfully expounds its virtues. EDF had largely succeeded in promoting its views within the PEON Commission despite the relative pluralism of powers. It succeeded because it was able to make the case that the LWR produced cheaper electricity than the gas-graphite design. Whether this argument was right or wrong is of secondary significance; the available information was probably not adequate in any case. The important point is that by means of doubtful cost analyses EDF could carry the technical Commission, reinforced by support from the industrialists. The CEA's most powerful arguments, of security of supply and independence, fell outside the true competence of the PEON Commission; they formed one of the elements of the problem as seen by the source of the final political sanction, but as de Gaulle's influence waned and as political life was preoccupied by other matters the final political sanction was postponed.

The report of the Commission was finished in April 1968 and published in December 1968, but it was not until 12 November 1969, after several postponements, that the Council of Ministers came to the following four decisions:

1. The CEA would continue its studies on the gas-graphite design.
2. The studies of the fast reactor would be pursued actively.
3. After 1970 EDF would launch a programme of diversification in reactors using enriched uranium.
4. The necessary components of industry should be encouraged by the State to regroup and restructure.

In the matters of 3 and 4, EDF achieved everything they wanted. Decision 1 was a concession to the CEA; it was of no practical significance because EDF, the only client, had declared itself quite uninterested and had received permission to build other reactors. Shortly afterwards EDF passed the order to Framatome for two PWR nuclear boilers for the Fessenheim site, work to start in 1970 and 1972 respectively.

Ths existing nature of the CEA was increasingly questioned after these events. For some time there had been suggestions that the CEA be reorganized; these were now implemented, as described elsewhere, and the CEA was converted to an organization suitable for its new role of industrial entrepreneur. These events mark a turning point in the relationships of CEA, EDF and the industry. Beforehand the CEA, reporting directly to a sympathetic Prime Minister, was the strongest influence on nuclear policy in close control of the industrialists and challenged only by EDF. During this debate on reactor choice EDF imposed its view, hastening the reorganization of the CEA and substituting itself for the CEA as the industrial overlord.

The new role for the CEA no longer overtly conflicted with that of EDF, but was complementary; for a short and critical period the influence of these two bodies reinforced and met with little opposition. Again the events within the PEON Commission are an accessible and clear record of this.

146

In December 1969 the *Ministère de l'Industrie* asked the Commission for its advice on the consideration that should be given to nuclear energy within the Sixth Plan. The Commission esteemed that the competitiveness of large LWRs with electricity generated from fuel oil would soon be achieved; this event could be brought forward by a sufficiently audacious initiative in the Sixth Plan which would permit the usual economies of manufacture. The Commission proposed that the Sixth Plan should provide for a total of at least 8,000 MW(e) of new nuclear generating capacity in seven or eight units. The representatives of the *Ministère des Finances* disagreed with the majority view and doubted that the programme was compatible with the financial constraints of the period of the Plan (1971–1975). They recommended a programme limited to three LWRs. It is clear that, with this new coincidence of interests between CEA and EDF there was now virtually no restraint on the enthusiasm of the PEON Commission for an ambitious programme of nuclear developments. The resistance of the *Rue de Rivoli* was a token resistance; they were junior members of the Commission and had little weight; they had other ground to fight on.

The propositions of the Commission PEON were taken up by the committees associated with the *Commissariat du Plan*. The committee concerned with electricity production, the *Comité d'électricité* was dominated by EDF; the material, the discussion, the solutions to current questions are almost identical with the contents of the *Contrat de Programme* and the reports of the PEON Commission. Not surprisingly, the report is peppered with dissensions from the *Ministère des Finances*. The same propositions concerning electricity production from nuclear sources were adopted by the main energy Commission of the Plan – the *Commission Energie*, and eventually the 8,000 MW(e) target was made part of the overall plan and approved by the Government and Parliament. It is a particularly clear example of how the propositions of the Plan concerning nuclear energy actually originate from the EDF–CEA axis as represented in the PEON Commission and are in fact little modified by the synthesis supposedly carried out by the institutes of *Le Plan*.

In practice, EDF ordered in 1971 and 1972 three reactors of 900 MW(e) (Fessenheim II, Bugey II, and Bugey III); after allowing for its contractual engagements to export part of the output these reactors represented an input of some 2,100 MW(e) into the national network. This rhythm of orders was slightly below that foreseen which on average was equivalent to 3,200 MW(e) in two years.

The relative costs of electricity from oil and nuclear fuel had moved as a result of the Teheran-Tripoli Agreements. This conjunction of circumstances prompted the Government to ask the Commission again for its views on the future of the French nuclear programme.

The Commission considered that the competitiveness of nuclear electricity in France was undeniable. This fact was reinforced by the uncertainties of supplies of fossil fuels and by the belief that all future developments were likely to favour the nuclear option, e.g. the economies of scale and series, technical developments in nuclear power, increases in oil prices, and desul-phurization of oil. The circumstances justified, in the view of the Commission, a massive resort to nuclear energy. The Commission recommended an acceleration of the programme to the extent of recommending that 13,000 MW(e) of new capacity be ordered in the five years 1973 to 1977.

A remarkable aspect of this report is the extent to which the massive nuclear programme which was to be authorized after 1973 is foreshadowed in the deliberations of the PEON Commission in late 1972. But the most remark-able aspect of all is the agreement of the *Ministère des Finances*; this is stressed (subtly) in the final section where one normally expects to find the reservations of the *Rue de Rivoli*, but which in this instance innocently observes that the report has been unanimously adopted by the Commission.

This report was published in April 1973, and shortly afterwards the petro-leum market suffered violent changes. The Commission was reconvened by the *Ministère de l'Industrie* with the job of deciding whether an even bigger programme would not be desirable and of determining in particular what constraints there might be to nuclear developments within the next two years.

The Commission gave as its view that practical constriants prevented con-struction to be begun on more than 13 nuclear sets during 1974–1975. This restricted to 20,000 MW(e) the nuclear generating capacity that could con-ceivably be operating in France by 1980. To achieve this would require that the construction industry increase its capacity to some 8 or 10 sets a year, without as yet having amortized its previous investments. As the industrial representatives made clear, it could only do this if there was a reasonably assured internal market. Without being definite the Commission suggested that in 1976 and later, an ordering programme of seven sets a year would be reasonable, leading to an installed capacity of some 35,000 MW(e) by 1985 plus that dedicated to enrichment capacity. The consequence of this pro-gramme together with the likely evolution of demand was that nuclear sets would eventually be replacing fossil fired sets that had not come to the end of their useful lives. This implicit decision was recognized and considered economically sound.

The Commission recommended unanimously that EDF be authorized to begin the construction in 1974–1975 of 13 units of 900 MW(e) each and that EDF be authorized in future years to pass similar multiannual contracts in order to offer industry adequate incentive to undertake the necessary new investment.

It is difficult to attribute the initiative for this programme to any particular source. The instruction from the *Délégation Générale à l'Energie* to the Com-mission was clear enough, i.e. calculate the biggest practical programme. But the true initiative had been that of EDF in the years after 1967 as they pushed their ideas in every conceivable way and prepared the ground in their rela-tionships with government and industry. They had already broken through and the October War simply accelerated a process that was well underway.

The compliance of the *Ministère des Finances* is probably explicable by the speed of the operation and the feeling of near panic that gripped the French Administration in the months following the December 1973 rise in oil prices. Certainly, the *Ministère des Finances* was to stage a comeback.

The proposals of the PEON Commission were put to the Council of Ministers on 5 March 1974. The Council decided to authorize EDF to begin the construction of 13 sets of 900 MW(e) (11,700 MW(e) in total) during the two years 1974–1975. *Le Monde* wrote about this Council Meeting:[4]

> President Georges Pompidou was already seriously ill. Opposed to the *Délégué Général à l'Energie* and the Minister pleading the dossier of EDF, there was no one. Monsieur Poujade, who might have defended the environment, had just been replaced, forty-eight hours earlier. His successor, Monsieur Peyrefitte, was helpless. It was finally the Prime Minister, Monsieur Pierre Messmer, who decided. France would accelerate the construction of power stations and direct herself towards the horizon 2000 with the all electric, all nuclear.

In November 1974 the *Ministre de l'Industrie* requested the Commission to make another review of the nuclear programme and propose future guidelines. This was the time when the *Ministre des Finances*, horrified at the immediate financial consequences of the Commission's deliberations, endeavoured to have his representatives elevated to the status of members by right. The almost unresisted domination of the Committee by EDF was to be challenged.

An alliance between industry and EDF wished EDF to be authorized to order in 1975 at least 20,000 MW(e) of plant, not to be begun immediately, but to be spaced out over several years. The firm commitment would be an especial advantage to industry, which would be relieved of the risk attending its investments; it would also represent a degree of freedom for EDF, from the continual obligation to present its investment programme to the *Ministère des Finances*. The Ministry, not surprisingly, disagreed and proposed that EDF should be restricted to 8,000 MW(e) in 1975. The willingness of EDF to take on this enormous responsibility, and the fact that it pushed the idea within the Commission, demonstrates that it was by no means responding to pressure from the DGE but, on the contrary, that the massive nuclear programme still expressed the expectations of EDF.

The *Ministère des Finances* also disputed the forecasts of future electricity demand; it proposed a figure some 20% below the mean estimate by EDF for 1985 and stressed the financial constraints. The Commission was completely split. The representatives of the *Rue de Rivoli* proposed a programme of 5,000 MW(e) per year for 1976 and 1977, of which 8,000 MW(e) could be ordered in 1975; the other members recommended that 20,000 MW(e) should be ordered in 1975, of which 14,000 MW(e) would begin construction in 1975–1976.

The dispute was mediated by the *Conseil Central de Planification* (essentially the Council of Ministers under a different name), who authorized EDF to order 12,000 MW(e) in 1975 for construction to begin in 1976–1977. This

149

was a mean value between the extremes proposed by the conflicting groups within the Commission. An effective, but not overwhelming, check had been made to the initiatives of EDF and the DGE.

It is in the nature of things that EDF should, in the present circumstances, be the most powerful force within the PEON Commission. The choice of reactor was a topic on which the industry and the CEA had much to contribute. The matter currently in dispute is much less the direct affair of these other participants. It is up to EDF to make forecasts of future electricity requirements and then to calculate the economic consequences of introducing reactors of specific characteristics into the power system. It is EDF that will buy and operate the reactors; there is little natural opposition except from those responsible for finance; they have little technical expertise, but they have done, and are doing, their best to achieve the necessary standard. The *Ministère des Finances* now has its own model of the electricity supply system on which it can try out alternative strategies; it is much simpler than the EDF model and is the source of some scorn in the house of that enterprise, but it is a valuable part of the equipment for facing up to EDF.

The basic mechanism at work is clear. The *Conseil des Ministres* pronounces on proposals from the DGE based on work carried out by the State enterprises. An independent institute of energy studies in Grenoble said of the events described above:[5] 'this process shows to what point the arbitration of the state is deficient.' It goes on to quote from a report of the *Assemblée Nationale* on petroleum companies operating in France:[6]

> The Government have let themselves be abused by demonstrations determining the price of energy to one hundredth of a centime. The search for least cost and the conclusions of specialists have taken the place of an energy policy.

This, says the Institute, is as true of nuclear energy as of oil. But this interpretation is almost certainly false. It is not that Ministers simply accept technical conclusions in place of an energy policy; many Ministerial pronouncements have made clear that French energy policy is aimed at providing secure supplies of energy even at a premium. Ministers are not capable of following or criticizing the technical arguments, but they know they have certain priorities – to reduce the imports of oil, to reduce the balance of payments deficit. If a technical basis can be found for proposals that fulfil these political aims, then the Ministers will accept them. EDF and the CEA know what the political priorities of Ministers are, and if they do not, then the DGE most certainly does. It is therefore true to say that neither side imposes its guidelines on the other; the process is more akin to collusion. The ambitions of CEA and EDF are presented in a way that demonstrate them to satisfy the broad political preoccupations of Ministers.

The final question proposed for identifying the source of initiative was – who benefits? Evidently the proponents of a particular strategy are bound to argue that the State and the people at large will benefit. To be confident of that requires an appraisal of the merits of the case in a detail that we do not yet wish to make. The clear beneficiaries are, of course, EDF, the CEA and Framatome, behind which is Creusot-Loire and the Baron Empain – a restricted group.

EDF benefited from the strategy so far as it clearly fulfilled the expectations of the 'new commercial turning' sketched above and permitted it in a large measure to move towards the total control of its environment, postulated earlier as the most pervasive motive of such an enterprise. In one respect the strategy misfired. The enormous financial burden that the strategy placed on EDF was too much to allow the *Contrat de Programme* to be continued or renewed. As a result the *Ministère des Finances* has been able to reimpose the previous regime of controls, with heavy emphasis on those of an *a priori* character. That battle EDF will have to fight again, with the *Ministère des Finances* forearmed with a knowledge of the consequences.

The benefits to industry are by no means certain; the profits will only begin to accrue if and when contracts are signed. The industry believes this will happen, so they believe they have benefited. But there is little evidence that French capitalism, or le Baron Empain, has been an architect of the nuclear policy. The French Left allege that the policy has been imposed by the holders of capital, but there is little sign of it. What is true is that a bloody battle was fought by the industrialists for the fruits of the policy, but that is another matter. The convincing winner of this struggle was an outsider. A brief sketch of the process is too interesting to omit.

Up until the age of 30 the Baron Empain, of Belgian nationality, appeared to have no interest in the affairs of the great industrial dynasty of which he was the heir. The fortune dated from his grandfather, *le Général* Empain. It was the result of an accumulation of successful undertakings. In each new affair the General risked the acquisitions of all previous ventures. He created Heliopolis in Egypt, he invested in the Congo, he invested in electricity supply and public transport all over Europe. He was owner, or part-owner, of tramways in France, Brussels, Madrid, Tashkent and Cairo. He was a shareholder in electricity supply companies in Belgium and France. In 1963 the group, directed by the father-in-law of the present Baron, sold the greater part of the holdings in electricity supply in Belgium; the consequent availability of large sums of money coincided with the death of Charles Schneider, without heir.

The Empain Group was attracted by the prestige of the Schneider empire; it acquired one-quarter of the capital. In 1967, the present Baron took over from his father-in-law. De Gaulle had imposed as President of Schneider M. Roger Gaspard, out of a deep concern that one of the most celebrated of French companies was passing under the influence of foreign capital. The young Baron would not tolerate the tight dependence of the company on the various Ministry *tutelles*. He removed the President and shortly afterwards took on the job himself. His initial intention was to divest himself of much of his interests in heavy industry, which he saw as unprofitable and too much tied to the State as monopoly buyer.[7] His proposals were resisted by M. Pompidou, in particular his attempt to sell *Jeumont-Schneider* to the American

151

Company Westinghouse. The Baron gave in to these demands, but he refused to marry the company to the *Compagnie Générale Electromécanique*, presided over by M. Ambroise Roux and impeccably French. Thereafter he decided to reinforce the heavy engineering components of the group. One of these components was Framatome, with a PWR licence and experience at Chooz. The ambitious programme of investment described in Chapter III, undertaken in anticipation of the nuclear policy, assured him the leadership of the nuclear construction industry. The Baron is now well placed to emulate in nuclear engineering the achievements in tramways of the grandfather whom he so obviously admires.

At the time of the crucial decisions, the Baron professed to be ill at ease with the French politico-administrative milieu. His background (a playboy to the age of 30), and Belgian nationality, did not endear him to the closed and nationalist nature of the administration. His success at this critical time was the result of his entrepreneurial qualities. Subsequently he became the friend of Giscard d'Estaing, who is said to have helped him acquire definitive control of Creusot-Loire. Finally, he was invited to join the Council of the CNPF, the first time a stranger has been permitted to sit at the table of the high council of French capitalism; the event is viewed as a great concession throughout France and the ultimate mark of respectability.

2. ENERGY CONSERVATION POLICY

The French initiatives in energy conservation provide an equally instructive study. Before the October War energy conservation enjoyed the same empty respect in France as everywhere else. After the October War it was an obvious element in the energy policy of any consuming nation and the words were on everyone's tongue. For that reason it is impossible to attribute the initiative for the act of creating the *Agence pour les Economies d'Energie*. All one can say is that a broad range of opinion in the Government and the administration (both in the *Ministère de l'Industrie* and *des Finances*) supported the creation of such an Agency. It is also reasonably clear that a large part of this opinion saw the Agency as a means of persuading the public that conservation formed an element of the energy strategy whilst remaining extremely sceptical about what the Agency might well achieve. In fact the Agency is beginning to exercise considerable influence on energy policy. This slightly unexpected result depends on the character of the man appointed to direct the Agency. The Director of the Agency is M. Syrota, a relatively retiring and reflective, but extremely tenacious man. With a small team he began seriously to investigate the economics of energy use. From these studies there came some sensible proposals for legislation and financial incentives that would encourage the more efficient use of energy. Of more immediate interest is the fact that, as the Agency began to investigate the costs of performing certain tasks with different forms of energy, so it began to undermine the French nuclear programme. The Agency quickly convinced itself that the heating of houses and other domestic dwellings by electricity was either expensive (direct resistance heating) relative to other fuels or, as with electric storage heating, did not provide a satisfactory degree of comfort. Having established this to its own satisfaction, the Agency rapidly converted a portion of the *Délégation Générale à l'Energie* to this view. Ever since, a certain sense of schizophrenia has prevailed in the DGE; a profound belief in the necessity of nuclear energy being challenged by a compelling economic logic that demonstrated the impediments to the introduction of this source into what was technically the most accessible market.

M. Syrota quickly succeeded in interesting the *Ministère des Finances* and in persuading the Ministry to allocate him a budget. The Ministry recognized that the funds were a profitable investment and was happy to support an institution which could help reduce the size of the nuclear programme. Little by little, forecasts of future demand began to drop; the estimated contribution from nuclear energy began to fall and that of oil began to rise again. The Agency became the main channel for reasoned opposition to the size of the nuclear programme.

The technique of the Agency has not been dissimilar to that of EDF; skilful work within technical committees combined with continuous lobbying in the *Ministère des Finances*. Details are obscure, but there is considerable evidence that the negotiations have been a pretty hot-blooded affair. One interesting example is the history of the working group on the *Pénétration de l'Electricité*. This obscure working group of the *Commission de l'Energie* of the *Commissariat Général du Plan* was the scene of vigorous conflict. It was set up during the course of elaboration of the Seventh Plan at the instigation of the *Ministère des Finances*, which in doing some sums had noticed that the penetration of electricity into the space heating market, as envisaged by EDF, amounted to 100%. The observation may well have been whispered to *les Finances* by the *Agence pour les Economies d'Energie*. The move is characteristic of the rearground operations fought by *les Finances* in matters where the high level political arbitration has gone against it. Having been saddled with a nuclear programme which it considers too large, *les Finances* will seek all possible ways of delaying, reducing or casting doubt on the programme. The working of the Commission appears to have been bizarre. Cynical reports allege that when EDF was obliged to table its calculations within the Commission, it was immediately apparent to all concerned that EDF had underestimated its costs by some 20%, but although such a phenomenon may be apparent that does not permit a rival to challenge the results. Consequently the gas industry and the oil companies formed a common front and agreed to underestimate their costs by the half of EDF's margin. The working group was chaired by a representative of *les Finances* who was aware of what was going on but powerless to prevent it. The outcome of this manoeuvring was that the group recommended that some two million new houses be equipped with electric heating by 1985, corresponding to a penetration of the order of 40% and that the penetration for gas should be about 35%; the remainder, principally comprising group heating schemes and large apartment blocks, was allocated to the oil companies. This account of the ganging up against EDF is similar to the stories current of activity in other working groups and notably the *Commission sur la Valorisation de Chaleur* on combined heat and power. The flavour of the anecdotes, if not every fact, is almost certainly true.

Further evidence of the extent and vigour of the conflicts stimulated by the *Agence pour les Economies d'Energie* is provided by their troubled passage through the *Conseil des Ministres*. The usual practice in France is that propositions put to the *Conseil des Ministres* have already been agreed between the departments concerned and the secretariats of the President and Prime Minister. The approval of the Council is normally a formality. The French press are generally briefed before the Council meeting takes place; *Le Monde*, coming out as it does in the afternoon, often reports the results of the Council meeting as a *fait accompli*. Comparisons of the official communiqué with the press reports based on the press briefing forms a useful technique for distinguishing those decisions of the Council which are a surprise to the administration. On this test it appears that the conservation of energy has been responsible for more than its fair share of surprises. This is all the more remarkable in that conservation of energy is not normally thought of as a topic to set ministries against each other. To date the most spectacular divergence between the results considered acquired, and the outcome, took place in the Council meeting of 23 February 1977. Because of the persistence of the external trade deficit, the Council was supposed to approve a number of measures suggested by M. d'Ornano, the *Ministre de l'Industrie*, designed to economize energy and other raw materials imported from abroad. The proposals for economizing energy included the *encadrement* of the consumption of gas and electricity by industrialists, as already practised for heavy fuel oil; financial and technical aid for methods of heat recovery; contracts with the automobile manufacturers to reduce fuel consumption of their vehicles; a reduction of the penetration of electric heating. *Le Monde* reported in great detail that the following measures 'had been taken'.[8]

1. The *encadrement* of gas and electricity consumption after 1978. This meant that users of these services would be constrained to use no more than a specified amount probably related to past consumption. The use of quantities in excess of the prescribed limit would attract a financial penalty.

2. The conclusions of the report of the Committee on combined heat and power were to be applied. In particular the State would create an institution for the finance of heat recovery from power stations and combined heat and power in industry; settle particular outstanding points of law; and undertake studies in certain localities.

3. The *Ministère de l'Industrie* would seek to sign contracts with the manufacturers of automobiles which would engage the manufacturers to introduce vehicles with a better performance.

4. The Council was to confirm that the development of electric heating should be slowed down. Action was to be taken to bring home to the user that although the initial investment was lower the running costs of electric heating were more severe.

These ideas almost certainly originated in the *Agence pour les Economies d'Energie*; it is difficult to see them being generated anywhere else within the DGE. They were designed by the Agency for energy saving and associated with the balance of payments deficit in order to make them more popular with the Prime Minister and *les Finances*.

The measures had been discussed and agreed the day before in preliminary meetings between the interested Ministries, the Secretariat of the *Hôtel Matignon* and possibly the Prime Minister himself. The Secretariat of the Council was sufficiently certain that agreement had been reached to present them as decisions that had been taken. In the event none of these topics appeared in the Communiqué of the Council. [9]

The *Agence pour les Economies d'Energie* abandoned its proposal for *encadrement* and constructed a different proposition with a somewhat similar effect. It envisaged that a tax of 2% should be applied to the expenditure on energy of the 5,000 largest consumers in the country; the consumer could escape from the tax if he invested greater than a related amount in energy conservation. A company buying energy worth 1,000 MF would be obliged to pay 20 MF per year or make investments equal to some 70 MF. The new *Ministre de l'Industrie* announced this proposal in the *Assemblée Nationale* during the debate on the budget. It was presented to the Council of Ministers on 30 November 1977 along with the proposals concerning combined heat and power; [10] the Council refused the propositions and did so again at the following meeting on 7 December. [11] It is now believed in the Ministries concerned that the measure has been lost indefinitely.

This unpredictable behaviour is not typical and is most probably the result of a vigorous and evenly matched struggle behind the scenes with unexpected last minute changes in the balance of power. It is known that industry is strongly opposed to *encadrement* and to any measures of the parafiscal type. There can be few measures more likely to galvanize lobbying from industry than one which discriminates against almost all of the 5,000 largest firms; such a measure has a guaranteed, inbuilt opposing lobby. The lobbying proceeded through the instrument of the *Confédération Nationale du Patronat Français*; the object of the lobbying is less certain; the natural terrain would have been the *Ministère de l'Industrie* but that was the source of the initiative. The rejection of the proposals after apparently being agreed in February by the Prime Minister suggests that the *Elysée* may have been one target; the *Ministère des Finances* was most likely another.

The *Ministère des Finances* was lukewarm and possibly opposed for another characteristic reason. To pay for the resources necessary for the work it was proposed that the Agency be allocated a supplementary budget of 200 MF, which the *Rue de Rivoli* insisted was not to be found.

The decision of the Council of Ministers is contrary to the recommendations of the Seventh Plan. The Plan foresees that by 1985 the economies in energy use will be equivalent to 45 million tonnes of oil equivalent; this target is estimated to require investment at the rate of 5,000 MF a year up to 1985, of which 2,000 MF a year would be invested in industry. In practice less than 2,000 MF were invested in 1977, of which less than 1,000 MF went into industry. The idea of the Agency was that the proposed tax would cause industry to invest something like 1,500 MF a year, the remaining 500 MF to be provided by the State, through the Agency in the form of low interest loans, repayment of interest and similar measures. After the latest setback these targets can no longer be taken seriously. The 45 million TOE expected from conservation is roughly equivalent to the energy expected from nuclear power in 1985, but the amount of investment required to achieve this is some 72,000 MF in electricity during the Seventh Plan and at the most 25,000 MF a year for conservation.

The story illustrates several points. The preoccupation of the *Ministre des Finances* which causes it to resist expenditure on nuclear energy simultaneously causes it to resist expenditure on conservation that would reduce demand for nuclear; there is not necessarily a coherent philosophy of austerity. The event also illustrates how the *Conseil des Ministres* and particularly the *Ministre des Finances* are not constrained in practical decision-making by whatever recommendations there may be in the Plan. Finally, the story shows that although the *Agence pour les Economies d'Energie* was able to find sufficient backing for its proposal that the installer of electric space heating equipment should pay for a slice of the power station to run it, despite fierce opposition from the powerful EDF, nevertheless the Agency could not find support for its proposals, in a somewhat similar spirit to restrict consumption, sufficiently to balance the power of industry and the CNPF. It is interesting as being one of the few relatively clear cases of private industrial lobbying having an effect on French energy policy; this lobby which one would expect to be effective in this area is not in fact often detectable.

3. PETROLEUM POLICY

In contrast to the relatively transparent decision-making procedure in the nuclear policy where reports are prepared by committees, the contents frequently leaked and occasionally published, where the actors are sufficiently in need of support from a wide constituency to bring their conflicts out into the open, decision-making in French petroleum policy is extremely opaque. The reason is that the nature of the policy has not in the past hinged on technical choice or market forecasts; it has always been formed by age-old political considerations, innocent of any complexity, such as control and sovereignty. The policy has been directed towards control of sources, control of processing, control of transport, distribution and markets; the aim has been to ensure independence. Traditionally, certainly up to 1970–1971, petroleum policy has been intimately linked with French foreign policy.

De Gaulle divided the functions of government in practice into two not easily distinguishable parts. One part comprised international affairs with a bearing on the role and influence of France in the world – matters such as defence, foreign affairs and relations with the former French colonies in Africa. The second part comprises domestic matters. In the latter part initiative was generally left to others, the President acting as arbitrator. In the former part initiative for policy often, and indeed generally, lay with the President or his politically trustworthy men whom he had placed in dominant positions. Under de Gaulle foreign policy was the preserve of the President; this principle still persists, but in a much less comprehensive form. It follows that, oil being intimately bound up with foreign affairs, defence and relationships with the African colonies were of prime importance to de Gaulle, and one can safely assume that the grand strategic decisions were sanctioned by him. The Gaullist actor on whom de Gaulle relied for the initiative, elaboration and operation of policy was, of course, M. Pierre Guillaumat. A good example of how the President intervened directly to facilitate the task of his collaborators is the appointment of M. Guillaumat to the *Conseil d'Administration* of CFP described in Chapter III.

Pierre Guillaumat had been appointed by de Gaulle to be the *Directeur des Carburants* in 1944, which post he held until 1951 when he became *Administrateur Général* at the CEA; in 1966 he became the first *Président-Directeur Général* of ELF-ERAP and continued in this job until his retirement in 1977. Throughout this period M. Guillaumat was the principal adviser to de Gaulle on energy policy and especially petroleum policy, both when de Gaulle was in and out of power. The great structural changes in the State sector of the oil industry since the Second World War were made exclusively while de Gaulle was in power. The BRP (*Bureau de Recherches du Pétrole*) was created in October 1945; this was the critical decision which attributed to a State organism the mission to prospect for oil 'in the exclusive interest of the nation'. The UGP was created in 1959; this second crucial decision created a vehicle for the commercialization by the State of the *pétrole franc* and strengthened State involvement in the downstream sector. ERAP was created in January 1966; this third critical decision gave the State the means of translating the national policy of *pétrole franc* (and particularly the close co-operation envisaged with Algeria) into still more vigorous action in the market. The creation of ELF-ERAP and the nomination of Pierre Guillaumat as President was never voted by Parliament but was established by decrees signed by Georges Pompidou, the Gaullist *Ministre de l'Industrie*, M. Michel Maurice-Bokonowski and M. Giscard d'Estaing. These initiatives were very largely the intellectual property of M. Guillaumat; they were brought into being by the great personal authority and constitutional power of de Gaulle.

A fourth example of a substantial change in the structure of the State sector of the oil industry, again conceived by Guillaumat and promulgated by decree without resource to Parliament, but under a different President, is the Union of ERAP and SNPA.

If a few people are effectively to control a huge sector it is essential to ensure that key positions are held by people sympathetic to the cause in hand. This principle was indeed a characteristic of M. Guillaumat's technique. Important posts in the DICA and in ELF-ERAP, and to a lesser extent elsewhere in the energy sector went to Gaullists whom Guillaumat had encouraged and helped in their careers. There has never been any question of posts being given to politically sound men of dubious talent, but the encouragement of these protégés, known in France as colts or foals (*poulains*), had certainly given the State sector of the oil industry certain characteristics which are echoed in the energy sector at large. The most influential of these *poulains* was M. André Giraud; he was *Directeur des Carburants* from 1964 to 1969, before going to the CEA. During these five years State petroleum policy was created by Guillaumat and Giraud with the political backing of Pompidou and de Gaulle. It is difficult to provide convincing logical justification for the BRP-ERAP line of development parallel to the CFP line. The latter originated after the First World War from similar ideas of what should constitute French petroleum policy to those which provided the political rationale for the BRP after the Second World War. The necessity for two organizations has never been clear. But once formed, and in front of the brilliant results achieved in Algeria, the exclusively State institutions were developed by a select few, sharing a common and restricted view of their task, into an inflexible and peculiar instrument of a well-specified and equally narrowly based petroleum policy.

It is tempting to conclude that this peculiar evolution of ELF-ERAP and its dangerously strong association with a single supplier was encouraged by the decision-making structure which confined the formulation, evaluation and choice of policies to a small group of people of a particular and special political outlook sharing a particular view of the place of France in the world, believing intensely that a secure supply of petroleum was an essential, if mundane, part of the vigorous, independent economy that was a prerequisite for France to fulfil its vocation among the countries of the world.

This élitist decision-making mechanism, controlled by men with powerful political motivation, has in many respects deteriorated since 1970-1971. There have been two reinforcing causes of this, which are probably related on a higher plane; they are the attenuation of Gaullism at the pinnacle of power and the collapse of the policy of *pétrole franc* as a result of the nationalization of French investments in the oil industry in Algeria. The consequence has been that ELF-ERAP has been obliged to try to operate more like a multinational oil company with a diversity of sources.

As the vision faded of a symbiotic relationship between France and Algeria, isolated from external influences, and as the fortunes of ERAP came to be determined almost exclusively by the laws of the international petroleum market and not the dealings of diplomats, so technical and financial factors have become more important in the life of the company. As demonstrated in a previous sector, the mechanisms of government control of ERAP and the CFP have been modified; instead of depending almost exclusively on the

DICA they now depend equally, and in practice more strongly, on the *Ministère des Finances* and its newly formed *Mission de Contrôle des Sociétés Pétrolières*.

The set of questions proposed as a test of the sources of direction for a policy were: who initiates policy, by what political processes was it brought about, who benefited from the policy? The gist of the preceding discussion is that the answers are: a few men sharing a particular political outlook, who exploited the great power of the executive and in particular of the President to design a petroleum policy which they perceived as benefiting the French State.

In recent years French petroleum policy has been characterized by untypical indecision and an absence of direction; it has been formed by a defensive response to events.

G. Energy and the President

The influence of the President on energy policy is potentially very strong as it is with any other concern of government. A full account would require access to information about the relationships between ministers which is not available to me, but it is worthwhile briefly to sketch the role of the President.

The President has controlled the Council of Ministers throughout the Fifth Republic; M. Pompidou even managed to remove M. Chaban-Delmas as Prime Minister after the latter had received a vote of confidence for his policies from the National Assembly, and M. Giscard d'Estaing successfully contained M. Chirac until their relationship became intolerable. The dominance of the President has held up until now because he has been acknowledged the head of the majority parties.

But there are contradictions between the evolution of the powers of the Presidency and the personality and beliefs of the present incumbent. The commonly accepted view in France and abroad is that, from de Gaulle to Pompidou to Giscard d'Estaing, there has been a monotonic decline in the personal prestige of the President. A judgement of this nature is logically deplorable; it is most unsatisfactory to express so simply the result of multitudinous comparisons of interacting personal qualities and talents at work in a variety of strictly incomparable situations. Nevertheless, it is the vulgar view. But perhaps to offset this decline in personal prestige and to consolidate the dominance of the Presidency, built as much on the audacity of the general as on the provisions of the constitution, his epigoni have appropriated crucial practical powers. De Gaulle reigned over France, leaving to his prime ministers a considerable margin of initiative, more in some fields than others, but never disguising the true source of authority. The division of power between the Prime Minister and the President that might have been allowed by the constitution was relegated to the status of an academic possibility by the personality of de Gaulle. M. Pompidou, as President, benefited temporarily from the prestige of de Gaulle, but he recognized that this would not endure and set about resolving the potential conflict of power between the *Elysée* and the *Matignon* by concentrating powers in the Presidency and by making an example of M. Chaban-Delmas. M. Giscard d'Estaing continued the work. As *Ministre des Finances* for many years he was well acquainted with the powers of the Ministry; this knowledge and breadth of personal contact and influence was in itself a great source of power, but he chose to add to it by transferring to the Presidency from the Prime Minister the authority to arbitrate the final division of the budget. After the preliminary negotiations between the spending ministries and *les Finances* it inevitably happens that the sums demanded by the ministries exceed the total of the budget as fixed by *les Finances*; up until 1974 the Prime Minister arbitrated between them. This power was important because it represented one of the few means by which the Prime Minister could exercise control over the allocation of real resources. Transferring the authority to the Presidency reduced at a single stroke the power of the Prime Minister relative to the other ministers, but especially relative to *les Finances*, and at the same time reinforced the powers of the President. M. Giscard d'Estaing has also redefined the relationship of the President to the national plan, enabling him to intervene more formally than previously as President of the *Conseil Général de Planification*. Of greater import than the formal modification of structure, the incumbent President has also shifted the emphasis of planning from the process of collaboration into the justification of politically inspired objectives formulated by the body over which he presides.

It is psychologically likely that the successors of de Gaulle have concentrated formal powers in the Presidency precisely because they were aware of their inability to fulfil by strength of personality alone the expectations of autocratic rule which de Gaulle had created in the hearts and minds of the French. Practical as this response may be in the short term it is bound to reduce the stability of French political life as a gap appears between the powers of the Presidency and the esteem in which the incumbent is held.

These opposed themes – declining personal prestige of the President and a reinforcement of the powers of the Presidency – are joined by a third theme of a quite different nature which greatly extends the possibilities for poignant contradictions. The third theme originates in the personality of M. Giscard d'Estaing, who has many times exhibited and professed a liberality of thought that is at odds with the actions of the President and the State. In his book, *Démocratie Française*, he treats extensively of the notion of pluralism of power and in an interview he referred to the idea of pluralism as being his greatest personal contribution to the development of French political thought. But in no sense do his actions bear out the idea. At the highest level, power continues to be concentrated in the Presidency and, in matters of more immediate popular appeal, there is virtually no scope for the citizen or affected groups to contribute their views or influence the outcome; examples within the energy sector are the decision to amalgamate ELF-ERAP and SNPA, and the elaboration of the nuclear policy. For the purposes of the nuclear programme the usual procedures of public inquiry (*déclarations d'utilité publique*) are practically suspended; the courts fail dramatically to give a satisfactory impression of independence; protests are summarily rejected and violently put down. All this appears to make the President genuinely uneasy without deflecting the policy of the nation. In April 1974 he declared 'Nuclear power stations will not be imposed on populations which refuse them', but on any reasonable interpretation of events that is what has been done. Similarly in an interview in January 1978 he said, 'Since I have been President I have advocated a new growth which economizes energy, which avoids massive employment of a foreign workforce, which revalues manual labour, which responds to aspirations of a more qualitative nature.'[13] In the same interview he said, 'The development of nuclear energy will be reasonable, mastered and balanced.' The reality was the elaboration of a nuclear programme that was beyond the resources of the nation and whose residue is probably still excessive, but which is at least under way. And in contrast the most important aspects of the legislative programme for energy conservation have been lost.

The book *Democratie Francaise* is full of statements of principle which contradict the historical fact of Giscardian politics. To take one example, on writing about nationalization, the President argues that:

> Such a system has grave drawbacks on the strictly economic level. *But more importantly, it is in contradiction with the democratic principle of pluralism of power.*
> A society in which the great enterprises, by virtue of nationalization and authoritarian planning, are directly subjected to the political power and to its bureaucracy, ceases to be a pluralist society. Power is concentrated to such a degree that it is inevitably oppressive. If economic power coincides with the power of the State, who will protect us from the economic powers? (Reference 12, page 102, Presidential italics).

The President advances this analysis as an argument against further nationalization. But in many ways his criticisms apply to the existing system, at least as far as energy is concerned. The policy chosen is precisely the policy which potentially will satisfy the economic and political powers. The mechanism by which this coalition triumphs is different from that about which Giscard d'Estaing is warning the French people, but the end result is similar.

In more general terms, but still with a bearing on energy policy, the principles contained in this quotation directly contradict the increasing assumption of powers to the President, as sketched above.

These observations on the contradictions between the thoughts and actions of Valéry Giscard d'Estaing are not criticisms of the man. By that mysterious mechanism which gives validity to the most outrageous politician, the President of the French Republic reflects the contradictions of French society. France has made considerable progress towards the modern industrial society and the international political role that was the aim of de Gaulle, and the justification of his Fifth Republic and his paternalistic manipulation of the apparatus of centralized administration. In the view of many French people it is now the time to reduce the extent of the intervention of the administration into their lives, to shift the emphasis of social objectives from the quantitative to the qualitative, and to render unto the Frenchman the semblance (or illusion) of political self-determination, especially in local government, enjoyed by his neighbours.

But M. Giscard d'Estaing is aware that economic and political power in the international community are not yet completely achieved and have always to be maintained. The perilous path to the goal as formulated by the President – ' . . . to rejoin the camp of the strong, that is to say Germany and the United States, and not that of Italy and Great Britain'[14] – is by no means finished. The President is also keenly aware of the constant requirement to reassert the international political position of France if it is not to be lost. In a recent television interview he replied to the question why France presently enjoys this international influence:

> I would say firstly that it is incontestably due to the personal prestige of General de Gaulle and the dimension which he gave to French diplomacy. And it is further due to the policy that has been pursued . . . of having an imaginative attitude towards the subjects of the moment and of expressing points of view which are not egoist but which seek objectively for the solutions to problems. . . . *This represents an effort and, as with all efforts, the results are never acquired; they must be constantly conserved and protected.*[15]

M. Giscard d'Estaing's perfect understanding of the precarious reality of France's political and economic power confronts his genuinely held beliefs in ecology, a new form of growth, diverse aspects of liberalism, and pluralism of power; the products of this confrontation are the self-evident contradictions between thought and deed. The heavy responsibility of the President for the security of the nation inevitably means that when it comes to the crunch liberal principles take second place; this selection of priorities is reinforced by the character of the administrative structure which makes it easy for a President to authorize an impressive programme of nuclear construction but difficult for him to introduce effective policies for energy conservation.

The President has great and, in many ways, increasing authority over the design of broad policy guidelines. This concentration of powers is belied by an increasing reluctance of the community to accept a Presidential/Monarchic rule, which casts some doubt on the stability of the system in the future. But the power even now is exercised within considerable constraints. The Presidents of the Fifth Republic without exception have given the highest priority to an almost ostentatious concern with the industrial development of France and its political weight. The concentration of power has helped make it possible to maintain this as a priority in the face of the perpetual demands from all sides for the resources of any nation, but the objective has in turn constrained the use of the concentrated power.

The second constraint is that the existing institutional structure allows some Presidential initiatives/sanctions to flourish and assures that others wither. The President has only to sanction the nuclear programme and existing skilful institutions like CEA and EDF will do everything in their power to see the policy implemented because it fits their own objectives. There is no existing institution that will commercialize energy conservation in a comparable way and it would be difficult to devise an institution with objectives that would stimulate talented and ambitious men to the production and marketing of energy conservation as others are dedicated to the production and marketing of electricity. Nuclear power requires only a sanction from the President, but if he were thoroughly determined to force through a programme of energy conservation it would require a commitment in time and effort that would be quite unrealistic. So, great as the power of the President is, it is the power to select which of the available competing institutional forces will be released, and is therefore the power to choose among the possible states attainable by the release of those *institutional* forces; it is not the power exactly to fashion the forces necessary to achieve the preferred state from among all those which might be *technically* attainable.

The third constraint is related to the second. In certain areas the President can initiate the construction of specific institutional forces or direct their development by creating organizations and nominating their leaders. This possibility applies only to the supply of energy not to its use. Le Gaulle put oil policy into the hands of Pierre Guillaumat and he created the post-war state oil companies which were Guillaumat's instruments. The power to nominate the head of a state enterprise is of considerable significance and the President will try to ensure that the man of his choice will take the enterprise in the direction which he requires. But when strong and brilliant men like M. Boiteux and M. Giraud take over an enterprise like EDF or the CEA, they develop their own ideas and seek to extend the power and influence of their enterprise. It is not that they will refuse to adopt the expected road, but not being responsible for maintaining the overall balance in the aims and achievements of the nation they will inevitably try to push the policies of their enterprise beyond the interest of the community. To put the matter melodramatically, the President chooses men he can trust and assigns them the powerful instruments of state enterprise, but thereafter he risks perpetually to become the victim of a technocratic monster that he can no longer control. As an official of the DICA ironically observed to me, 'No one could say Guillaumat was controllable.'

H. Epilogue

After the manuscript of this book was completed the French announced changes in the structure of the energy policy machinery within government and changes to the celebrated *dirigiste* regime of 1928. These changes bear out the themes developed in the preceding chapters and they further expose some of the underlying conflicts of interest which we have identified as contributing to the dynamics of French policy making. But in some respects the changes contain surprises and, like any new event, contain evidence of fresh motivations. Rather than revise the whole manuscript, these new developments will

163

be discussed in this epilogue, giving the reader the opportunity to decide for himself the extent to which they are a surprise-free extrapolation of the past analysis and the extent to which they demonstrate shifts in the balance of power between the interested parties.

In April 1978 M. André Giraud was nominated as *Ministre de l'Industrie* in the second Barre cabinet, succeeding M. René Monory. Monory himself had succeeded M. Michel d'Ornano in the same month of the preceding year; Monory is by origin an industrialist, and a man in whose opinion the industrial future of France depends on the existence of vigorous, prosperous companies. The logical prerequisite for this happy state of affairs is a return to free pricing permitting the companies sufficient profits to finance their expansion. Monory publicly defended this point of view on several occasions. This appointment was a manifestation of the economic liberation of Giscard d'Estaing and Raymond Barre and a preliminary to later unexpected events.

The appointment of Giraud in April 1978 was in many ways a manifestation of a quite contrary current; *Polytechnique* and *corps des mines*, friend of Guillaumat, Giraud was in the classic technocratic mould of the men who have dominated French energy policy. A few months after his appointment, Giraud proposed changes to the organizational structure of the *Ministère de l'Industrie*; they were approved by the *Conseil des Ministres* in August 1978.

The *Délegué Général à l'Energie*, M. Paul Mentré de Loye, was obliged to give up his post and the functions of his *délégation* were attributed to a new *Direction Générale de l'Energie et des Matières Premières* (raw materials), headed by M. François de Wissocq, at that time *Directeur des Mines*. The motives for this reorganization were twofold; it stemmed partly from an adjustment to the personality and background of the new Minister and in part it facilitated policy changes that were to come later. Mentré is a highly political and powerful figure who behaved in many ways as a Minister for Energy; he is close to Giscard d'Estaing (he was *directeur-adjoint* of Giscard's cabinet at the *Ministère des Finances*) and Michel d'Ornano. During d'Ornano's time at the *Ministère de l'Industrie*, the potential ambiguity of responsibilities caused no problems, similarly with Monory who had no special knowledge of energy. But when Giraud, with his strong energy background, arrived at the *Ministère de l'Industrie*, the ambiguity was no longer tolerable – 'two stars keep not their motion in one sphere'.

Underlying the superficial personal manoeuvring is also the perennial power struggle between the *grands corps*, especially the technical corps of the *Polytechnique* and the finance related *corps*. Mentré, an *inspecteur des finances*, was the first head of the DGE, or of the preceding *Sécretariat Général*, not to come from the *corps des mines*. His appointment was a considerable success for *les Finances*. Although a prime mover of the nuclear programme, Mentré's enthusiasm was not equal to Giraud's; he was susceptible to the reservations of *les Finances*. The flavour of the negotiations is detectable in Giraud's appreciation of Mentré – 'a financier by origin, his new functions as financial adviser to the French Embassy in Washington should match his abilities perfectly'.[16] With M. François de Wissocq, *Polytechnique, corps des mines*, the traditional preserves have been re-established.

But the reorganization also had a basis in energy policy. Putting energy in with raw materials suggested a shift in emphasis away from market regulation towards monitoring of supply. Also helping to nudge the administrative structure into this shape was the diversification of the interests of the State oil companies into other materials – especially uranium and coal.

The related policy changes were announced the following month.[17,18] Much of the 50-year-old system was dismantled or made obsolete. The new proposals covered three relatively distinct matters – import quotas, price control and the responsibilities of the French oil companies.

The principle of a delegated State monopoly was confirmed and the A10 and A3 licences will persist, but to obtain an A3 will be relatively easy, in keeping with the recent trend. The system of quotas was abolished. The effect is that once a company has a licence there is no restriction on the volume of petroleum it can import. So, although the mechanisms of the 1928 policy have been kept because they were there, the spirit and purpose have been largely lost.

The principal mechanism of control by the public authorities is now based on a supply programme elaborated by the DICA. The programme aims at diversification. As has been discussed earlier, the DICA and the Quai d'Orsay have tried since 1973 to influence the origin of imports by bilateral agreements with producers in the interests of security of supply; they have had little success because political requirements run counter to the logic of the refining industry; there must, therefore, be some doubt about whether they will succeed in enforcing a supply programme.

The prices of heavy fuel oil and naphtha were freed on 7 July 1978 as part of the general lifting of restrictions on industrial prices. The prices of petrol, diesel and domestic fuel oil are still controlled, but will be progressively released and completely freed on 1 January 1980. From 1 September 1978, an ex-refinery posted price for these latter products will be calculated according to a formula taking into account the price of crude and the dollar exchange rate. The price of crude appears with a 45-day lag and the dollar rate is changed every two months. This price, plus taxes and VAT, will define a ceiling price.

For domestic fuel oil and diesel, any discounts to the consumer will be permitted, but discounts on petrol will be restricted. For several years the lobby of small garage owners has succeeded in persuading the Government to restrict discounts to 5 and 6 centimes/litre for ordinary and super petrol. The big chains attached to supermarkets would like to make larger discounts and they already give (illegal) discounts of up to 15 centimes. The maximum discount has not yet been fixed (September 1978), but will probably be between 10 and 12 centimes.

The falling franc during the first nine months of 1978 increased the difference between the ex-refinery price of petrol and the retail price, therefore increasing the profit to the distributor. This benefit will in future be taxed away. The amount of tax on a litre of super (costing Ffr. 2.68) will rise from Ffr. 1.75 to nearly Ffr. 1.82. For the last three months of 1978, the incremental tax (worth Ffr. 500 M) will be used to finance the activities of the *Agence pour les Economies d'Energie*. Afterwards it will pass into the revenue pool of the State and may be used to compensate for OPEC increases in crude prices, thereby avoiding a rapid down-and-up movement in retail petrol prices.

The objective of 50% of the product market for French companies has been abandoned. The objective of controlling production equivalent to the national needs also appears to have passed into oblivion; it has not been achieved for the last 10 years. (In 1969 French companies were producing 80 Mte against a national consumption of 70 Mte. By 1977 they were producing 74 Mte, although national consumption was nearly 120 Mte.)

The losers of the new policy are without a shadow of doubt the French oil companies. The *Union des Cadres et Techniciens du Pétrole*, the principal management union in the industry, has expressed itself 'stupefied' by the proposals which it alleges will lead to 'an aggravation of the operating losses in oil refining in France. A whole industrial sector of strategic importance will be abandoned to international competition'.[19]

This is presumably the Prime Minister's intention. But the risk is high. The financial difficulties of the French oil companies have been discussed earlier; they are in no position to resist increased competition. The companies are likely to have to cede part of their market share to the majors and/or close their less efficient refineries, bringing the French companies' share of refining down from the present 51%, and/or to accept subsidies from the State.

French officials are already suggesting exploration subsidies from the *Fonds de Soutien aux Hydrocarbures*, but this remedy will increase the dependence of the companies on the State. Part of the intention of the policy is to force the French companies to become more efficient; State subsidies are evidently contrary to the spirit of the policy.

The adoption of this policy is a remarkable success for the protagonists of economic liberalism; it runs counter to the long established French economic tradition. In these respects the petroleum policy is only a special case of Barre's decision to relax price controls over industry. The proposals appear to have been worked out by M. René Monory while he was *Ministre de l'Industrie*, and they are certainly consistent with his liberal economic philosophy; it also appears that M. André Giraud was not a supporter of the changes; in the Gaullist tradition he would have preferred to see some continued protection for a commodity of incomparable strategic importance. It is indeed surprising that the oil companies with their influence were not able to prevent these developments. It is clear that Giscard d'Estaing and Barre have considerable political will to liberalize the French economy. How the introduction of this new element will affect French policy-making will be fascinating to watch.

References

1. *Rapports de la Commission Consultative pour la Production d'Electricité d'Origine Nucléaire.* Ministère de l'Industrie.

2. Marcel Boiteux. Press conference at the opening of St. Laurent-des-Eaux – verbatim account in *Energie Nucléaire*, Vol. 11, No. 7, October 1969.

3. 'Les Travaux de la Commission PEON. Interview de M. J. Couture,' *Energie Nucléaire*, January 1969.

4. 'Le pari nucléaire,' *Le Monde*, 22 November 1974.

5. *Alternatives au nucléaire.* Institut Economique et Juridique de l'Energie, University of Grenoble, Grenoble, February 1975.

6. *Assemblée Nationale, Rapport sur les sociétés pétrolières opérant en France* (so called Schwartz report).

7. Interview with the Baron Empain. *L'Expansion*, September 1970.

8. 'Le gouvernement prend de nouvelles mesures d'assainissement économique' *Le Monde*, 24 February 1977.

9. 'Le communiqué officiel du conseil des ministres.' *Le Monde*, 25 February 1977.

10. 'Les économies d'énergie,' *Le Monde*, 1 December 1977.

11. 'Le communiqué du conseil des ministres,' *Le Monde*, 9 December 1977.

12. Valéry Giscard d'Estaing, *Démocratie Française*, Fayard, 1976.

13. 'Un entretien avec M. Giscard d'Estaing,' *Le Monde*, 26 January 1978.

14. Remark attributed to Giscard d'Estaing by Françoise Giroud in *La Comédie du Pouvoir*, Fayard, 1977, p. 17.

15. 'L'interview télévisée du Président de la République.' *Le Monde*, 11 February 1978. Italics added.

16. 'La Réorganisation du Ministère de l'Industrie,' *Le Monde*, 28 July 1978.

17. 'Les difficultés des groupes pétroliers,' *Le Monde*, 31 August 1978.

18. 'La politique pétrolière,' *Le Monde*, 1 September 1978.

19. 'La nouvelle politique pétrolière suscite de vives inquiétudes, *Le Monde*, 2 September 1978.

167

VII

The Opposition to the Nuclear Policy

The structure of this chapter is designed to exhibit the logical sequence by which the nuclear programme generates an opposition to which the proponents of the programme themselves respond. The nature of these changes depends on the expectations and objectives of the groups involved and on the relationships between them. The significance of these relationships is in turn determined by the procedural framework which governs activity; the procedural framework is composed of formal elements (administrative, legal, constitutional . . .) and informal elements (traditional, social, taboo . . .).

The opposition to the nuclear programme can crudely be classified into three groups: first, there are those people who object to the construction of a particular nuclear plant because they believe that it interferes with the local life or some feature of the specific environment; second, there are those who object to all and every nuclear plant on general principles; and, third, there are those who object to the size or rate of the proposed programme, but not to nuclear power in general. To identify these three classes I have coined the titles: the local, universal and technical oppositions. They are not exclusive categories. They are simply convenient headings for discussion.

A. The Local Opposition

The nature and characteristics of the local opposition will depend on the kind of economic life existing in the region around a prospective nuclear site. The extent to which the characteristics of the opposition are reproduced from site to site will depend on the extent to which the technical specifications for nuclear sites are correlated with particular forms of socio-economic development. An essential first step in the appreciation of the local opposition to parparticular nuclear developments, is therefore an understanding of the factors determining the choice of site, the practical restrictions which these factors place on the planning programme and the extent, if any, to which they select for communities of a certain economic character.

The most elementary technical requirement is that the site should be capable of physically supporting the construction which supposes the conjunction of certain geological conditions. More interesting than this essentially static requirement are the dynamic requirements relating to the exchanges between the installation and the environment. Any thermal power station requires that the heat given up at the condenser (equivalent to two-thirds of the heat generated in the boiler) be evacuated by fresh or salt water or by the atmosphere; it requires also that the electricity produced be transported to the distribution system by a high voltage transmission line, and finally that the fuel be brought in by road, rail or sea and that the waste be taken out. For a fossil fuel fired station and a nuclear station of equivalent electrical generating capacity there is no difference in the requirements for transport of electricity; there is a substantial but not critical increase in cooling water requirement for the nuclear plant and there is a critical relaxation of the requirements for fuel transport. A fossil-fuelled station of 2,000 MW(e) might consume 5 million tonnes of coal equivalent a year, and the choice of a site will depend critically on trading off the costs of transmitting electricity to the load against the costs of fuel transport to the station. Usually the latter factor will dominate and a coal-fired station will be located on a coal-field or at a port and an oil-fired station will be over the wall from a refinery. The restriction is much less important for nuclear plant and as a consequence they will tend to be located in such a manner as to minimize the costs of transmitting electricity, i.e. they will be put near the load. In the United Kingdom a restrictive siting policy has caused nuclear plant to be built almost exclusively in remote regions to alleviate real or imaginary fears of chronic or acute radioactive emissions. In the French view this policy is exaggerated; EDF argues that the requirement to provide a flux for cooling is far more restrictive than the requirement to dilute radioactive emissions and that therefore these exclusively nuclear constraints are weaker than others common to both systems.

The view of EDF is that the planting of nuclear stations is less constrained by technical requirements than is the planting of fossil-fuelled stations and this relaxation of constraints will tend to cause nuclear stations to be planted nearer the loads, i.e. nearer large cities and industrial areas, than an analogous fossil plant. A good example is the fast reactor at Creys-Malville which is 30 miles from Lyon, 35 miles from Grenoble, 45 miles from Geneva and even nearer fair-sized towns like La Tour du Pin and Chambery. This tendency to siting near loads is aggravated within EDF by the onerous task of financing the nuclear programme. Finding the money for the power stations is evidently a *sine qua non* for the nuclear programme; this task is difficult enough in itself, and if the burden is amplified by the contingent necessity to finance transmission lines to bring power from remote regions, then the chances of successfully fulfilling the programme are correspondingly reduced. Planting stations near load centres minimizes the investment in new transmission lines and frees funds for generating plant.

169

This conjunction of technical and financial circumstances is reinforced by another practical constraint arising from the necessity to obtain consent to the construction of power stations and transmission lines. Obtaining consent for the construction of a power station involves negotiation with relatively few parties; it is feasible for EDF to invoke support from central government, to offer swimming pools to the local community and in other ways to smooth the path. Obtaining consent for transmission lines involves negotiation with many parties; EDF finds it more difficult to concentrate its forces; there is more scope for local opposition to develop because more localities are involved and a greater variety of interests are threatened, and the whole business favours the decentralized organizations and guerrilla tactics which characterize the environmental opposition. A rapid programme of nuclear development will also for this reason tend to avoid remote sites.

The technical factors can be resumed as follows:
France has a favourable geology for siting power stations; there is little seismic activity; she has a long coastline in the north and west with many suitable sources of cooling water; she has several large river basins with favourable hydrology.
Planting of stations at the coast is generally more expensive because of high transmission costs; this applies especially to the west coast.
The most favourable sites are those near loads on large rivers which will sustain once through cooling and do not require cooling towers.
When the above sites are exhausted the choice must be between coastal sites with high transmission costs and inland sites with cooling towers. For the reasons sketched earlier EDF has chosen the latter.
As a consequence the development of nuclear power will be concentrated in the existing industrial areas of France especially along the Rhône. There will be severe limitations on the amount of power available in the present less-developed regions. This will reinforce the already severe regional imbalance in France, broadly between the west and the east. This is evident from the map of sites.

In addition to the factors which determine the technical suitability of the site, there is a group of socio-political factors which relate to the chances of the site being accepted by the local community.
A variety of interests may be threatened by the planting of a nuclear station; the principal sources of genuinely local opposition have been the owners of second homes, people engaged in the tourist industry and agriculturalists, especially peasant farmers. The owners of second homes are rumoured to exert a strong influence on siting decisions and there are stories of sites being abandoned by EDF as the consequence of well-directed letters from senior *polytechniciens* with property nearby. It is difficult to prove or disprove allegations of this nature; certainly EDF recognizes that the influential owners of second homes do contribute significantly to the forces forming their decisions. This class is not, however, to be seen in the demonstrations on

170

the streets and I have been unable to gauge the consequences of their clandestine operations.

Farmers and people making their living from tourism are closely related groups in rural France. Their opposition is founded partly on fears that the installation of a nuclear station will disturb the practice of agriculture and prevent people from coming to the region, but more strongly on the fact that the plant will disturb their traditional communities and lives without bringing them any commensurate benefit. Typical of this attitude is a peasant farmer at Malville who complained that as a result of the fast reactor he would no longer be able to drink at the well where his father and grandfather had drunk before him.

There is also a party political dimension to this group of determinants. Broadly the Communist Party and the parties of the political majority support the nuclear policy. The Socialist Party has reservations; these specific reservations, plus a general tendency to frustrate on principle the measures of a government of different persuasion, cause Socialist local councils to oppose the implementation of nuclear plant in their communes. This is particularly true of the stubborn, proud, contrary councils of places like Languedoc and Brittany. Privately, officials of EDF maintain that these councils are in practice easily 'bought' by the material attractions of the *patente*. The *patente* is an annual tax to which is subjected anybody exercising a profession in France and which is paid by EDF to the commune where an installation is sited. But this claim is probably a way of casting doubt on the integrity of the opposition; the practical evidence points to strong and sincere opposition at those sites as will be sketched later. There is a tendency for these difficult councils to be in the declining agricultural regions where the other socio-political and technical determinants reinforce to inhibit nuclear developments. Again the effect is to aggravate the regional unbalance in France.

B. The Universal Opposition

This is the title which I have given to that part of the opposition which broadly objects to the development of nuclear power at any place and at any time in the foreseeable future. The complexity of this movement as expressed in the often conflicting expectations and objectives of different components – the grave dissensions about the means to be employed, the differing relationships perceived between the anti-nuclear movement and other contemporary topics of political significance, the association with a search for new forms of organization and lifestyle, the wide range of social backgrounds from which the members are drawn, and the sheer number of groups comprising the movement – almost defies taxonomy. But some attempt at classification is essential; the most helpful qualities for distinguishing between the participating groups are the balance struck between individualism and the necessities of the group and the attitude to violence as a means of persuasion. These qualities are useful in practice because they are behavioural characteristics

171

which can be observed, and they are useful in principle because the participants in the anti-nuclear movement go from extremes of violence and non-
violence and form themselves into anything from rigidly hierarchical to
chaotic organizations. The classification is shown below in the form of a
matrix with some groups entered in the appropriate positions.

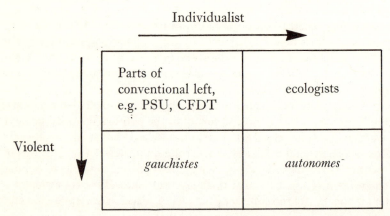

I stress again the limitations of this classification; it is evident that the
difference between the PSU and the *gauchistes* is not simply that the latter is
more violent. The terms 'violent' and 'individualist' must be interpreted with
care. It is difficult to establish the boundaries and there are many other
qualifications to be introduced, but provided that these cautions are heeded
the classification is useful because it does distinguish four principal streams
making up the movement, which broadly are characterized by the qualities
suggested.

1. THE CONVENTIONAL LEFT

Of the conventional left the PSU is the only political party of national significance to have taken up a robustly anti-nuclear attitude. This attitude is faithfully reflected in *Le Nouvel Observateur*, a journal that was formally linked to
the forerunners of the PSU and which is still closely associated with the party.
The PSU on the whole rejects the use of violence, although a few of its members do not. It is rare in publications of the PSU to find a denunciation of all
nuclear developments; there are generally qualifying phrases such as 'at a
rhythm and under such conditions as to deny the most elementary requirements of prudence'. But these qualifications do not loom large; the bolthole is
there, but it is not advertised. On any and all particular nuclear ventures the
PSU contributes to the opposition. It is especially hostile to the fast reactor.
The arguments of the PSU are essentially that the nuclear programme is
unacceptable because of the deleterious environmental effects, because of its
risks for the workforce and the population, because of its irreversibility,
because of the type of society which underlies it, still more centralized, more
secret, more repressive, more heavily political, more militarized. The PSU,

as is only reasonable in a party of the left, pays especial attention to the aspects of the nuclear programme which reinforce the deficiencies that socialists customarily perceive in the capitalist system. It is greatly concerned with alleged deteriorations in the working conditions in the factories of the nuclear industries. The reprocessing plants at La Hague and Marcoule are said to be run with inadequate respect for the health and safety of the workforce in order to maintain the activity of the plants at profitable levels (as discussed in Chapter III). The workers in the factories belonging to Framatome are allegedly submitted to an incessant police control. Certainly the work done is subjected to most stringent quality controls for the purpose of ensuring safe and reliable operation of plant, but these controls are also perceived by the PSU as a deterioration of working conditions. The PSU tends to avoid wondering whether things would not be better under a socialist system and if then whether nuclear developments at a slower pace could be permitted.

The general attitude of the PSU and the broad basis of its arguments are similar to those of the CFDT. Officially, the CFDT seeks to avoid violent confrontation with the public authorities; the majority of its elected representatives respect and repeat that line, but a minority of militants from regions where nuclear plant is planned or under construction are probably to be found at meetings and manifestations not sanctioned by the union. The similar argumentation of the CFDT to the PSU does not prevent them from reaching slightly different conclusions. The CFDT faces up to points which the PSU overlooks and arrives at a more coherent analysis; it proposes a moratorium on nuclear investment for three years, during which adequate resources would be devoted to studying the possibilities of economizing energy use and developing alternative methods of supply, so that at the end of the period it would be possible to make a reasonable assessment of how much nuclear generating capacity is actually needed. The period of the moratorium would also be put to use to improve the conditions under which nuclear energy is eventually to be developed. This would involve, *inter alia*, nationalization of the nuclear industries to remove the conflict of interest between safety and profit, the institution of an independent agency for inspection of nuclear installations, the elaboration of laws governing the production of nuclear energy and the initiation of public debate.

Although the policy sketched above is the official policy of the CFDT, it would be wrong to conclude that this large and powerful body is monolithically opposed to the nuclear programme. My impression is in fact that the vast majority of the CFDT finds the topic esoteric, is preoccupied with compelling matters like unemployment and salaries and essentially is fed up to the teeth with the nuclear question. The persistent opposition of the CFDT is animated by a relatively few extremely sincere, well informed and active members, some from the CEA and other nuclear companies.

Finally, I should add that both the PSU and the CFDT regard the nuclear programme as having been imposed by the State on EDF at the instigation of French capitalism. This is not my impression.

173

2. THE GAUCHISTES

Moving down the first column of the matrix brings one to the box labelled *gauchistes* which comprises the revolutionary parties of the French left. The term does not include the PCF, both traditionally and reasonably, because to describe the PCF as revolutionary would be to suspend disbelief beyond acceptable limits. *Les gauchistes* are to be found in a motley variety of Trotskyist and Maoist groups. In France, as elsewhere, their names and philosophies can be distinguished only by the connoisseur. *L'Union des Communistes de France Marxistes-Léninistes*, *Les Communistes Marxistes-Léninistes de France*, and *L'Organisation Communiste de France (Marxiste-Léniniste)* are all independent organizations (and this is only to begin the list). On the whole, but by no means exclusively, these organizations favour violent (revolutionary) action not only against the nuclear programme, but also to achieve their other objectives. These groups are not opposed to nuclear energy *per se*, so much as to its quality as the most perfect expression of the sacrifice of the people to capital. To stop the nuclear programme for these parties is a secondary objective to destroying capitalism. In some cases their anti-nuclear attitude is a straightforward cynical and opportunist attempt to exploit a topic of insignificant direct interest but which they perceive rouses hostility in the populace; in other cases the anti-nuclear attitude is an integral part of a Marxist analysis which has identified broad range of ecological abuses as a principal contribution to the oppression of the people. But the question of sincerity or cynicism is really irrelevant; the essential fact is that, whatever the reason, the anti-nuclear struggle is a small part of the struggle to overthrow capitalism. Naturally enough this ranking of priorities comes across most strongly in conversation and in the battle cries; but it is not difficult to perceive it in published sources. One can read:

> In fact, the mass anti-nuclear movement in which participate many classes of the people, the peasants and the young especially, transmits through the energy question, fundamental questions about the revolution in our country.[1]

> However, it is possible to achieve good conditions of safety in nuclear stations. The only real obstacle in our society is the search for maximum profit. . . . That is why one must ensure that the struggle of the people, of the town workers as of the peasants against the installation of nuclear plant should exhibit this anti-capitalist dimension.[2]

> Our enemies are not coal nor the atom, which science will eventually tame; they are the 'coal barons and the railway barons' and their successors, the technocrats of EDF, the bosses of Creusot-Loire and Framatome. As blinkered capitalists, they only see their narrow interests; what counts for them is profit.[3]

The strongest and the most highly organized group of the extreme left is the *Ligue Communiste Révolutionnaire* (LCR) of the Trotskyist persuasion. Officially the group rejects the tactics of violent confrontation because of the low probability of success. In practice a fringe of the LCR makes a substantial contribution to the sources of violent demonstration. This inconsistency appears to cause considerable and genuine displeasure to the authorities of the party; it arises from a profound philosophical split within the extreme left which is by no means confined to nuclear policy. The material manifestation of this split is the development on the margins of the extreme left of the *autonome* movement, which I shall come to shortly.

These extreme left-wing groups are about evenly divided on the question as to whether nuclear power in a Marxist-Leninist system would be acceptable. Those groups who believe that it would be acceptable tend to be those who are exploiting the anti-nuclear issue in a cynical and opportunist way.

Though not strictly relevant here, I might add that the majority of these groups regard the U.S.S.R. as being every bit as unpalatable as Western capitalism. The notion which has recently been put about that the anti-nuclear movement is being encouraged by the U.S.S.R. to embarrass the Western world, although possibly true in a few cases, is unlikely to be true in any general way. There are no facts to support the proposition, and to anyone who has ever bothered to make the most superficial study of anti-nuclear movements it is most implausible.

3. LES AUTONOMES

In the rapidly changing, undocumented and often ill-expressed life on the margins of the extreme left it is not easy to make historical analysis. It is plausible to say that the historical origins of the *autonome* movement can be traced back to the events of May 1968 even though few of the *autonomes* of today would have been more than 15 at the time and took no active part. But if the movement is seen as part of the anarchist tradition, then the development can be taken much further back.

In the aftermath of May 1968 many of the young participants, especially the students, developed or reinforced a contempt of the left, moderate and extreme. May 1968 they saw as a confirmation of the futility of party political organizations within which individual political expression was perverted or annihilated. This rejection of organized political life fomented several unconventional lines of thought, including the ecological ideas which I shall come to later. Where the rejection coincided with a natural tendency to the extreme left the *mouvement autonome* was born. The *autonomes* have finished with ideologies; Marxism, Leninism, Maoism are repudiated; the adherents of these beliefs are reviled and treated as 'widows of Mao' (*veuves de Mao*). The U.S.S.R. and China are despised as strongly as Western capitalism – more so in many cases because of the sense of betrayal. The hostility of the *autonomes* to the extreme left is no gentle fraud; the offices of the LCR have been attacked several times and its members assaulted. The broad origins of the *autonome* movement are similar to those of groups such as Baader-Meinhof in the Federal Republic of Germany; there is appreciable international communication and sympathy between French, German and Italian movements and no doubt others. And the lore of the *autonomes* treats as much of Baader-Meinhof as it does of Malville.

For a long time after 1968 the movement existed in the shadow of the extreme left. It is only comparatively recently, since 1974, that the *autonomes* have attracted the attention of the general public and indeed that they have attributed to themselves the elements of an identity. The nature of the movement makes it difficult to consider it as having an identity. The *autonomes* have virtually no structures to provide an identity; they have condemned any political organization which would impose the same divisions as does capitalism (those who think, those who act, those who serve); they refuse to acknowledge leaders and they have renounced democratic decision-making as enthusiastically as they have renounced autocratic decision-making. The individual, or a group of like-minded people, is responsible for and answerable to itself alone. This attitude has unattractive ramifications; in a large gathering of *autonomes* I saw a boy violently assault a girl without a single remonstration from the crowd, and scarcely a glance.

The nearest thing to a means of identification is the proliferation of broadsheets and reviews produced often by a handful of people, but which serve as kernels for the movement. *Front Libertaire* was formed in 1976; it is produced by the closest approach to an organization within the *autonome* movement, an old anarchist group renamed the *Organisation Communiste Libertaire* (OCL). *Marge* was started in 1974 and originates from the University of Paris, *Camarades* was formed in 1975.

A part of the reason why the *autonomes* flourished in the mid-1970s is the 'proletarianization' of students consequent on the heavy unemployment among those leaving university. Again the extreme left was unable to respond to the problem of student unemployment, to satisfy the expectations of the unemployed and to incorporate them into its organizations.

As far as one can attribute precisely formulated objectives to the *autonomes*, an indication is to be found in the edited record of the '*Assemblée Parisienne des Groupes Autonomes*'.[4] They are to repulse repression and to defend the true freedoms; the true freedoms are expressed in a telling concept as *les libertés des espaces de lutte*. This untranslatable phrase I take to mean the freedom to use the media (interpreted generously) to liberate man. So when the *autonomes* squat in unoccupied houses, they regard it as the liberation of a lifespace. The radio-piracy which they practise they regard as the liberation of radio space, the space of radio waves; work obviously is boring and alienating; possessions are incompatible with freedom (and also likely to be destroyed by the police) so they live with a minimum of goods and money, and do not exclude stealing. By picking and choosing among the aims and according to the exact interpretation, there is the potential to live like a saint or a criminal parasite. I have no means of judging how the *autonomes* are distributed between these extremes, but it is impossible to refuse to recognize some genuine and creative aspects of the movement which it might be more convenient to ignore, the easier to reject the whole phenomenon. The obsession with information by the printed word and by illegal radio transmissions is an attempt to provide local communities with means of communication which are otherwise denied them. *Télédiffusion de France* (TDF) is a State monopoly which is generally thought to present a particular view of events; in any case if all radio and television is controlled by a single organization, however generous and catholic (a reproach that is rarely made to TDF), it can hardly reflect the details of all the currents of modern society. Control of information is to an *autonome* part of the violence and repression of the State which must be destroyed. So out of the movement have sprung a variety of clandestine radio stations. In conformity with their views the operators of these stations rarely impose the contents of the emissions; as technicians they simply make available the means by which immigrants, ecologists, regionalists, feminists and other groups can diffuse their views.

The first private station to come on the air was *Radio-Verte*; this station, principally concerned with ecological matters, first broadcast on 13 May 1977. Others have followed, including *Radio-Fessenheim* in Alsace with a particularly strong anti-nuclear vocation. The emissions are jammed by TDF with more or less success. The radio-pirates do not emit regularly because that practice would make them easy targets for TDF's experts in jamming, but they choose hours when the experts are unlikely to be there. As they point out with joy the experts are civil servants and they eat at regular hours. One must wonder whether, emitting at irregular times, the radio-pirates have an audience other than the jammers of TDF, but that thought does not seem to worry either side.

The *autonomes* are obliged to tolerate violence and some have made it an essential element of a struggle to prevent the movement becoming a conventional defence of rigid ideas. But it is impossible to live the life of an *autonome* without becoming hardened to violence. Squatting is not encouraged by the French authorities; squatters are regularly driven out in the early morning by the CRS and the *gardes mobiles* using extremely violent methods. At times the evictions have developed into pitched battles fought with barricades, Molotov cocktails, pick handles and iron bars. There is no doubt that in French law the squatters have no rights, but nevertheless the authorities do little to restrain the violence of the para-military forces and there has developed an intense mutual hatred between the forces of law and order and the *autonomes*. This hatred is probably an inevitable theoretical consequence of the belief in the violence of the State and the desire to expose and make this violence manifest, but one cannot emphasize too strongly that it does exist in practice also, unmitigated by any trace of the friendly compact that is sometimes read into the word *flic*.

It is to this layer of the anti-nuclear movement that the gross acts of violence are mostly to be attributed. Among many are the bomb attack on the home of M. Boiteux, arson practised against offices of EDF and the sabotage of machinery having a relation, if sometimes remote, with the nuclear programme. As far as I can see, a typical *autonome* is rather badly informed about almost all aspects of nuclear power, but does not find this a hardship. His opposition is sufficiently grounded in the idea of nuclear power as a perfect incarnation of the violence of the State, imposed without consultation, propelled by lies and force, irrelevant to the true freedoms and requirements of society. Another contribution to the interest of the *autonomes* in nuclear matters may be the desire to have a crack at the CRS under circumstances where a degree of tolerance and support from respectable citizens ensures slightly more equal odds than those which prevail at 6.00 a.m. in a Paris street as the *autonome* is chased from his squat. Again one should make it clear that the notion that these acts of violence are inspired in any systematic way by the U.S.S.R. is not to be taken seriously; they have their origins in the extremes of a discontent with modern society which stands in continuity with quite common and moderate forms of protest throughout the Western world.

THE ECOLOGISTS

The discontent of disappointment in the left and extreme left after the events of May 1968 was not confined to those who abandoned the extreme left to sow the seeds of the *autonome* movement. Another part of the left withdrew from traditional political formations and began to develop a new political movement without real coherence or formal structure, but held together in practice by three themes: feminism, anti-military sentiments and opposition to nuclear power. The first stage in the evolution of the ecological movement in the years following 1968 was tranquil; considerable work was being done to gather documentary evidence and to prepare analyses. *La Gueule Ouverte*, one of the most influential ecological magazines, was begun. The first anti-nuclear demonstrations of significance took place at Fessenheim in 1971, attended by 1,500 people, and at Bugey, attended by 2,000 people. In 1972–1973 there were many anti-nuclear demonstrations and an anti-military demonstration at Larzac where much the same thoughts and people were in evidence.

But, up to the end of 1973, the anti-nuclear movement was a marginal movement in French society. The second stage of development began with the energy crisis which caused, and what is probably as important, attracted attention to, a dramatic acceleration of the French nuclear programme. Many small local protest groups sprung up around the chosen sites. These caused EDF considerable irritation because they obliged the enterprise to enter into a multitude of small legal actions. As a result the Government in collusion with EDF decided to put the confrontation on a more traditional basis and to consult the local democratically elected representatives of the people. In January 1975 three groups of scientists called on the elected representatives not to engage in negotiations with EDF on this basis because they had not been supplied with adequate information. This deficiency arose in the view of these scientists partly because EDF did not itself have adequate information. The Government could at this point no longer sustain the idea that it was acting democratically.

EDF made up a brochure of 40 pages which it sent to all interested parties and the scientific groups made up a counter brochure. The dynamic was released. The elected representatives in the affected areas organized referenda, although the Minister of the Interior pointed out that the referendum is unconstitutional for this type of problem. Only one (Flamanville) out of five or more, showed the local population to accept the installation of a nuclear plant. The preoccupations of the ecologists then began to combine and reinforce with a growing concern within the trade union movement. The trade unions are important to the ecologists because they provide an efficient method of circulating information, texts and documents which eventually will reach the administration, EDF and local branches of the trade unions in places where EDF plans to install nuclear stations. The information is diffused by many channels but converges at the site.

As a result of this effort, the ecologists have animated the latent opposition of many parties and there have been demonstrations all over France. In many respects the opposition has shown a rich cultural quality; each regional committee has its own magazine often in an attractive style, typically French – witty and elegant. A variety of ingenious and gentle ways have been found to raise money, by the sale of balloons at free fêtes or the sale of anti-nuclear stickers and posters. The humorous surface of the ecological movement should not be permitted to obscure the deep conflicts between the State and the individual which lie beneath – that is why it is a radical movement.

The third stage in the development of the ecological movement is characterized by its entry into conventional politics. In the elections of 1974 René Dumont stood as a candidate for President. He did not expect to win; he presented himself as a suppliant. The chief practical gain was that for the first time in France environmental propositions were diffused by French radio and television and, to a lesser extent, in the press. The message which Dumont's campaign transmitted was authentically ecological; it was well constructed and significant; it dealt with that which people did not wish to see – the other side of growth, the results of contempt for the environment, in the home, in the town, in the countryside. For the first time the French public were exposed to the complete ecological *problématique* and sensitized to the problems.

The ecological movement committed itself again to conventional politics when it entered the municipal elections of March 1977. The decision to do this was not taken lightly; it was a more important commitment than the presidential election because it cost more money and because it required a substantial commitment from the body of the movement, not simply from an individual and his aides. A perpetual current of debate in the ecological movement in France, stemming from the relationships implicit in the matrix formulation of the anti-nuclear movement sketched earlier, is whether to stay within the confines of existing political institutions and modes of conduct. Or from another point of view, whether to connive in an illusion of democracy. The balance of opinion was yes. The means to contest the elections were available, given the participation of allied or peripheral groups such as peasants, farmers, cyclists, fishermen. The objective again was to sensitize the populace, not to take control of Paris. The French ecologists, like their brethren in other countries, have no comprehensive political programme, a fact for which they are much reproached by conventional political parties.

One result was that the other candidates immediately turned 'green' in an attempt to capture the ecological vote, with the exception of M. Chirac and his *Rassemblement pour la République* (RPR). M. Giscard d'Estaing suppressed the Paris Expressway from his programme and made other conciliatory gestures and speeches. As *La Gueule Ouverte* put it,

> Their eyes riveted on the blue line in 1978 [the legislative elections], the parties discover a sudden love of nature and flaunt trees on their posters whilst shamelessly pillaging the ecological programme, with two exceptions – nuclear [energy] and [the distribution of] power . . . the two key matters which distinguish the ecological society from any other.

This is essentially a correct record of events; none of the principal political parties was tempted to turn anti-nuclear or espouse decentralization of power.

Alsace was certainly the region where ecological themes received most support from the public. The station at Fessenheim was about to be commissioned, the anti-nuclear campaign in the region was gathering strength and was drawing an increasingly wide consensus within the region. A variety of movements had given their support to the campaign and 107 pastors and priests of Alsace had just signed a declaration concerning the human implications of the nuclear industry.

The results of the municipal elections in the 'atomic communes' were variable, but in about three-quarters of the cases indicated hostility to the nuclear stations. At Flamanville and Gravelines the results were broadly favourable to the supporters. At Fessenheim the opponents obtained nine seats out of 17; elsewhere at Erdeven, Pellerin and Saône-et-Loire the opponents scored notable successes, either directly by electing their own representatives or indirectly by influencing the result between the other two parties in a way favourable to their views. *Le Monde* analysed the results of the elections in 24 nuclear communes and concluded that only six had remained faithful to the councils which had agreed to the installation of nuclear plant and 18 had supported new or old teams which were hostile to the projects.[6]

Among the ecologists who had supported the intervention in the municipal elections there was dissension about the value of the outcome. The majority thought that they had succeeded in strengthening the democratic nature of the elections, had contributed to a demystification of science and had laid upon others an obligation to declare themselves. A minority considered that the intervention had failed because it had been too costly and because the results were not commensurate with the effort. In any case the movement decided to persist with its intervention in the democratic process by contesting the legislative elections in March 1978.

Preparation for the legislative elections confirmed the division of the ecological movement into two main currents, signs of which had been visible in March 1977. One side, regrouped under the title *Collectif Ecologie 78*, was an attempt to constitute a united front of ecologists independent of political parties; the alliance was constructed exclusively for the legislative elections as the title makes clear and was to be disbanded the morning after. In principle, it was neutral between the main political parties which it viewed as equally committed to growth and to the nuclear programme. The other pole of the ecological intervention was formed by a union of regionalist, ecological and feminist groups along with MAN (*Mouvement pour une Alternative Non Violente*) and the PSU. The union known as the *Front Autogestionnaire* was to provide a new socialist and ecological party. The priority of this alliance was to minimize the possibility that the ecological intervention would harm the chances of the Left. The defection of the ecologists to the PSU under its new title was small; most assembled under the *Collectif Ecologie 78*.

The intervention of the ecologists in the legislative elections was nothing like the success of their intervention in the municipal elections. They polled 2% of the vote on the first round, but much more significantly they failed almost completely to bring ecological and anti-nuclear matters into the election debates. The voters who were persuaded that ecological arguments were relevant to their choice of local representatives could not be convinced that the same arguments were significant in the management of the country.

The other great schism in the ecological movement arises from the other quality which I used earlier to help categorize the nuclear opposition – the attitude to violence. It demonstrates the imperfections in the taxonomy because the ecologists continue to exhibit to some degree the full range of qualities that were employed in the categorization. There is a whole spectrum of attitudes in the ecological movement from the entirely pacific, passing through an ambivalent mixture of ruse and passive resistance, to full-fledged violence. Most of the violence originates with the *autonomes*, but there is a violent fringe to the ecologists and the boundary between the two groups is far from distinct. In a sense the ecologists were the first *autonomes*. They were the first people to go to the political parties with new ideas which did not fit into the well established lines of political battle. They were among the first to be repelled by the established parties, to be told that their preoccupations were secondary to traditional elements of the political scene; they were among the first to reject the political parties and to become 'autonomous'. Although the ecological movement as a whole has since developed distinct characteristics, the links with the *autonomes* remain. There is for example an ecological magazine originating in Grenoble, known as *Casse-noix* which regularly publishes recipes for Molotov cocktails, which encourages the creation within the ecological movement of an anti-nuclear militia, which instructs on the manufacture of gas masks and on the techniques for listening to and jamming police broadcasts. It once wrote:

> Among the companies which work for Malville, the camps and convoys of CRS, the anti-nuclear guerrillas need not lack targets, and if that is not enough we must strike higher and aim at the decision making centres.

On another occasion it published photographs of members of the police force at Grenoble, one of whom was circled by a target with the title 'not to be missed'.

The activities of the intermediate stage of ruse and passive resistance could take many forms: the sabotage of lorries carrying material; the reduction of payments owed to EDF by 15% as a gesture of refusal to contribute to the finance of the nuclear programme; the payment of 10 centimes too much, which is reputed, implausibly, to gum up the computer-managed accounting system; the distraction of the CRS by demonstration at one site whilst sabotage takes place elsewhere. The possibilities are limited only by the powers of imagination.

Most ecologists, including many of those who preach and practise non-violence, are convinced that the only way that the movement can succeed is if its activities contain a violent component. In their view the courts of justice are in the service of the State; the quality of life is not an adequate legal argument; the ecologists have lost every court case except one at Malville, on a formality that was quickly reversed.

C. The Technical Opposition

The ephemeral public debate on the nuclear programme which began in January 1975 was not instigated by the Government. It was imposed on it by a combination of local agitation around selected nuclear sites, aggravated by the ecological movement and supported by the work of a few scientists and professionals. The notion of professional responsibility is perhaps taken more seriously in France than in the United Kingdom, and dissension among professionals is less frequently exposed to public view. At the origin of these tendencies, and reinforcing them, is the concept of the expert which prevails in France: disagreements occur not because of fundamental conflicts of interest but because people are misinformed; given access to the technical information, there is only one view that can be held; it is necessary simply to assemble the right experts to ensure the correct interpretation of the facts; those who disagree are just badly informed. An excellent demonstration of this attitude is to be found in the record of a debate on the fast reactor (Super Phénix) organized by the *Conseil Général de l'Isère*.[6] The experts of the EDF and the CEA reiterated throughout the proceedings that if only the experts on the other side would come and see them they would put all the facts before them and there could no longer be any disagreement. There is a lot to be said for this belief and I have no intention of denigrating it, but this deeply held understanding of what it is to be an expert does inhibit professional people in France from proclaiming publicly conclusions which they have drawn from a study that must, by the nature of things, be less profound and less comprehensive than the work of the experts of EDF and the CEA. The consequences of this sociological condition are amplified by the great involvement of the French State in the scientific life of the community. This involvement takes the form of hierarchical structures and *a priori* controls which not only ensure that the particular view of the responsibilities of experts is remembered, but also facilitates reproof of whomsoever may forget.

In these ways the growth of professional opposition to the activities of the State is nipped in the bud. The State is thereafter able to present a choice of a fundamentally political character as a technical decision best made by the disinterested and impartial scientific experts. Any objection can be rejected as obscurantist and perverse. The highly technical nature of the decision pre-empts any democratic control, and the citizen is obliged to trust in the specialists. This has led commentators in France, as in the United Kingdom, to conclude that the nuclear choice is incompatible with democracy.

In this social context the entry of professional groups into the contest at the beginning of 1975 is all the more remarkable. Within two weeks three distinct and unconcerted attacks were launched on the nuclear programme, provoked by the brochure distributed by the *Ministre de l'Industrie* for the purpose of informing the locally elected representatives of affected communes of the consequences of a nuclear station. The most publicized of these attacks came from the *Groupement des Scientifiques Concernés* based at the *Collège de France* in Paris, bearing the signatures of 700 scientists.

Three hundred scientists in Alsace, based on a research centre of the CNRS in Strasbourg, produced a counter-brochure of their own which they sent to their local elected representatives. The most elaborate criticism, augmented by a detailed definition of an alternative strategy, was produced by the members of the *Institut Economique et Juridique de l'Energie* (IEJE) – the sole independent institute in France specializing in energy.

The following year the *Commission Physique du CNRS* (constituted in half by members elected from among university staff and in half by nominees of the Government) produced a report criticizing especially the safety precautions taken for the fast reactor.

None of this activity, and other initiatives from similar groups, has received any direct acknowledgement from the Government which professes to believe, and probably does believe, that independent technicians have nothing to add to the work of EDF and the CEA. These technical criticisms have been more effective when they have been mobilized by the ecological movement and used to aggravate the worries of the local communities in the vicinity of a proposed installation.

D. The Response to the Opposition

The response of the interested parties to the opposition to the nuclear programme is composed essentially of six elements: reassurance, information, consultation, compensation, recuperation and repression. The proportions of these elements will depend on which of the various parties is involved.

Broadly, the elements making up the reaction of EDF, the political parties and the State are distributed as follows:

	EDF	Political Parties	The State
Reassurance	×	×	×
Information			×
Compensation	×		×
Consultation			×
Recuperation		×	
Repression			×

EDF's response is based on reassurance and compensation. The local communes around a nuclear site receive an annual payment (*patente*) from EDF as they do from all professions practising on their territory. The *patente* is intended to finance the provision of infrastructure for the construction work, and generally there is a margin left over for the commune, which in a small community can represent a substantial fraction of the local budget. For example, St.-Laurent-des-Eaux received 5 MF from EDF in 1974; this benefit permitted the commune to construct three heated swimming pools which are the pride of the *département*.[7] The fact that the swimming pools were electrically heated did nothing to allay criticism.

There is obviously considerable scope for interpretation of these payments. Certainly they form an important part of the arguments advanced by EDF in its negotiations and no doubt they have an important influence on the outcome. To a classical economist it is not unreasonable that a community which is disturbed by an installation which benefits almost exclusively other people should be compensated/bribed. A conventional economic line of argument in opposition to this would be that the proposition only holds if the local population is properly informed of the consequences and properly understands them. The argument then shifts to whether or not the populace fulfils this condition. A less rigidly analytical and perhaps more emotional line of opposition which is the most widespread among critics is simply that it is immoral to bribe a local population to accept an installation dangerous to them and the community at large; as presented here this line of thought begs certain questions. There are, one should add, practical difficulties arising from the procedure of buying off the opposition. Whereas some people may find an electrically heated swimming pool inadequate compensation for becoming a nuclear site, others may find it excessive. There is likely to be considerable jealousy of the manna falling on a small number of French communes, particularly from those communes near enough to the station to be affected by it, but not near enough to touch any of the benefit. This jealousy is likely to be a small, but unpleasant side effect of the events.

The other tine of EDF's two-pronged attack is reassurance. This is provided by an active policy of convincing the public of the need for, and the benign character of, nuclear power. Representatives of the company take part in debates. Many documents are produced and circulated and information centres are set up on the future nuclear sites. Critics complain that the information is inadequate and biased. Certainly the documents prepared for public consumption are brief to the point where it must be doubtful that they are adequate – the brochure prepared for the proposed station at Ponteau comprised two pages, and that prepared for the fast reactors at Creys-Malville ran to only six pages. A brochure prepared by EDF specifically about nuclear power and the environment made no mention of thermal pollution, although heating of the great rivers and especially the Rhône must be one of the principal and incontestable sources of environmental damage associated with the nuclear policy as a whole.

The response of the State is closely co-ordinated with the response of EDF. There are areas such as the repression of violent manifestations and the consultation of elected representatives which are the prerogative of the State, but in other areas the efforts of EDF and the State combine. This is especially true for the provision of reassurance and information; in this function it is difficult to disentangle the State and the enterprise. The public powers indisputably control what can be said on the subject of nuclear energy on the radio and the television; they control also the organization of the material presented to the local communities in the vicinity of a proposed site. Behind the State lies the CEA and EDF. It is EDF which prepares all the reports for the *Ministère de l'Industrie* concerning the construction of stations (the preliminary, preparatory and final reports). There does exist a small body of some 20 professional staff, under the hierarchical control of the Minister, whose job it is to ensure standards of security are elaborated and observed for each site, i.e. the *Service Central de Sûreté des Installations Nucléaires* (SCSIN). But the supporting staff to SCSIN, comprising several hundred engineers are supplied from the Nuclear Safety Department of the CEA. It is perhaps eminently reasonable that the monopoly of the work of appraising sites should lie with the professional staff of the CEA and EDF. Nevertheless, whether this is reasonable or not, the contention is certainly true that at all levels of control one finds the engineers of the CEA and EDF – judges and suppliants.

The State monopoly of information has by an inexorable process caused to develop the non-conventional means of dissemination of information which have already been sketched.

From time to time the Elysée has shown signs of being uneasy about this near monopoly of information enjoyed by the State. The most recent manifestation of this unease was probably helped along by the extent of the demonstrations at Malville and their brutal suppression (to be described later). Shortly after these events the President of the Republic announced the creation of the *Conseil d'Information Electronucléaire*.[8] The Council is composed of 18 members; it is attached to the Prime Minister and has the task of 'ensuring that the public has access to information on the questions relating to electronuclear energy in the technical, health, ecological, economic and financial areas'.[9] The requirements of military and industrial secrecy are not to obstruct the work of the Council without due cause. The members comprise the *Maires* of four communes where a nuclear station will be built, six representatives of ecological organizations (of the more moderate character) and others with qualifications in the energy field. There are no representatives from the CEA, EDF or the DGE; the nearest is M. Jean Couture, one time President of the PEON Commission.

Considerable scepticism exists among opponents of nuclear power about this committee; it is probably justified. It took six months from the announcement that the Commission would be created to the nomination of its members; not a sign of undue haste. The nuclear programme has not been, and will not be, modified to await the deliberations of the Council, which in any case exists to advise on how people should be convinced of the benefits of nuclear energy and not to judge whether there are benefits. The Council is seen as a typical Giscardian gesture; liberal words and superficial activities designed to calm the opposition, whilst the provoking acts are prosecuted with the same determination as before. Indeed the interim announcement of details of the committee coincided with an assertion by M. Monory, *Ministre de l'Industrie*, that there could be no question of a moratorium, nor of a referendum, nor of a modification of the programme.[10]

This is the third attempt to initiate public debate on the nuclear question, the other two having failed ignominiously. In 1975 the *Délégation à l'Information* announced the publication of a white book comprising the views of 25 persons for and against the nuclear programme. The texts were prepared, but the project was squashed by the *Ministère de l'Industrie*, presided over at the time by M. d'Ornano, now *Ministre de l'Environnement*. In May 1974 M. Giscard d'Estaing, as candidate for President, had promised the creation of a national ecological committee with the task in particular of studying the appropriate precautions to take with nuclear power. In October 1975 the *haut comité de l'environnement* was indeed enlarged and reanimated, but it never grappled with the nuclear question. In the face of this past history, and the general context in which the *Conseil d'Information Electronucléaire* has been established, it is certainly most plausible to consider it a smokescreen.

The response of the political parties has been varied. The Gaullists have not modified their views to the smallest extent, nor have the Communists. For the Communists it is not permissible to cast doubt on the integrity of State enterprise. The attempts to recuperate the ecological vote have come from the socialists and the centre parties of the majority. The PS proposed a moratorium on nuclear construction after a period of distinctly ambiguous policy; it is generally thought, by its industrial and ecological critics alike, that this proposal is eyewash and will never be imposed if the PS were to be elected the principal party in a government of the left. Within the left-wing parties there are special commissions as for all subjects including energy. The Commission within the PS which considers energy policy is composed three-quarters of employees of EDF and CEA. EDF in particular has a strongly left-wing membership and a substantial part even of management belongs to the CGT. It follows then that, quite apart from the will of the senior management of EDF, there is considerable pressure on the leaders of the PS to see the advantages of nuclear energy. The impression one has of the PS is definitely that of a party which has adopted an ambiguous opportunist line and prefers to criticize the decision-making procedure rather than to decide on the programme itself. The PS protests that the policy has never been debated in the National Assembly, a contention that is not true. The topic was debated in May 1975 in front of a handful of deputies among which was a smaller handful of the left.

E. Authorization Procedures

The technical factors determining the siting of nuclear power stations and the socio-political origins of the opposition have been sketched. The outcome of these conflicting interests will be influenced not only by the nature and strength of the forces at work, but also by the administrative framework in which they interact. An account of the procedures for obtaining authorization is therefore necessary for a complete understanding.[11]

Nuclear installations in France can only be begun after the authorization has been obtained in the form of a decree based on a report by the *Ministre de l'Industrie* with the consent of the *Ministre de la Santé Publique* (public health). The application for authorization is first directed by EDF to the Minister responsible for atomic energy who then informs those of his government colleagues who may be concerned. The application is then sent to the prefect of the department where it is planned to site the installation. The prefect organizes a form of public enquiry, i.e. *Déclaration d'Utilité Publique* (DUP). A representative of the prefect informs the public and consults the local authorities, in particular the mayor of the commune directly concerned. The procedure of the DUP is far more one-sided than that obtaining in a public inquiry in the United Kingdom which has, although not originally intended, an adversarial quality; both sides put a case before an arbitrator. In the French scheme the State, through the prefect, *informs*. The municipal council must give its opinion within one month. The conclusions of the inquiry and the views of the local representatives of the competent government departments are sent to the prefect, who passes them on with his own opinion to the Minister responsible for atomic energy.

During the course of the DUP a preliminary safety report on the application is made, in principle, by a committee of experts, in practice by EDF. This report is appraised by the safety department of the CEA and passed on to the SCSIN which prepares the authorization decree.

Up to 1973 the procedure operated fairly slowly but without hindering the relatively small French programme. Successive accelerations of the programme have made it necessary to find many sites rapidly and put sufficient strain on the procedure to contribute to the delays. In some cases this delay

187

has caused EDF to begin work on a site without the DUP; whether this is legal seems to be a controversial point; but there can be no doubt that it shows considerable confidence in a successful conclusion to the inquiry.

The imperative necessity to try to ensure that the programme is not delayed by a lack of sites threatens to make siting an important element of the critical path of the overall programme. The development of the programme was originally seen as follows:

Date of Commissioning	Locality	Output MW(e)	Cumulative MW(e)
1976	Fessenheim 1, Fessenheim 2 Bugey 2	2,700	2,700
1977	Bugey 3	900	3,600
1978	Bugey 4, Bugey 5, Tricastin 1, Gravelines 1	3,600	7,200
1979	Gravelines 2, Tricastin 2, Dampierre 1	2,700	9,900
1980	Dampierre 2/3, Tricastin 3/4, Gravelines 3	4,500	14,400
1981	Gravelines 4, Dampierre 4, Chinon B1, Blayais 1/2, St. Laurent B1/B2	6,300	20,700
1982	Chinon B2, Malville 1(R), Fessenheim 3, Paluel 1, Cruas 1, Cattenom 1	6,100	26,800
1983	Cruas 2/3, Fessenheim 4, Cattenom 2, Paluel 2, Flamanville 1	5,800	32,600
1984	Cruas 4, Nogent 1, Flamanville 2, St. Alban 1	4,000	36,600
1985	St. Alban 2, Nogent 2, Le Pellerin 1, Saône 1(R), ? 1	5,200	41,800
1986	Le Pellerin 2, Belleville 1, Saône 2(R), ? ?	5,000	46,800

R—fast reactor.

There were many options and uncertainties which have been suppressed for brevity, but the sketch faithfully reproduces the essential aspects of the programme.

188

In principle EDF would like to ensure that the availability of sites should never retard the programme. That means having not only enough sites for the programme envisaged but also a few in reserve to cope with unexpected events. To achieve the programme sketched above, EDF would require to begin work on 10 sets of 900 MW(e) and two sets of 1,300 MW(e) in 1976–1977 at: St. Laurent, Gravelines, Dampierre, Fessenheim, Blayais, Chinon, Cruas, Cattenom, Paluel, Flamanville and Creys-Malville; then in 1978–1979 to begin five sets of 900 MW(e) and five sets of 1,300 MW(e) at perhaps: Paluel, Flamanville, St. Alban, Nogent, Le Pellerin, Fessenheim, Cruas and Cattenom.

EDF has obtained most of the sites it required in 1976–1977 with the exception of Cattenom on the Moselle. The DUP has been granted at Cruas, but there is considerable local hostility. It must be less likely that the enterprise will obtain the sites it wants in 1978–1979; there is strong hostility at Le Pellerin, Cattenom, Nogent, Cruas and St. Alban and a reluctance to see an expansion at Fessenheim. Siting has not until now been a significant restraint on the problem because of the fierce resolution of EDF. The years 1978 and 1979 will show whether, as seems likely, it will be a restraint in the future.

The fierce resolution of EDF has caused it to start work without the DUP at Creys-Malville and Flamanville. Whether this is legal seems to be a nice point,[12] but it does demonstrate considerable confidence within the company that the inquiry will be favourable.

F. The Representation of the State in the Region

To describe fully the origins and dynamics of the opposition to the nuclear policy it is necessary to introduce an account of the balance of powers between central and local government. Strictly the account should begin at least with Charlemagne, but the *ancien régime* offers a compromise between brevity and completeness. In the theory of the *ancien régime* the king was the state, sovereignty belonged to him and his will was law. The system was perfected under Louis XIV who demanded the passive obedience of all on the basis of the doctrine of *l'absolutisme d'essence divine*. The administrative system was highly centralized and hierarchical. The powers of the representative of the State in the provinces – the *intendant* – were strengthened. In practice despotism was never complete; the church, the law, the nobles had appreciable autonomy, but this pluralism of powers was arbitrated by an undisputed authority. It was also undermined by varying degrees of venality in the monarch. The slowness of communications obliged much discretion to be left to the *intendant*. The Revolution, by transferring sovereignty from the king to the nation and at the same time undermining the other sources of power, effectively destroyed the *de facto* pluralism. The power vacuum was filled by the administration.

Napoleon Bonaparte put the pieces together. Bonaparte drafted the constitution of 1799 which gave him absolute power. The executive power belonged to the First Consul and his nominated ministers. The legislative power belonged to four Assemblies, essentially nominated by the First Consul. The judicial power was exercised by judges nominated by the First Consul. Government of the provinces descended directly from Bonaparte through an administrative structure of *préfets*, *sous-préfets* and *maires*. By carefully synthesizing aspects of the Revolution and the *ancien régime*, Bonaparte constructed a system which attributed unprecedented power to the head of state. This concept of local government – 'central power and local opinion' – persists to this day; it is evident for example in the procedure of the DUP sketched earlier. Much of the administrative structure by which the central power was enforced in the provinces also persists. The little it has lost has been amply compensated by the invention of the telephone.

An excellent account of the powers of the contemporary *préfet* and *maire* is given by Ridley and Blondel.[13] These authors divide the powers of the *préfet* into four categories. He is the representative of the State, and as such he can in emergencies exercise considerable powers on his own initiative. He is the representative of the whole government and officially the head of all government services. He is the 'eyes and ears' of the Government in the province and periodically produces a report on the morale of the population. He is the representative of the *Ministre de l'Intérieur*, the Minister responsible for supervising local authorities. As such the préfet supervises the activities of the *maires* and the local councils. He is also the chief executive of local government at the level of the department. The *préfet* is appointed by the Government, generally from the prefectoral *corps*. Some of the ablest ENA graduates choose the prefectoral career; they join the lowest class of *sous-préfet* on secondment and then after serving for some time it in are established as members of the *corps*.

The *maire* is a representative of the State at the level of the commune, and as such he is under the hierarchical control of the *préfet*. In the Napoleonic system the *maire* was appointed by government; a reform in 1882 permitted him to be elected by the municipal council. The *maire* is therefore also a representative of the people. The *maires* of large towns like Paris and Grenoble often have the resources to stand up to the *préfet*. In rural communes where the electorate may only be a few hundred the *maire* can exercise rather little power over real resources.

G. Case Studies

We have sketched the interests involved and the framework in which they are constrained to operate. It is helpful to study these interests in conflict at some of the sites where EDF is working.

1. LE PELLERIN (LOIRE-ATLANTIQUE)
EDF sought at the end of 1974 a site on the Loire estuary. The regional councils of the *Pays de la Loire* had unanimously accepted in principle the siting of three stations in the region. EDF investigated four possible choices

on the lower Loire before settling on a site near a small town called Le Pellerin on the left bank of the river about 15 km from Nantes. More than 440,000 inhabitants live within a radius of 20 km; construction of the station would take 280 hectares of land out of cultivation, and in the view of many people there are enormous uncertainties about the effects of liquid and gaseous effluent on Nantes and of the disturbance which would be caused directly and indirectly to the agricultural equilibrium of the surroundings. When completed, the station would be the largest in France, having four sets of 1,300 MW(e) each.

From the beginning, the proposal has been the object of vigorous contestation securely based on a large part of the local population, especially the peasants, and faithfully translated by the elected representatives of the 12 communes concerned. Equally EDF is almost desperate for the site if it is to meet its plans for 1985; the delays in finding a site on the Loire leave the enterprise little room for manoeuvre; the stage is therefore set for a violent clash of interests.

The process of the DUP was installed soon after EDF had decided on the site. The procedure requires that registers be left in the *mairies* of the affected communes to receive a note of any observations that the population may care to make. On 31 May 1977 the prefectorial office began the operation. In the majority of communes the *maires* refused to allow the register into the *mairie*; in some cases donning the *tricolore* sash of office and bodily preventing the entry of the bearer.* In these acts the *maires* were faithfully representing the wishes of their constituents who had, a few weeks previously, elected them to office on the basis of anti-nuclear programmes. Nothing daunted, the ingenious *sous-préfets* summoned prefectorial vans which they parked alongside the *mairies*, dubbed them *mairies-annexes*, installed the registers for the DUP and left them in the care of the *gardes mobiles*.

The registers, and the fashion with which they had been forced on the people became the symbol of the station and the violence with which it was to be imposed on the community. Two days later, on market day, in the village of Coueran, between 35 and 40 local peasants stormed the *mairie*, broke into the room where the register, guarded by three *gendarmes*, was chained to a desk, overwhelmed the *gendarmes*, tore out the register, took it into the market place and burnt it. Five peasants were recognized by the *gendarmes* and later arrested.

The affair was widely publicized; the arrested peasants received considerable support from the French scientists who had produced the cautionary tracts described earlier. One of them, the Director of the Laboratory of Particle Physics at the *Collège de France*, gave it as his view that the site at Pellerin was 'one of the worst in the world'.[14]

On 10 June the five peasants were brought before the tribunal at Nantes and charged under *la loi anti-casseurs* (of which more later). The President of

* *Allez dire à votre maître que nous sommes ici par la puissance du peuple et qu'on ne nous en arrachera que par la puissance des baionnettes.*   Mirabeau

the tribunal paid no heed to the claims by an assembly of independent scientists that the defendants had only behaved reasonably in refusing to accept a nuclear station until they had been properly informed and had achieved a clear perception of the risks. 'There has been violence,' said the President. 'If there has been violence,' said the defence, 'the first violence is to impose a station on a population who do not want it.' The local *maires* and their aides attested to the collective refusal of the station. The defendants were sentenced to eight months in prison, of which six were suspended.

Two hours later the *mairie* in a neighbouring commune was entered by a group of 30 demonstrators who destroyed the register and demanded to be charged. During the following days the local branches of the trade unions organized demonstrations in front of the *préfectures* at Nantes and Rennes to protest against the 'police repression'; about 2,000 people attended. An appeal was launched and signed by 200 technical experts in energy and nuclear physics, essentially on the theme that the local population had been inadequately informed. The local *maires* protested formally to the *préfet* against the severity of the sentence and against the 'escalation of violence consequent on the conditions under which the DUP is being performed under the protection of imposing forces of police, constituting a permanent challenge to the population which, in great majority, had refused the proposal to site a station at Le Pellerin'. The traditional forms of protest in agricultural communities were not neglected; in one commune the prefectorial van which performed the office of *mairie-annexe* found itself unable to park in its usual place, which overnight had been transformed into a depot for old agricultural equipment.

In the face of the fierce protests, the Appeal Court at Rennes reduced the sentences, freeing one man completely and extending the suspension of sentence to eight months for the others, thereby in practice releasing them also. But the President of the Court could not resist the sibylline observation: 'I cannot see honest farmers undertaking such acts of violence without being pushed by others.'[15]

Subsequently the communes have resisted the enquiry by a variety of means, laying complaints against the *préfet* for abuse of power, incompetence, and non-conformity to the law.[16] A petition of 30,000 signatures was presented to the *préfet*; this latter esteemed the number 'few with regard to the population from which the signatures were collected'. The *maire* of Nantes described the enquiry as 'a parody of consultation', a description which the *préfet* found 'especially inappropriate'.[17]

The procedure continues. The example shows, and it is characteristic, how the *préfet* acts as the local agent of the State. Accordingly the hostility of the discontented is focused on this convenient symbol rather than on a nebulous target in Paris (as the United Kingdom directs its wrath at 'Whitehall'). Formally the *préfet* may appear to consult the local populace, but when it comes to the crunch, the channel between the community and the State quickly shows itself one way. Many *préfets* make little pretence even in normal times. Evidently the system does little to assuage local discontent; the sense in the local communities of being governed is undoubtedly a part of the cause of the rapid recourse to violence.

2. FLAMANVILLE (MANCHE)

Of all the projects of EDF Flamanville is the most spectacular. The same strong current that carries away the radioactive effluent from the reprocessing plant at Cap de la Hague at the extremity of Cotentin continues along the western shore of the peninsula and passes by the village of Flamanville about 15 km to the south. There is no shortage of cooling water for four sets of 1,300 MW(e) apiece which EDF plans to install. But there is no place to put them; the sea touches the granite cliffs which line the coast. To plant the reactors, a section of the cliff 700 metres deep is to be removed, and the emplacement so created extended seawards by a platform of granite debris. The whole is to be protected from the sea by a 100,000 tonne barrage. The artificial site will cost 400 F for each square metre.

The physical determinants of the site are good, but difficult; the socioeconomic determinants are also, in their own way, mixed. The area has some of the ideal characteristics of the receptive location; it is experiencing the slight industrial decline which concentrates the minds of the community and its elected representatives on jobs, investment and the proceeds of the professional tax. The very site of the station is a disused iron mine; the blasting of the granite and the handling of the material is work that suits perfectly the one-time miners of the locality. On the other hand, industrialization is local; the majority of the surrounding communes depend on agriculture and tourism. As is to be expected in this environment the reception of the station has been much more ambiguous than at Le Pellerin.

The municipal council agreed to the project on 20 December 1974. The *maire*, himself a one-time miner, is reported as describing the decision as a 'return to the good old days' of the iron workings.[18] But from the beginning the commune was divided. In April 1975 the *maire* organized a local referendum which he won by 425 votes to 248. The opposition instigated a march to protest at the result and apparently to their surprise attracted the support of some thousand people from the region, although not the immediate locality. From this was founded the *Comité Régional d'Information et de Lutte Antinucléaire* (Crilan); periodically smaller groups have broken off from Crilan to organize protest with a distinctive emphasis – groups of fishermen, farmers and groups of militants unhappy with the non-violent philosophy of Crilan. But on the whole the Crilan has formed the nucleus of protest in the region.

EDF formally presented the request for the DUP on 18 February 1976. The commissioning of the first two sets on the site was planned for 1983 and 1984; the construction time was unusually long because of the difficulties of the terrain and the additional complexity of 1,300 MW(e) sets. This timetable required work to begin during 1976.

Crilan animated the region with anti-nuclear propaganda. Autonomous local committees flourished, anti-nuclear balls, anti-nuclear fêtes, films, magazines, posters and stickers multiplied. Debates were organized with representatives of the EDF; the emotional arguments of the opposition, the prevailing relationships of force in the debating chambers and the technically unsophisticated audiences provided Crilan with sweeping victories. The strike of the workers at La Hague and their allegations about the risks of nuclear power also made an impression on the locality. The peasant farmers set up a fund to purchase the land of colleagues threatened with expropriation; they intend by this means to resist the demands of EDF more successfully than they could singly. This initiative was modelled on a similar undertaking at Larzac and further back on the methods employed by Swedish, German and American anti-nuclear movements. The public enquiry was finally opened at the end of 976. The commissioners gave a favourable opinion subject to the condition that the route of the transmission lines from the nuclear station carrying the output to Brittany and the area of Paris should be presented to the enquiry during the first quarter of 1977. The DUP was not officially granted but EDF needed the site urgently and they began work at their own risk.

When the civil engineering contractors turned up to begin the work, they found their route blocked by a barricade of rocks manned by their opponents. The terrible divisions in the community were exposed by the intervention of the *maire* on behalf of the contractors, backed by the shopkeepers, mineworkers and craftsmen of his commune. For them the station represented 3,000 jobs during construction and the eventual prospect of 400 permanent jobs as operators with EDF, plus an annual revenue of some 100 MF from the *patente*. Against them, on the barricade, were teachers, students and above all farmers with nothing to gain from the construction work and for whom the fruits of the *patente* (widening of roads, swimming pools, sports club) held no attraction. The contractors withdrew, but the following day at dawn, bulldozers escorted by *gardes mobiles* surprised the occupants of the site and destroyed the barricade. Some 800 demonstrators arrived too late to change events and so descended by car on Cherbourg where in retaliation they created considerable trouble for several hours and prevented the circulation of traffic.

In the municipal elections in March 1977 the results of the referendum in April 1975 were repeated. The 436 votes obtained by the outgoing *maire* were almost exactly the same as the 'oui' in 1975; the 'non' polled 230 as they did two years ago. In this part of France people do not change their minds easily. During the elections there was little sign in the neighbouring communes that the station was of compelling interest either way.

A month later Crilan organized anti-nuclear Easter hearings intended to attract militants from all over France and Europe. Between 1,000 and 2,000 people attended, participated in debates and demonstrated peaceably on the cliff. In the afternoon about 100 members of the extreme left coming from outside the region arrived by coach and destroyed a part of the boundary fence to the site; they rolled blocks of granite down onto the workings from the top of the cliff and destroyed some of the machinery, but they dispersed before the arrival of the *gardes mobiles*.

During the summer of 1977 there were sporadic assaults on machinery and a few more blocks of granite fell down the cliff face. A peaceful demonstration and anti-nuclear fête was held in August. But there has certainly been nothing that EDF and the authorities cannot take in their stride. The leaders of Crilan are committed to non-violent methods, a commitment strengthened after the events at Malville. They count on a national debate in the framework of the legislative elections in March 1978 to further their cause.

The opposition to the nuclear station at Flamanville has failed to make the site a significant centre of protest. The sociology of the community is not favourable. There is a strong anti-nuclear sentiment in the region especially among the agriculturalists, but it does not predominate. This conjunction weakens the legitimacy of the movement and prevents a collective refusal comparable to that expressed at Le Pellerin. At the same time the early efforts to make Flamanville a national and even international centre of protest failed; the attempts appear to have been abandoned now for fear that if successful they would lead to a violent confrontation in the spirit of Malville.

3. CREYS-MALVILLE (ISÈRE)

There can be no prettier spot for a fast reactor than Creys-Malville. Downstream from the fort of Mérieu and a string of wooded islands, the Rhône briefly widens its course. To the east is the Château St-André and in the distance the foothills of the Alps; on the west bank is a forested plain at the edge of which is the village of Malville. North-west of the village is the construction site, surrounded by a triple fence of electrified barbed wire, patrolled by police and guard dogs; at night the perimeter is illuminated by batteries of powerful lamps.

The French fast reactor programme began in 1953 at the CEA; in 1967 the fast reactor Rhapsodie at Cadarache diverged for the first time; the output of the plant was 40 MW thermal. In August 1973 the fast reactor Phénix at Marcoule diverged; its capacity of 250 MW(e) is connected to the grid. There is no doubt about the success of the CEA in fast neutron technology; the French claim to be, and probably are, ahead of the world in this undertaking. The intention to push ahead at full speed to a still larger design had no connection whatsoever with events following the October War; it orginated in part from the natural enthusiasm of technicians who lead their rivals in a difficult challenge, in part from the desire of the CEA to capture for France a high technology market and in part to a curious French desire to show that they are capable of the determined and coherent development work required to convert brilliant technology into a commercial triumph. For so long the world has thought of France as being incapable of practical application; the

Maginot Line, the liner *France*, the Secam colour television system and Concorde are the examples usually cited of ambitious French technology come unstuck. It would be dangerous to underestimate the extent to which the CEA, EDF and Government were motivated by the passion to show that they can commercialize a technological line going back to Madame Curie. (They are as convinced that Madame Curie was French as they are convinced that the PWR is a French design.)

The next technical step in the fast reactor programme after Phénix was seen as the construction of a design at 1,200 MW(e). EDF were as conscious as anyone of the poor historical record of commercial competitiveness of advanced French technology; the enterprise therefore attempted from the beginning to associate the potential clients with the development of Super-Phénix. An agreement to commercialize the French designs was therefore signed in May 1971 between EDF, its Italian analogue, ENEL, and a private company for the distribution of electricity in West Germany, the RWE. The official ratification of the agreement was delayed by certain aspects of the legal status of EDF, but the date of this agreement, which itself followed lengthy negotiation, shows quite clearly that the rapid development of the fast reactor line was predicated on quite other grounds than the strategic weaknesses disclosed by the 1973 War in the Middle East.

One legal obstacle to the international agreement came from the law nationalizing the electricity supply industry in 1946; the law attributed to EDF the monopoly of the production and distribution of electricity in France; a joint company with foreign partners would infringe the monopoly. Another legal obstacle was a law of 1967 which required that any company be comprised of a minimum of seven legal personalities. It was necessary to create an exception for a company comprising EDF, ENEL and RWE.

The importance of these legal points is that they obliged the Government to request Parliament to authorize the new company. Without this legal accident the project to construct a fast reactor would never have been debated by Parliament – an astonishing lack of democratic participation. The left opposed the motion, not from any compelling opposition to the fast reactor, but because they disapproved of the precedent of diminishing the monopoly of EDF, especially to the benefit of a private German Company. Nothing prevented Westinghouse, argued the left, from acquiring shares in RWE that would allow them access to the secrets of Super-Phénix. But the motion was passed and the new company authorized by the law of December 1972. In 1974 the *Société Centrale Nucléaire Européenne à Neutrons Rapides* (Nersa) was created, to own and operate a fast reactor; the capital was distributed among EDF (51%), ENEL (33%) and RWE (16%). After safety analysis had been made (by the CEA) the construction of Super-Phénix in France was authorized by a restricted Council of Ministers presided over by the President of the Republic in April 1976.

EDF had decided in 1971 to install Super-Phénix at Malville; the site had been chosen because of the proximity of the German and Italian electricity networks which were to take the electrical production of the plant in proportion to the capital holdings. The siting predicated by the requirements of international co-operation in development, was also to facilitate and encourage an international anti-nuclear opposition. The request for a DUP at Malville was made by EDF in July 1973. It was granted by the *Conseil d'Etat* in November 1976 despite indignant complaints by the local elected representatives that neither they nor the population had been consulted.[19]

Indignation and resignation dominated the reactions of the local community – not the stuff of spontaneous action but abundantly productive material for outside agitation. Up until the summer of 1976 the fast reactor was a taboo subject; the local population was in large part uneasy, but few if any could speak of the matter with knowledge. There had been meetings, and tracts had been distributed, but on the whole they had had no real audience among the people of the region, who found the opponents of the fast reactor as foreign as they found the subject of the contestation. But at the beginning of July members of a variety of organizations assembled at Malville for an 'anti-nuclear fête'. Most came from outside the region, from all over France and some from Switzerland, Italy and Germany. They came to demonstrate, to develop the arguments against the fast reactor and to demand a referendum among the population of the region. The demonstrations of 3 and 4 July 1976 took place without any turbulence. The organizers had formally denounced all violent confrontation with the authorities; they succeeded in achieving this aim and in controlling the small proportion of *Gaullistes* and other groups of a revolutionary character. About 2,000 to 3,000 people attended the demonstration, camping in fields made available by local farmers. The weather was fine as it was the drought of 1976, and many of the demonstrators stayed on, mostly young, some couples with children, resolutely non-violent, improvising dances and music. During the afternoon of 8 July, as the majority of the occupants were sun-bathing and giving more attention to the 'fête' side of things than to the *anti-nucléaire*, the CRS cleared the site by dropping tear gas grenades from low-flying helicopters. In panic the occupants took refuge in the woods, some in bathing costumes, one woman with blood on her face. A stubborn group reassembled and on 10 July, with the assistance of some of the local *maires* and the participation of local farmers with their tractors, held a demonstration at the village of Bouvesse. There followed a march towards the reactor. In the evening the demonstrators improvised another camp at Mérieu about a mile from the site. As night fell several hundred CRS moved in on the ground to clean up (*nettoyer*). The demonstrators were chased from their camp with gas grenades and *matraques* (clubs); their tents and equipment were destroyed and scattered; they dispersed into the woods and fields and were sheltered by peasant farmers, stupefied by the behaviour of the CRS.

The indiscriminate brutality of the forces of law and order in France on occasions like this does have to be seen to be believed; it was, in this particular case, in striking contrast to the restraint of the demonstrators.

The violent intervention of the State against the peaceful demonstrators made a deep impression on the local people and their representatives; it aroused latent hostilities and was directly responsible for the decision of the elected representatives of the Isère to organize for themselves two days of hearings on Super-Phénix. The proceedings of the hearings have been published. In the Preface the *Président du Conseil Général de l'Isère* makes this connection quite clear. Other participants made the same point. Some quotations from the proceedings give an idea of the reactions of the local elected representatives and a flavour of the character of French local government. The *maire* of Bouvesse on the events in his village on 10 July alleged:

> ... there was a brutality without precedent which so overcame the population of our commune and neighbouring communes that I told the *Commandant* of the CRS when he came to see me on 13th July: 'If you had not sensitized the population before, you have done so today.' He replied: 'It was necessary to strike hard to put an end to it or it would have gone on for a long time'. Then I told him: 'It was the one thing not to do because in that way you have sensitized a population who up until now did not know the strength of the CRS'. They have learnt to know it.

Another of the elected representatives had some perceptive observations on the evolution of the relationships between the demonstrators from outside the region and the local population:

> I studied the attitude of the population. At first it was very prudent, reserved, even hostile to the *contestataires*. Imagine our farmers of Morestel with their feet solidly anchored in the soil from which they live – more or less, well, I might say in passing, because of the drought – face to face with these *gauchistes*, these *écologistes* and other names in *istes!*
> Then to my great surprise I saw the doors of these same farmers, their ears, and even their hearts, open. In a few days these young people, shattering the fetters of official information, had brought the populations to see the other side of this realization, to comprehend, across the megawatts and kilowatts, the problems of safety, of reliability, of cost, of lifestyle, even, why not, of civilization.
> ... how great was my surprise to notice that a union, a symbiosis, had been made between these farmers, of whom I was just speaking, and these *contestataires* and I saw to my great surprise several dozen farmers participate in the demonstration and then file off towards Malville, all – I bear witness – in the most absolute calm and dignity.
> I will tell you here of the emotion that I felt as an elected representative, as a man, in front of this crowd of several thousand people. It made me think – I am a teacher of history – of the pilgrimages made to avert the end of the world in the year 1000. I am not preaching catastrophe, reassure yourselves, but this thought came to my mind.

Others of the elected representatives present bear witness to the non-violence of the demonstrators, the brutality of the police and to the manner in which this conjunction of attitudes brought home to the local population the fact that the fast reactor had been imposed on them without consultation.

Indeed the most revealing aspect of the hearings was the disconcertion exhibited by EDF, CEA and the Government; there were numerous hesitations about the role of the delegates who should be sent and a continual debate about the order of the speakers and in particular who should have the last word.

The hearings themselves lasted only two days and were necessarily superficial. The audience was clearly disconcerted by the disagreements between the experts of EDF and CEA and other scientists not belonging to the industry; it was equally out of its depth in the technical discussions, although overjoyed that at last they were able seriously to question the technocrats; it was happiest debating political matters, principally whether or not the construction companies should be nationalized. At the end of the debate three motions were proposed, one each by the socialists (19 members of the council), communists (10 members), and the presidential majority (15 members). Each motion faithfully reflected the position of the political parties in the country as a whole. The members of the presidential majority supported government policy and the development of Super-Phénix. The communists denounced the participation of private enterprise, reaffirmed its demands for nationalization of all the industries concerned, but avoided saying what should happen to the fast reactor project. The socialists broadly agreed with the communists, deplored the absence of democratic debate and the contemptuous treatment of the local populations; they requested the Government to suspend the fast reactor project until their objections were met. None of the groups was opposed to the nuclear policy or the fast reactor in principle.

The socialist motion was adopted by the general council and communicated to the Prime Minister. There was no reply – not even an acknowledgement that the communication had been received. But a month later Nersa was authorized to put out the first orders to Novatome, for the steam generators.

The vast movement of sympathy unleashed by the behaviour of the police during the events of July 1976 at Malville did not stop at the borders of the Isère. The ecological magazines made much of the events as was only to be expected, but the reaction of the national press was also on the whole sympathetic. Marc Ambroise-Rendu, a persistent but restrained critic of nuclear policy, wrote in *Le Monde*: 'To the legitimate unease of thousands of citizens, who ask simply that democracy should function, they reply with the most summary and least legitimate force.'[20]

Comités Malville began to flourish all over France; they were established to provide nuclei for the growth of the campaign against the fast reactor. Three series of committees are distinguished; local committees from villages in the immediate vicinity of the site, committees from towns in the Rhône-Alps – Grenoble, Lyon, Geneva, and committees from more distant parts of France. In practice the co-ordination is dominated by groups from the large towns in the Rhône-Alps, especially Grenoble, with large populations of young, eloquent, active people near enough to be affected. The only qualification for a group to be a *Comité Malville* is an assertion that it is one and attendance at the appropriate meetings. The movement has therefore been easily infiltrated by the revolutionary margins of the left. As is often the case, a small number of people have been able to direct events by dint of determination, organization and persistence.

An extensive propaganda campaign was launched by the *Comités Malville* aided by their journal, *Super Pholix*, and a clandestine radio station, *Radio Active*. Early in 1977 the assemblies of the departments of *Isère* and *Savoie* called on the Government to suspend the construction of the fast reactor. In February 2,000 to 3,000 people attended a meeting in the village of Morestel, near the site of the reactor, to define a programme of action for the future. Four propositions were approved; they comprised the reduction of electricity bills by 15%, pressure on the legislative and municipal elections, sabotage that avoids physical injury (e.g. burning of lorries, burglary of Nersa offices, blocking roads to prevent convoys reaching the site) and finally a demonstration at Malville on 30-31 July designed to attract 100,000 participants. This assembly was, and is to this day, the greatest manifestation of the anti-nuclear movement in France and probably in the world. The programme foresaw a series of forums on 30 July, designed to permit the participants to advance their ideas about nuclear power and to define new means of struggle. On 31 July the assembly would march on the site.

But then and during the intervening months, a passionate debate split the co-ordination of the *Comités Malville*. Pacifism, non-violence, violence or paramilitarism? The main stream argued that what would stop the fast reactor project was not the damage that could be committed but the political effect of the assembly. To achieve the greatest political weight it was necessary to attract as many participants as possible and to encourage scientists, unionists, farmers and local politicians to come and support the movement – or at least to see and appreciate its extent. Consequently the assembly had to be peaceful so that everyone could come. On the other hand it was vital to assure that the demonstration have a substantial impact on the national conscience and to avoid a purely symbolic gathering. The proponents of this view envisaged reconciling the requirements by a number of marches converging on the site, avoiding the police by perpetual withdrawal and re-formation – a sort of peaceful guerrilla or hide and seek – quite impractical in fact in the difficult terrain around the site, marshes, woods, cultivated fields, hills and tiny country roads. A minority dreamt of quasi-military actions and occupation of the reactor site, like the West German anti-nuclear movements had recently managed at Brokdorf. The profound split was patched up by a purely verbal contrivance; the demonstration was christened *une marche pacifique offensive* – an offensive, peaceful march. Although the official organizers continued to call it a peaceful or non-violent march in all their literature and publicity, they went into the event quite aware of the determination of a few to do their utmost to turn the march into a violent confrontation.

The demonstrators began to arrive in force on 29 July. Four camp sites had been foreseen in fields provided by sympathizers on the outskirts of the villages of Montalieu, Courtenay, Poleyrieu and Morestel. Participants were directed to sites following the place of their origin; all foreigners were assigned to Morestel. Normally in France camping is freely permitted without any authorization other than that of the owner of the land, providing the camping does not exceed six shelters and 20 people. The large encampments were therefore probably in contravention of the law. The *Préfet de l'Isère* had in addition forbidden by decree all camping in a generously defined area around the site. The *Préfet de l'Isère* had also forbidden the march itself, or more precisely he declared that it would be forbidden as soon as it crossed the Route Nationale 75 which runs north-south roughly parallel to the Rhône and about 5 km west of the river. Several roads and bridges were blocked, including for a short time the N 75 itself although the problems caused by the fabulous holiday traffic in France at the end of July soon required it to be reopened. On many other roads only the local inhabitants were allowed to move. But the most important consequence of the prefectorial prohibition was that it made every single participant a likely criminal offender because any person participating in a prohibited demonstration at which criminal violence is committed by a third party can be charged under *la loi anti-casseurs*.

The participants were almost all young; few were more than 30 and the great majority were probably between 18 and 25. They had come to enjoy themselves; long-haired, unshaven and unwashed, they carried the circular loaves of the region threaded on to the arm and held in place by litre bottles of wine. The local tradesmen rose to the occasion; there was no shortage of bread or wine. The moderately well off carried a sleeping bag but many had no luggage other than a packet of *Gauloises*. Petty violence and thieving was not rare.

The international camp site at Morestel was dominated by West Germans, probably about 500 strong, who took over the organization at an early stage. Preserving national characteristics even in the heart of the international ecological movement, the West Germans were distinctly quieter, cleaner and more efficient than their hosts. There were also many Swiss, Italians, Belgians and Dutch. Anti-police, ecological and political slogans were bellowed out over the loudspeakers – *vive la révolution, vive la nature!* They mingled with the sound of guitars, songs and folk dances. There was gaiety and surly aggressiveness. The music was quickly extinguished by a cold rain – it had rained heavily for the three preceding days and it rained throughout the night of 29 July.

At dawn some 500 CRS in full riot gear surrounded and raided the camp sites at Montalieu and at Morestel. At Morestel a small resistance was quickly subdued. The intention of the CRS was to ransack the camp, but the *maire* of Vasselin, President of the association of elected representatives against Malville, intervened and prevented the destruction of the camp. He obtained permission to bivouac – to put up a tent at nightfall and remove it at dawn, never spending two nights in the same place. The CRS searched the sites and examined papers. The total arsenal discovered in the two camps comprised some 30 crash helmets, about as many gas masks and assorted knives and forks. The small number really bent on violence were not for the most part in the camp sites, but were sleeping rough in places where they could prepare and equip in secret. Keys of vans that had been providing a free ferry from the village to the site were taken away.

The day of forums on 30 July never materialized. Most participants spent the time drinking or sleeping. There were a few political sideshows and buskers. The CFDT held a meeting at Morestel attended by at the most 100 people and the militants prepared their Molotov cocktails in the safety of the woods. But the tension never ceased to mount. Helicopters circled over the surroundings, the N 75 was blocked, communications between the four villages were almost entirely cut and the villages all but isolated. Frogmen in dinghies mounted guard over the banks of the Rhône. The prohibition of the march and the consequences for all participants of the inevitable violence weighed heavily on the minds of those who had come prepared for a peaceful march. The presence at Morestel of some hundreds of West Germans permitted the *Préfet de l'Isère* to declare: 'For the second time Morestel is occupied by the Germans.' This observation by the representative of the State in the department did not fail to impress some of the local inhabitants already disturbed by the presence of so many foreigners and so many paramilitary forces.

Towards evening the participants assembled in the villages to have the tactics of the following day disclosed. Instead the minority with violent ambitions reopened the debate about what the march would do when it came across a barricade, and whether there should be four marches or one was again put in question. Confusion was total. At Morestel drunken French anarchists broke into the *mairie*, around the steps of which the crowd gathered. They broke some windows and waved some French flags from the mansard before ejected by a group of West Germans who then mounted guard over the *mairie* on the grounds that they would be blamed for any damage. Sure enough in the morning the *préfecture* announced the wrecking of the *mairie* at Morestel by West German commandos.

At Morestel the decision of the meeting was overwhelmingly in favour of a single march by all four villages, resolutely peaceful and excluding all of violent intent. The decision was to be carried by a devious route to a meeting with representatives of the other villages; the communal decision was to be announced in the morning. In the meantime some 5,000 people who had come with the intention of camping at Morestel had to find somewhere to sleep. Unwilling to risk the prepared camp site again, the mass of participants descended on the village; they pitched tents on every patch of land, slept on the pavements, in the market square, in barns and disused buildings and in the grounds of the ruined castle dominating the village. The inevitable music and dancing began, ecologists in hobnailed boots waltzed to an accordion, but the atmosphere was very strained and soon the entertainment ended.

By seven in the morning the roads around the villages were swarming with confused demonstrators. At Morestel the organizers announced that the participants should join their colleagues at Courtenay. An impressive column of minibuses, cars and vans ferried what must by then have been 6,000 or 7,000 people to Courtenay by the secondary roads, the RN 75 being still blocked by the police. The objective of the organizers, still at this time secret, was to liberate the village of Faverge in the forbidden zone. The plan seems to have been known to the police who had concentrated forces of *gardes mobiles* and CRS at this point during the night. The disposition of the forces of order comprised two lines of resistance. The outside line followed the forbidden area as defined by the *préfet* and guarded the principal means of access to the reactor site; it was abandoned as soon as it came under pressure. The second line contained only some 500 hectares of ground around the site and was supported by large mobile units, about 3,000 men in all; it was considered impregnable.

The first demonstrators arrived from Poleyrieu, the nearest of the encampments, at about 10.00 a.m.; they requested from the officer in charge of the *gardes mobiles* permission to occupy a field outside the second line of defence overlooking Faverge. The permission was granted. Some demonstrators began to dance, a difficult operation on the sodden ground. A heavy glacial rain began in the morning and continued until late afternoon.

Between 11.00 a.m. and 12.00 noon the body of the marches began to arrive, containing the principal organizers and a few of the elected representatives of the locality – there to try to restrain the marchers and to act as intermediaries. The organizers, seeing that the march could go no further without a battle, called on their adherents to avoid confrontation and asked the partisans of violence to leave the march. At 11.30 some hundreds of demonstrators wearing helmets and masks and armed with iron bars, clubs, slings and Molotov cocktails advanced across the fields towards the village; they had almost reached the first houses when the *gardes mobiles* opened fire with gas grenades and concussion grenades. In principle the gas grenades are intended to be fired in the air so as to reduce the chances and effects of a direct impact with the device. In practice, after the first few salvoes they were often fired at individuals with careful aim. A West German demonstrator had his hand blown off in attempting to throw back a concussion grenade under the impression that it was a gas grenade. A Molotov cocktail set fire to a car hired by a journalist. The exchange of grenades and Molotov cocktails continued for over an hour. A concussion grenade exploded before being thrown taking off the hand of the gendarme and severely injuring two of his colleagues. Another West German lost a foot in trying to extinguish a concussion grenade. The extent of the skirmishing began to spread as small groups of well-equipped and violent demonstrators began to move parallel to the line of defence.

Pacifists attempted to breach the defences by a non-violent movement, but were driven back quickly. Italian revolutionaries charged with cries of '*lotta, lotta*' (struggle). In the afternoon the CRS relieved the *gardes mobiles*, and at 14.10 they passed to the attack. They marched forward, stopped, fired a salvo of grenades and then repeated the cycle. The order was to clear the hill completely. The demonstrators withdrew but not fast enough for the CRS who charged, hand to hand fighting began, the tiny roads to Faverge were blocked with demonstrators still arriving and therefore the withdrawal was slow; the groups engaged in a rearguard action with the CRS were driven back into the mass of non-violent demonstrators, one of whom was killed by the explosion of a concussion grenade on his chest. A minority of anarchists, West Germans and *autonomes*, continued to fight in the maize fields around improvised barriers and in the tiny village of Le Devin on the road to Faverge. At 15.30 the firing of the grenades stopped and the CRS ceased to put pressure on the retreat. The demonstrators gathered briefly at Poleyrieu. Representatives of the co-ordination revealed that their objective had been to gather the demonstrators on the hill overlooking Faverge for a peaceful occupation; they reiterated that they had never had any intention of entering into a conflict with the forces of law and order; they had been overwhelmed by small groups beyond their control. Under a heavy rain, soaked, cold, filthy and tired, the demonstrators returned to Courtenay and Morestel.

By 8.00 p.m. a semblance of calm was restored, the N 75 was reopened, holiday traffic was guided through the difficult crossroads at Morestel by a young man with a whistle overjoyed at the opportunity to mimic with great talent the more extravagant gestures of an especially formal traffic policeman. Eventually he was replaced by a convoy of genuine gendarmes. Convoys of CRS passed through on their way back to the garrisons; a bottle was thrown but fell short. Soon afterwards the traffic stopped again and the gendarmes left. The CRS prepared to *ratisser* (rake) the town. Squadrons of CRS formed up at the principal entries, each unit disposed in something like 10 lines, 10 abreast. The front line charged with raised matraques, carrying shields and gasmasks. They howled as they ran; they stopped, and a second line moved up behind them carrying rifles with gas grenades. In this way they proceeded 100 yards at a time up the street. At the crossroads they were met with a shower of the wine bottles which densely littered the streets. The rear ranks fired gas grenades, under cover of which the front ranks could use their matraques. The CRS struck at anything which moved. Resistance was generally slight. Some cars registered in West Germany had their windows broken with rifle butts and their tyres slashed; there was especially severe damage to West German cars parked in one of the farms on the outskirts of Morestel. Farms sheltering demonstrators were entered and searched. A disused farm on the edge of town where some participants had spent the night was the scene of fierce fighting. After 30 minutes the CRS ambulances went in and brought back the injured demonstrators, to have, as the official report put it, their papers controlled.

There are different views about what incident prompted the CRS to clean up the town. In some accounts it was the bottle, others allege that a few gendarmes had been cornered in the town and were being stoned and attacked with bottles. I saw nothing of that if that were indeed the case. But to identify the seminal incident is an academic exercise; the confrontation was sought by both sides. It is known that the cleaning up was not authorized by the *préfet*.[21] The squadrons of CRS involved were those that had borne the brunt of the attacks at Faverges; they had not had enough; they were also clearly prepared for the operation. Any real or imaginary incident would have sufficed.

Estimates of numbers vary enormously. The public authorities estimated 20,000, the organizers estimated 60,000. I estimate that about 20,000 people camped overnight on 30 July, but they were joined by many others on the morning of 31 July who had come from parts of the region within one or two hours' drive. It is almost impossible to assess the number who arrived on 31 July; many of them never got near Faverge, but I would say that the grand total was nearer 60,000 than 20,000. Some 2,000, at the most, were determinedly violent, and as many again carried helmets and sticks as a show of romantic bravado. The West Germans could hardly have exceeded 500; their motives were difficult to decipher; they expressed little wide-ranging political commitment, but were certainly amongst the most determined to reach the reactor site; they were well equipped and organized.

One man died at Malville, five were seriously injured, all by concussion grenades, and about 100 demonstrators had lesser injuries, mostly scalp wounds from projectiles.

This lengthy essay in local history is of intrinsic interest as an account of the largest anti-nuclear happening in the world to date. The events also illustrate extremely well the interaction of the varied and contradictory currents of the anti-nuclear movement. But the main reason for studying the event is to learn about the strategy of the French State.

The main effect of the reaction of the State is to criminalize the anti-nuclear movement. This effect depends in turn on three main features: the provocation of the violent elements, the intimidation of the peaceful participants and the implication of the latter in the deeds of the former. This main theme of criminalization conflicts with a minor theme of the reaction of the administration, which is to avoid making martyrs. Superimposed on the combination are the attempts by the Elysée to recuperate parts of the movement.

The provocation of violent elements by the authorities was contingent; the propositions about the character and nature of the West German participants were undoubtedly provocative, but appear to have been a personal obsession of the *préfet* rather than an essential part of the strategy. Other actions designed to intimidate the non-violent participants were also described as provocative by the co-ordination, but again that was an incidental aspect. The truth is that those who had come with violent intent needed no provoking.

Although, in my view, the authorities made no systematic effort to provoke participants, they certainly made every effort to intimidate them, by shows of force, by harassment, by destruction of co-ordination and communication and by sinister threats. The low-flying helicopters (which on other occasions had been used for dropping gas grenades), the convoys of heavily armed

CRS which circulated in the region, the road-blocks and controls of cars were enough to unnerve a large proportion of the participants. The raids on camp sites and the accompanying threats increased the tension. The non-violent majority was afraid that they would be caught up in uncontrollable and violent events, afraid that the prohibition of the peaceful march would expose them to prosecution and the possibility of violent repression. Their fear was reinforced by the announcement of the *préfet* that if the march crossed into the forbidden territory the repression would be without pity. The almost complete absence of co-ordination and communication and the sense of isolation in the four centres exacerbated the feverish atmosphere. The acts of the public authorities contributed to this also; one of the principal members of the co-ordination of the *Comités Malville*, a Swiss national, had been expelled from France before the demonstration began, under suspicion of intending to disturb public order. His special task was to co-ordinate the groups from across the Rhine and to keep their participation within a peaceful framework. This absence may well have made it easier for the violent West German and Swiss elements to repudiate the authority of the co-ordinating committee. One cannot be sure. It is certain that the systematic attempts by the police to prevent communication between, and co-ordination of, the four centres undermined the precarious control of the co-ordinating committee. It is also certain that the intimidation inhibited the more fearful of the non-violent demonstrators and caused them to take up the rear of the procession and to hang back from the scene of conflict rather than to expose themselves to retaliation. As a result, events were easily dominated by small highly disciplined and uncontrollable groups with clear objectives. Without the intimidation and harassment they might have been less successful. One cannot know. I have no view on whether the strategy adopted by the State was right or wrong; it is simply my aim to distinguish the elements of that strategy. I am not even extremely sure whether this effect I have called criminalization is intended by the public authorities or whether it is the largely unforeseen result of leaving the CRS with a large degree of autonomy in their handling of the operations. It is known that the *ratissage* of Morestel was an initiative of the CRS; it is also known that there was no representative of the administration at the site of the conflict, but that information was transmitted directly from the CRS to the *préfet* at La Tour-du-Pin, 18 km away.[22] There can have been minimal administrative control over the operations under these conditions. The CRS naturally treated the affair as the sort of riot, civil disturbance or other quasi-military operation for which they were trained, with consequences that may not have been intended.

The tendency of the authorities to incriminate the peaceful participants by association with the deeds of the violent breaks down when it comes to making arrests. A criminal affair conducted in such a public manner can hardly go by without arrests, but the authorities have tried hard where possible to avoid making anti-nuclear martyrs. This contradiction is at the origin of one of the mysteries of the whole affair. The police came out of this violent event with only 12 people whom they wished to charge and only eight of whom were convicted, on very slender evidence. It was an extraordinary outcome, given that the CRS and *gardes mobiles* had ample occasion to take prisoners in flagrant offence at the scene of the conflict. There were also reports from the *préfecture* of isolated West German commandos penetrating the second line of defence and being arrested after a struggle at the perimeter of the reactor site, West Germans again being arrested after attacking gendarmes with Molotov cocktails from cars, and of unyielding West German groups being surrounded in derelict farms. The prisoners from these and many other incidents were apparently released. It would appear that rather late in the day someone noticed that they had omitted to justify, by the number of arrests, the propositions of the *préfet*, placing the responsibility for violence on the foreigners and especially on the West Germans. This may have been another reason for the *ratissage* of the village of Morestel and of farms throughout the region.

Le Monde[23] published extracts from the transcript of recordings of exchanges between the forces of order, captured by a radio receiver during the conflict. The whole thing is fascinating, but the passage of most significance in the present context is the following:

> We are told that the foreigners are moving towards Morestel.
> Wreck (*saccagez*) all foreign vehicles and arrest as many foreigners as possible.
> Order to disperse the demonstrators.

In the event only a dozen demonstrators were brought to trial; they had all been arrested outside the forbidden zone, some as far as 30 km away; none were in *flagrant délit*; none possessed helmets, gas masks, goggles, or scarves. The accusations rested entirely on the testimony of gendarmes present at the conflict that they recognized the defendants across fifty metres of teargas fumes and heavy rain. The trial itself caused consternation which there is not space to explore.[24]

Finally there is the slightly unexpected reaction of the President. With his liberal philosophy, Giscard d'Estaing appears to have perceived more clearly than other Ministers, or most of the administration, the unfavourable impression made by grenading peaceful demonstrators because of the presence of a violent minority. In addition the President claims great sympathy for ecological views, from which he excludes opposition to nuclear developments; he approves the passion with which French youth has adopted the ecological cause, providing it eschews violence. Reflections of this character probably contributed to his announcement shortly after Malville of the creation of the *Conseil d'Information Electronucléaire*.

H. Conclusions

The conclusions of this account address themselves to two principal questions. What will be the influence of the anti-nuclear movement in the future? What can be learnt about the alleged conflict between technocracy and democracy?

The future of the anti-nuclear movement will depend on whether it can continue to mobilize local support in affected sites and whether it can strike a balance in its use of force. Participation of the local community is an essential requirement if the movement is to have legitimacy in the eyes of the nation and the Government. This participation is jeopardized by the presence of indiscriminately violent groups. My impression at Malville, for example, is that although the local population are broadly hostile to the fast reactor they regard it as a lesser evil than a repetition of the events of July 1977. In short, they want out. Continuation of indiscriminate violence will reduce the anti-nuclear movement to a few cells easily handled by the public authorities. On the other hand it is essential to recognize the fact that in France there is little scope for popular pressure groups to influence public policy if they do not demonstrate considerable force. The optimum strategy of the anti-nuclear movement, therefore, will be to preserve a large peaceful participation whose support will provide a political perspective for particular and limited acts of violence which do not endanger human life; sabotage of equipment, burglary, burning of registers or whatever.

My own tentative assessment is that support for the anti-nuclear movement is waning. The opposition will certainly help delay the second pluriannual programme of nuclear installations by forcing more extensive and prolonged consultation. But eventually EDF will get the sites it wants. Subsequently, in my view, the nuclear programme will slow down anyway because of financial and construction constraints; this slow-down will remove the pressure on siting. Outside the affected areas popular interest in nuclear policy is declining fast. The ecologists in the legislative elections failed dramatically not only to poll many votes, but, more seriously, to make the nuclear policy an important aspect of the election debates. Even in Grenoble, the heart of the anti-nuclear movement, the electorate showed little interest and the anti-nuclear candidate polled less than 1% of the votes. 'Malville', said a voter from Morestel, 'that's all in the past.'[25]

What is there to be learnt about the alleged conflict between technocracy and democracy? The first element of a reply must be to assess the depth of sympathy in the country as a whole. In my view although there may only have been tens of thousands of people at Malville, there are hundreds of thousands who approve and probably millions who understand their motives and do not blame them.

Personal impressions are not the most convincing evidence. Statistical evidence comes from an opinion poll organized by *Le Nouvel Observateur* immediately after the events at Malville.[26] The poll comprised eight questions and the results of all were interesting. Perhaps the result which best supports my proposition is the answer to the question: 'Were the organizers of the assembly right to go ahead despite the prohibition by the *préfet de l'Isère*?' The answer was:

	They were right	They were wrong	Don't know
Total = 100%	40	48	12
Age			
18—24	54	37	9
25—34	53	37	10
35—49	43	44	13
50—64	28	60	12
65 +	26	59	14
Political Persuasion			
Communist	73	22	5
PSU/Extreme Left	73	15	12
Socialist	54	37	9
Presidential Majority	19	72	9

The most significant figure is the 53–54% of people under the age of 30 who considered it correct to continue with the prohibited assembly; this figure demonstrates considerable sympathy among the young for the broad idea that the administration restrains too strongly the activities of the citizen.

The importance of these silent millions is that they are in large majority the well educated and the university students, more questioning than the average and refusing to accept the objectives and assurances of their elders. What they want is to construct a future different from the one proposed to them. What it will be like they do not know.

The discussion is now touching on the second element of a reply to the question of technocracy and democracy. The anti-nuclear movement is not so much an expression of a simple opposition to nuclear power as an expression of a complex and confused dissatisfaction with society. The roots of the anti-nuclear movement in the events of May 1968 have already been sketched. It is interesting that Daniel Cohn-Bendit, when interviewed by *Le Monde* on the tenth anniversary of the events of May 1968 should have noted:[27]

In France, the movements at Lip, the feminists, the ecologists express this collective consciousness (*subjectivité*) which we lived without knowing how to formulate.

The argument that the anti-nuclear movement is a particular manifestation of a widely felt dissatisfaction of the whole development of society may seem to contradict the earlier assertion that it is a fading phenomenon. But it is not necessarily so. The obscure and ill-formulated dissatisfaction with the evolution of modern society, which underlies many specific and apparently unrelated events, will continue to develop for many years and one cannot know eventually what the consequences will be. Superimposed on this are explosive cycles culminating in events like those of May 1968 and the anti-nuclear summer of 1977. Directed at specific targets, these mini-revolutions rapidly gather support, but they have too narrow a base to sustain continuous action; they falter and collapse until after a time the underlying causes set off another explosion elsewhere.

It is tempting to try to explain this unstable behaviour in terms of the most fundamental contradiction in French life – the conflict between a radical political tradition and a conservative social structure; it can be detected at the level of the individual and at the level of the State.

At the level of the individual this conflict is frequently expressed in the aphorism: 'The French carry their hearts on the left and their wallets on the right.' The effect of the redistribution of wealth during the Revolution compounded by the Napoleonic laws of inheritance has been to make France a country of small production units. Despite the efforts of the Fifth Republic, this condition persists in large degree today. Distributing wealth among the people, instead of concentrating it in the State, led the children of the Revolution to see the advantages of the stability of society in the future. The property-owning peasants were used as a power base by Gambetta in his consolidation of the Third Republic; the revolutionary and republican tradition was thereby kept alive in a socially conservative class. This syndrome has been offered as part of the explanation for the slow industrialization of France;[28] industrialization was resisted by the peasants, small landowners and tradesmen, i.e. subsistence capitalists.

The same conflict is visible at the level of the State. The revolution asserted the elusive principle of the sovereignty of the people, but never in the history of French democracy has it been found possible to design political institutions which incorporated this principle. There was a permanent conflict between the ideal of the sovereignty of the people and the reality of centralized power inherited from the *ancien régime* and preserved by the social conservatism of the country.

Inevitably the administration arrogated great power. The hierarchical system required an extensive administration, and instability of the political institutions permitted it to become strong. Or from another point of view, strong governments enjoyed the powerful administration while weak governments could do nothing about it. The administration was, and is, staffed by a particular part of the upper middle class, its members having a common political, philosophical and social outlook.[29] The common origin and training of the *fonctionnaire* emphasizes stable government, law and order, stability of the community; he is encouraged to believe that there are no real conflicts of interest only technical disagreements; he is impatient with political controversy and instinctively anti-democratic; he enjoys enormous prestige. Inevitably, an administration composed in this manner will exhibit great scrupulousness in its own terms, but intolerable arrogance in establishing those terms. It will be impatient with the less able and less well informed. These characteristics are indeed visible in the French administration.

We now have the three elements needed to explain the explosive behaviour of French society; the arrogant administration, the tradition of political radicalism, and social conservatism. The arrogant administration irritates intolerably the quality of political radicalism, resentment builds up and eventually explodes. At that point the quality of social conservatism causes both parties to draw back; calm returns until the initial process begins to erode the dominant social conservatism and a new explosion occurs elsewhere.

It follows that the origins of the opposition to the nuclear policy lie not in an attempt to *prevent* technocracy, but in the elaboration and imposition by the *existing* technocracy. Its character as a small but topical part of a broader discontent means that it is not enough to convince that the nuclear policy is benign, nor alternatively would it be enough to stop building nuclear power stations. It is the extent to which it is possible for an individual to participate in the decisions that affect his life that is in question, not the contingent properties of nuclear power. A procedure has operated in Europe since the war whereby the citizen has been content for civil servants to design much of the society in which he lives. This has been more true of France than the United Kingdom, which explains why France has been materially so much more successful. The lesson of the anti-nuclear movement in France is that, even if it should itself fade away, underneath will still be growing the aspirations to feel less governed and to slacken the grip of the administration.

On a practical note, the greatest assistance to the nuclear opposition in stimulating local support has been the absence of provision for public debate, the apparent arrogance of the administration and public enterprise and the quite inadequate facilities for consultation with the local populations and their elected representatives. These failures are not easily remedied in France; they arise from the conjunction of the large and rapid nuclear programme with characteristic French social and political structures. The rapidity of the rhythm of installation has made it genuinely difficult to prepare the local populations. EDF and the CEA presenting themselves as arms of the State have tried to minimize debate with the public. The administration has not seen the necessity of explaining the decisions of the best experts in technology and administration to peasants and shopkeepers who could never understand the arguments or the stakes.

The United Kingdom is fortunate enough to have the oil and political traditions to permit it to afford a public debate. The French example should encourage the United Kingdom to continue on that line.

References

1. *Le Marxiste-Léniniste*, Supplément au No. 18/19, July/August 1977.
2. 'Nucléaire,' Special issue of *l'Humanité Rouge*, August 1977. Journal of Les Communistes Marxistes-Léninistes de France.
3. *Non au charbon*, July 1977, Organisation Communiste de France (Marxiste-Léniniste).
4. *Libération*, 21 November 1977.
5. 'Des centrales aux urnes,' *Le Monde*, 24 March 1977.
6. *Creys-Malville, le dernier mot*? Conseil Général de l'Isère, Presses Universitaires de Grenoble, 1977.
7. *Le Monde*, 12–13 January 1975.
8. 'M. Valéry Giscard d'Estaing annonce la création d'un conseil d'information électronucléaire,' *Le Monde*, 25 August 1977.
9. *Journal Officiel*, 19 February 1978.
10. 'Le conseil d'information électronucléaire groupera une vingtaine d'experts,' *Le Monde*, 6 October 1977.
11. *On the Conditions for a Community Policy on the Siting of Nuclear Power Stations*, European Parliament. Working Document 392/75/ANNEX. This document gives a useful, brief account of practice throughout the Community.
12. 'Les centrales nucléaires hors-la-loi,' *Le Monde*, 20 May 1977.
13. F. Ridley and J. Blondel, *Public Administration in France*, Routledge and Kegan Paul, London, 1969.
14. 'Le site nucléaire du Pellerin est l'un des plus mauvais du monde,' *Le Monde*, 10 June 1977.
15. 'Les agriculteurs anti-nucléaires du Pellerin sont remis en liberté,' *Le Monde*, 17 June 1977.
16. 'Le site du Pellerin,' *Le Monde*, 30 June 1977.
17. Polémique autour de la centrale du Pellerin, *Le Monde*, 1 September 1977.
18. 'La Guerilla Ecologique,' *Le Monde*, 14 July 1977.
19. See the preface by the *Président du Conseil Général de l'Isère* to reference 6.
20. 'La police au secours du nucléaire,' *Le Monde*, 13 July 1977.
21. 'Un entretien avec le préfet de l'Isère,' *Le Monde*, 4 August 1977.
22. *Le Monde*, 6 August 1977.
23. 'Un enregistrement des forces de l'ordre,' *Le Monde*, 9 August 1977.
24. *Le Monde*, 7, 8, 9, 10, 25 August 1977.
25. 'Le nucléaire a fait long feu,' *Le Monde*, 8 March 1978.
26. 'Nucléaire, ce que pensent les Français,' *Le Nouvel Observateur*, 14 August 1977.
27. 'Il y a dix ans, le 22 mars,' *Le Monde*, 23 March 1978.
28. D. Thomson, *Democracy in France since 1870*. Oxford University Press, 1969.
29. This is changing slightly; one symptom cf this change is the persistent restlessness at the ENA.

VIII

Appraisal

The broad objective of this study has been to ascertain to what extent energy policy in France is determined by material and technical factors and to what extent it is a reflection of French culture and institutions. A plausible argument can be constructed to suggest that French policy is a logical response to the material deficiencies in fuel supplies and the opportunities offered by available technology. I have tried to show that the special character of French institutions and the desire to exert political and industrial power in the world provide just as adequate an explanation as the theory of technological determinism.

Of course, energy policy is really a product of the *interaction* of material and institutional factors. We can see both these factors at work, but we cannot, from the study of a single country, assess their relative importance. The work described here is therefore being extended to other countries with different institutional structures.

Conclusions about specific aspects are scattered through the text. Only a few main points are resumed here.

Does the study provide any objective evidence in support of the hypothesis that there is a fundamental conflict between technocracy and democracy? Clearly France is undemocratic in the way it makes its energy policy. Whether there is a general correlation between resort to nuclear energy and undemocratic decision-making requires further evidence from other countries with different institutions and policies. If this correlation can be established, it can still be evaluated in two ways; it can be argued that resort to nuclear energy is only possible in undemocratic political systems or that we need authoritarian decision-making systems to impose this technique, essential for survival. This is a value judgement of the kind which I have tried to avoid.

The French system of indicative planning does not appear to have much influence on energy policy. The decisions which count are taken outside the Plan. The planning system has not helped divine the future; the planners persistently failed to appreciate the significance of petroleum until after the party was over. Technocratic control lies, in practice, firmly with the Ministry of Finance.

French energy policy is the result of a triangle of forces, made up of senior politicians (essentially the President, Prime Minister and Minister for Industry), public enterprise and the Ministry of Finance. If the priorities of these three actors coincide then the result is a very stable policy. This happened during the 1960s when the policy of cheap, French oil satisfied the expectations of the Gaullist politicians (independence), *Les Finances* (no public investment, cheap energy), and the State oil companies. The policy could not survive the French quarrels with Algeria. It has been substituted by a new, almost equally stable policy in which the public enterprise corner is filled by a powerful EDF-CEA axis. The only fly in the ointment is *Les Finances*. The Ministry is permanently trying to reduce the size of the nuclear programme. Only the effects at the margin are clearly visible. It is difficult to be certain how much of the programme the Ministry would like to keep. But one can be certain that the same triangle which operated for the policy of *pétrole franc* is the motor of the *tout électrique*.

The coincidence of the ambitions of State enterprise and the political authorities has produced an impressive effort in every branch of the nuclear industry. It is not clear if this effort will be rewarded. The construction industry has had considerable trouble with Fessenheim I; the later plants are now two years late. EDF is in considerable debt, the rising cost of nuclear plant and commissioning delays have caused its cash flow to deteriorate even further than was expected; worse is yet to come. The enrichment plant is another heavy investment that will not start producing cash until 1980. The difficulties with reprocessing enriched uranium fuel that appear to plague the plant at La Hague are reminiscent of the problems that have closed American plants. It may still be that the French will become the emirs of uranium; it is too soon to say. They are taking risks, they have not clearly won, but they have not clearly lost. The next few years will tell.

Domestic orders for reactors will certainly fall in the 1980s. The French investments will then need to find foreign markets. *Prima facie*, it seems likely that France will become a centre of nuclear proliferation; its sale of reprocessing plant to Pakistan is not a hopeful sign. There is no doubt at all about the efforts being put by Framatome and the Quai d'Orsay into the search for export markets for reactors. The Government claims that they will not contract to sell sensitive technology again in the foreseeable future. The generally callous attitudes of successive French governments to arms sales must oblige this protestation to be treated cynically. Nevertheless the intention is probably genuine. The priority of France must be to utilize its own investments in enrichment and reprocessing and to sell only the reactor. The main danger is that the probable over-capacity in manufacturing facilities for reactors in the 1980s will cause governments to offer reprocessing plant as an inducement to buyers. To prevent that sort of trade should be a high priority of the international community.

Index